The Puritan Revolution:

A Documentary History

The Puritan Revolution:

A Documentary History

Edited by
STUART E PRALL

LONDON
ROUTLEDGE & KEGAN PAUL

First published 1968
by Routledge & Kegan Paul Limited
Broadway House, 68–74, Carter Lane
London, E.C.4

Printed in Great Britain
by Eyre & Spottiswoode Portsmouth Limited

© *Stuart E. Prall, 1968*

SBN 7100 6378 4

CONTENTS

INTRODUCTION

Popular and scholarly interest in the era of the Puritan
Revolution has never been wanting, but the past half century
has seen this interest lead to an ever greater investigation into
the history of English life in all its complexities from the
mid-sixteenth century until the Restoration of 1660. The
day when England prided itself on achieving democracy by
way of evolution, whereas continental peoples were forced
to take the revolutionary road, is now passing. The multiplicity of revolutions since 1917 and the mass of literature,
both scholarly and journalistic, concerning them has been one
factor in helping historians of England to see similar patterns
in the later Tudor and early Stuart eras. Another reason for
the new interest in the Puritan Revolution has been the falling away of the old spirit of isolation and of the assumptions
of England's separateness from the life of the Continent.
Every great nation of the world has witnessed a revolution at
some point in the past two hundred years. Englishmen and
historians of England's history are now more than eager to
show that England too deserves a place in this modern revolutionary world. This new pride in having participated in one
of the great revolutions has led to the quiet abandonment
of the older name of Puritan Revolution, and also of the
term Civil War, and the adoption of the name English Revolution, not of course to be confused with the now under-
played Glorious Revolution.

Crane Brinton's brilliant study *Anatomy of Revolution*
marks the coming of age and the scholarly acceptance of this
current view that the Englishmen of the mid-seventeenth
century worked a revolution comparable in all important re-

spects to the classic French Revolution of 1789 and the nearly classical Russian Revolution of 1917. (It is interesting to note that the designation Russian Revolution has gained the ascendancy over the older term Bolshevik Revolution. In the past twenty years revolutions have ceased to be viewed as the work solely of the group or faction that triumphs, and are instead seen as truly national experiences which in the course of time are accepted as a real and good part of the nation's history—experiences to be shared, if not gloried in, by all good citizens.) Although accepting the validity of the term English Revolution, I use the older term Puritan Revolution throughout this essay primarily so that any confusion with the Glorious Revolution can be avoided, and because modern scholarship has really done nothing to undermine its essential accuracy.

To the student of history in the last generation or two the most intriguing aspect of the Puritan Revolution has been the century prior to 1640 plus the first years of the Revolution itself, up to the end of the war and the capture of the king in 1648. The period of the Commonwealth and Protectorate has been relatively slighted. Within the period from 1640–48, the Long Parliament and the roles played by its members individually and as members of one or another of the many subgroups are currently being most systematically investigated.

The vital question historians are trying valiantly to answer is what caused the Revolution? During the past three hundred years a variety of answers has been suggested, but none has as yet been found wholly acceptable for more than a generation or two. To Samuel Rawson Gardiner, whose many volumes covering the period from 1603 to 1656 constitute the classic history of the era, the Revolution was indeed a Puritan revolt against the Anglican establishment supported by the crown and the aristocracy, and at the same time a struggle for liberty against the encroachments of the royal prerogative. J. R. Tanner did not challenge this interpretation, but emphasized the constitutional aspects of the struggle. In his *English Constitutional Conflicts of the Seventeenth Century* the Puritan Revolution was seen as a violent period on the continuum leading from Tudor absolutism to Victorian parliamentarism. Since the interregnum went too far in the other direction, the Restoration was necessary to restore a balance so that the smooth evolutionary development of the constitution could be resumed.

These late nineteenth- and early twentieth-century religious, constitutional, and libertarian analyses were to be cast into oblivion by the work of R. H. Tawney. In his study of the gentry from the mid-sixteenth to the mid-seventeenth centuries he found that the economic and social rise of this new class was upsetting the balance of the old society and the constitution that reflected it. The Long Parliament could now be seen as representing new social forces struggling against the crown and church which stood for a way of life that was becoming anachronistic. Tawney's work has had a profound impact upon subsequent study of Tudor and Stuart history. The period he dealt with has even come to be called "Tawney's Century." H. R. Trevor-Roper has challenged Tawney's work, but not his fundamental point of view. He saw a divided gentry where Tawney had seen a united one. To Trevor-Roper the Revolution witnessed the clash between that part of the gentry that had successfully adjusted to the new techniques of making money—modern methods of estate management and sharing in the profits to be made by co-operating with the court—and the older type of gentry that continued to operate their estates in the old way and did not share in the riches available to those at court. Thus the declining gentry went to war against the rising gentry.

To these two variations on the same basic theme Christopher Hill added a more thoroughgoing Marxist touch. For Hill the Revolution was the point in English history when the new industrial and commercial capitalist bourgeoisie went to war to supplant the landed, feudal interest. Hill's theme was developed during the 1930s and has proved to be very short-lived, being abandoned by its own author in the 1960s. In his recent survey of seventeenth-century English history Hill has gone back to the old theme of court versus country: a theme that Trevor-Roper was actually expounding under a different name, and that both Gardiner and Tanner had been developing in their own ways.

Even though the recent economic interpretations are not

really out of line with the nineteenth-century Whig approach exemplified by Gardiner and Tanner, there is one fundamental difference. The willingness to see England as having shared the continental revolutionary experience is still with us. In his latest book, *Intellectual Origins of the English Revolution*, Hill assumes that as the French Revolution was preceded by the century of Enlightenment, or revolution in science and philosophy, so must the Puritan Revolution have been preceded by its intellectual revolution. Yet in his conclusion he says, "Although I left Puritanism out of my analysis of the intellectual origins of the English Revolution, a discussion of science, history, law, repeatedly brought us back to it." Thus we are in a way back to the position of S. R. Gardiner, although it must be admitted that Hill's use of the term "Puritan" connotes far more than the merely religious.

In editing this book, I have accepted the contention that England in the mid-seventeenth century experienced a true revolution. While I find it impossible to say with any certainty what caused the men of 1640 to resort to arms, once armed conflict began it unleashed forces that Tudor and early Stuart society had successfully kept locked up. By 1660, demands for reform or abolition in almost all aspects of English life had been proposed and even fought for. The monarchy, the peerage, parliament, courts, law, marriage, clergy and church, inclosures of land, tithes, centralization of government, imprisonment for debt, the jury system, the common law, the prerogative courts, probating of wills, the system of registering real estate transactions, taxation were all brought into question. Whether the intellectual revolution that Christopher Hill described really occurred is debatable, but there is no denying that once hostilities began all the ingredients for a social and intellectual revolution were at hand. The Restoration of 1660 is largely to be explained by the extreme nature of so many of the proposals for change in the twenty preceding years.

Whether or not one goes back to the mid-sixteenth century to begin the study of those social and economic changes that a century later were to lead to war, there is no denying that social and economic factors were joined by constitutional, political, and religious ones with the accession of James I to the throne in 1603. The fine balance that had been maintained by the great Queen during her last years was to be seriously upset within months of self-styled Solomon's arrival in England. A king almost from the moment of his birth, he had been educated both by some of the finest minds in the British Isles and by the poverty and near anarchy that were to be the economic and political sides of his inheritance. As king of Scotland he had reigned over an almost ungovernable people. Finding money to provide food for his household was a constant worry. It is no wonder that this precocious young scholar would turn to the tenets of divine-right monarchy for intellectual succor. His *True Law of Free Monarchy* with its assertion that the king was to his people what God was to mankind represents not his actual role as Scottish king but his goals as king of England. A lifetime of penury in Scotland led him to look upon England almost as an El Dorado. Little did he realize the role that parliament and the common law courts had already attained in England. Perhaps even less did he understand the great financial strain under which the English Queen had labored for most of her forty-five-year reign. Of the constitutional and economic realities of England he was in complete ignorance. While he was a scholar by nature, he was a king by birth and had in consequence a far greater interest in teaching his new subjects than in learning from them. The enthusiasm with which England greeted his accession soon turned to disenchantment. During the next thirty-seven years the fabric of Tudor society was sufficiently torn at the seams to make armed revolution possible if not inevitable.

It is how one looks at the increasingly disparate forces in society that determines the view one takes as to the causes of the Puritan Revolution. Therefore, rather than merely to recount the more important events of the reigns of James I and Charles I, it will be more useful to refer briefly to the various contending elements in English society and see how each stood on the eve of the convention of the Long Parliament.

Regardless of which interpretation of the Revolution one subscribes to, there is no denying that early Stuart England was in the throes of a constitutional crisis. The seventeenth century was an age of absolutism throughout Western Europe. The Tudors had brought the powers of the crown to a height never before seen in England. Where Henry VIII and Elizabeth I had wielded this great power with a sureness of touch that reflected their essential oneness with the peoples they ruled, the early Stuarts were totally lacking in the political and personal qualities necessary to maintain the equilibrium. The Tudors had brought parliament into the center of affairs, allowing it to discuss and take part in the determination of the most important matters of national concern. The Tudor crown never stood higher than when in parliament. The Stuarts neither understood the role that parliament had acquired, nor did they seem interested in learning. Where Henry VIII and Elizabeth had been able to provide leadership in both houses by seeing that their chief councillors were among the members, the Stuarts tended to let their leadership in parliament go by default. During the parliaments of James I and Charles I there emerged a small group of men sufficiently experienced in the ways of parliament, sufficiently concerned with the national welfare, and sufficiently capable of providing an indigenous leadership to be by 1640 in a position to confront the king with a coherent program of reform. The days of mere opposition were now over. Parliament had taken the initiative.

In addition to the crown and parliament, however, there was a third contestant in the struggle for sovereignty: the common law. In Elizabeth's reign the concept of sovereignty began to be discussed. (Such discussions were underway in France as well.) The sovereignty of king-in-parliament that the Elizabethans had accepted was now under attack. James I was championing royal sovereignty. In the early days of the Long Parliament, Henry Parker put forth the first defense of parliamentary sovereignty. But the real rival to James's claims was the common law itself. The common law judges, under the leadership and inspiration of Sir Edward Coke, were calling for a return to fundamental law. For Coke the whole body of the common law was sovereign, and the law was what the judges said it was. Neither king nor parliament could challenge this supremacy. With three contenders for sovereign power an alliance of two against one was to be expected. Prior to the civil war itself, the natural tendency was for parliament to ally itself with the law and the lawyers. (By the time of the interregnum, however, as we shall see below, the law and the lawyers were beginning to ally themselves with the institution of monarchy against the apparent usurpation of sovereign power by parliament.) The crown's use of the prerogative courts and its ability to manipulate the judges in the common law courts helped move the Parliamentarians away from reliance upon the law and toward open declaration of parliament's sovereignty. The Restoration was based upon the assumption that the Tudor constitution of king-in-parliament was to be reinstated in the seat of sovereignty.

At the root of the constitutional and legal struggle were the dire financial straits the crown had been in from the reign of Henry VIII. The days when the king could "live of his own" at least during peacetime were gone. The barest necessities of court, administration, and defense, not to speak of the settlement of debts already incurred, could not be provided for out of the traditional revenues from crown lands, customs, traditional feudal incidents, and church revenues impropriated by the crown since the Reformation. James I and Charles I were forced to seek new revenues either by an increasing reliance upon parliament or by a combination of reviving long dormant royal rights and creating new devices. In both of these latter cases the crown was dependent upon the co-operation of the courts. Since the Stuarts leaned toward the creation of new devices, taxation came to be by consent of the courts rather than by consent of parliament. This new twist to the constitution tended to alienate parliaments and the common lawyers.

Hand in hand with the breakdown of the Elizabethan constitution went the growing indications of schism in the Elizabethan religious settlement. Just as some historians of the period have emphasized the constitutional crisis, so others have dwelt upon the religious. Where James's political difficulties were partially caused by his ignorance of the English constitution, the same cannot be said about his difficulties with the church. His years of experience with Presbyterians in Scotland had taught him the great importance of preserving the episcopal structure of the English establishment. The Puritan had always regarded the Elizabethan Settlement of 1559 as a temporary stopping point on the road to Geneva. Yet as the years went by it had become increasingly clear to all that the queen regarded her church as a final settlement. By putting a stop to further reforms Elizabeth helped prepare a climate in which many men felt there was no recourse but to pursue their religious ends outside the framework of the establishment. The accession of James I renewed hopes for reform within the Anglican fold. The Hampton Court Conference of 1604 wrote finis to these dreams. James understood all too well the dangers to absolute monarchy that lurked under the name of Presbyterianism. Of course Elizabethan and Jacobean Puritans were by no means all Presbyterians. However, all shades of Puritan thought, plus that of the already separated brethren, were opposed to episcopacy as by law established. Since the church was already sufficiently Protestant in doctrine, the Puritans sought changes in organization, ritual, and the training of a preaching clergy.

The increasing disaffection between James and the Puritans drove the latter more and more into the arms of the Parliamentarians and the common lawyers. Before Charles I ever came to the throne, the ranks of the opposition were being welded together in a common front—a common front that would attract even more support in Charles's reign, and that would stick together until the vicissitudes of war drove a wedge into its membership. Charles's increasing reliance upon the Bishop of London, Laud, and then the latter's elevation to Canterbury, the Privy Council, and the Lord Treasurership simply threw great numbers of good Anglicans as well into the arms of the opposition. Once Laud and Charles succeeded in alienating Scotland, the unity of England was well-nigh destroyed.

Thus it was that the fabric of Elizabethan society, which had begun to show signs of strain in the queen's last years, not only was not restored to a healthy condition under James—the divisive forces became ever greater. The reign of Charles I was to be even more disastrous. Charles's personality and character differed significantly from his father's, but not necessarily for the better. Charles led a blameless private life, in contrast to the debauched life of his father, but both his view of his kingly office and his conduct of the office were to make this new reign even more shameful than the last one. James at least had the saving virtue of understanding issues even if he had not the will and the strength to act according to his understanding. Charles was not nearly so wise as his father. James's weakness of character allowed opposition to the crown to be expended against obviously corrupt advisers like Robert Carr and George Villiers. Public opinion was often given the opportunity to distinguish between the sovereign and his evil advisers, a distinction the English people were always wont to make when offered the opportunity to do so. This distinction was less likely to be made during Charles's reign, since the king's advisers were of a different type and were pursuing policies of a different nature. James's favorites certainly influenced policy, but their principal goal was private and family advancement. Charles's advisers were personally incorruptible, and devoted their efforts—with the king's ardent support—to the pursuit of public policies that were in opposition to the wishes and interests of a growing body of public opinion. By the time Charles was forced to bring eleven years of personal rule to an end and call upon parliament for money to force the Scots to accept the English Prayer Book, the opposition's hatred for his evil advisers—Laud and Strafford—was joined by a growing distrust of the king himself. Laud and Strafford could be attacked openly, the king could not. With the removal of his advisers, Charles was to feel the direct blast of public discontent and distrust.

During the eleven years of personal rule preceding the convention of the Short and Long Parliaments in 1640, Charles I had seemingly found the solution to the problem of how to create on a permanent footing an absolute monarchy. Parliament was non-existent, the courts—common law and prerogative—served the interests of the crown, and money began to come into the royal coffers in sufficient quantities, because of the acquiescence of the courts, as in the Ship-Money case. All that was needed to perpetuate the new system was peace. Internationally Charles maintained his father's policy of peace with Spain and France and the avoidance of involvement in the Thirty Years War. By a religious policy that was more confusing and upsetting to Protestants than to Catholics, any thought of the major Catholic powers uniting against England was made more remote (assuming that the end of the Thirty Years War would have made such a crusade possible). In the absence of a meeting of parliament, there was no institutional device through which concerted opposition to the crown could be organized. English society was still geographically too fragmented and insufficiently concerted to make a successful armed rebellion likely. As in the past, an uprising in one region would probably tend to remain a purely regional affair.

On earlier pages historians' willingness to accept the fact that mid-seventeenth century England had its true continental-style revolution was discussed. Because of the acceptance of the idea of revolution, the question of why it happened takes on new moment. Historians of the French and Russian Revolutions have long been in essential agreement as to the causes, but to accept the fact of revolution in England is to raise the question not only of what caused it but how and why it happened. Throughout English history there is a tendency for moderation and compromise. Why could not the disputes of 1640 be compromised? Whether the Puritan Revolution is thought of as a religious, political, economic, social, or regional conflict, the question remains. Why did war supplant debate and compromise as the solution? Were the issues insoluble any other way? Or had the old basis of consensus that had helped England through her earlier crises—and would help her through subsequent ones—ceased to exist?

It is in seeking answers to these questions that we can see why recent historians—since Tawney—have sought to find massive social transformations such as the rise or fall of the gentry, the crisis of the aristocracy (Lawrence Stone), the decline of the yeoman, or the rise of the bourgeoisie. If English society in the century before the Revolution had been radically transformed, then a sudden (violent) political and religious change would be necessary to create a new and harmonious society as soon as possible. As noted earlier, there is as yet no agreement among historians as to just what were the significant social and economic changes preceding the Revolution. To Tawney the chief factor was the rise of the gentry, to Trevor-Roper it was the question of which gentry were rising and which were falling, to Lawrence Stone it was not the matter of the gentry—rising or falling—but the efforts of the aristocracy to restore themselves to the commanding heights of society that they had occupied in the mid-sixteenth century, had lost by 1603, and had won back by 1640. To Mildred Campbell it was the decline in wealth and numbers of the yeomanry.

Whatever interpretation of the causes of the Puritan Revolution one may choose, there is the inescapable fact that the first year of the Long Parliament saw a very high degree of unity among its members in opposition to the crown and the church. The great cleavages that were supposed to be present in English society did not manifest themselves until after a good deal of reform had been achieved. Both houses were agreed that Strafford and Laud must be removed from the seats of power and be punished. Sir Edward Hyde (the future Earl of Clarendon and adviser to Charles I and II) was himself the member who introduced the bills to abolish the prerogative courts of Star Chamber, High Commission, etc. Therefore of more immediate concern to historians is the need to discover the reasons for the division into factions of this originally united parliament. Why and how was it that John Pym was able to lead about sixty per cent of the House of Commons and a few of the peers into armed rebellion while Hyde and about forty per cent of the Commons, together with a large majority of the peers, remained loyal to Charles? The truly interesting question, in fact, is not what were the causes of opposition to the king, but rather, what caused the emergence of a *king's party* during the first two years of the Long Parliament?

Since the publication of J. H. Hexter's brilliant study of *The Reign of King Pym* in 1941, several scholars have conducted a minute analysis of the members of the Commons, tracing their "party" affiliations, votes on key issues, religious preferences, and comparing this with their social, economic, educational, geographical, and genealogical backgrounds. The studies of Brunton and Pennington have shown that the only significant differences between Royalists and Parliamentarians are that the latter tended to be older men and had had more previous parliamentary experience. Those who have worked in the fields first plowed by Hexter have shown that within the Parliamentarian group there is a close correlation between religion (Presbyterianism, Independency, the sects) and the degree of militancy of opposition to the king, the church, the lords, etc. However, these later studies were concerned only with the intra-Parliamentarian struggles, not with the differences between Royalists and Parliamentarians. As yet there is no satisfactory answer to the question of what caused the Puritan Revolution, although it is beginning to be understood why, once armed conflict commenced, the Parliamentarians won and why one faction was willing to go to the extreme lengths of killing the king and abolishing the old constitution in both church and state.

It is my own feeling that the most satisfactory explanation of the cause of the Revolution is that which combines a little from all the various schools of thought. There was a struggle for power (or sovereignty) between the crown and the House of Commons. (As noted above, the Parliamentarians had had some previous parliamentary experience, and parliament must be thought of as an institution with a life and traditions transcending those of its individual members.) There certainly was a division between the Anglican and the Puritan religious persuasions. (Admittedly most Anglicans had been opposed to Laud, but with his fall the old Anglican loyalties could once again manifest themselves.) There was no social division, pitting the gentry against the aristocracy. The aristocracy was largely Royalist, and the gentry was split. The split among the gentry tended to be on lines of court versus country and of the North and Western counties against the South and Eastern counties. The North and West were less advanced economically and socially and were more Anglican and even Roman Catholic than the South and East. London went with the Parliamentarians, but many London businessmen individually supported the king. In all these divisions there were many exceptions. Even families were split down the middle, as in the border areas during the American Civil War. In fact, it is probably true to say that most of England was a "border" area, with each group and region merely leaning more to one side than the other.

Once armed conflict began, forces emerged to the surface that few had even suspected were there. Especially after the formation of the New Model Army, with the consequent expectation of victory by parliament, ideas from one extreme to the other, secular and religious, became the objects of debate and of conflict within the New Model Army and parliament. It was the decade from the mid-forties to the mid-fifties that saw England in the throes of a true revolution. The execution of the king in January 1649 and the subsequent abolition of monarchy, House of Lords, and Anglican Church were the high points of revolution in practice. Yet since these momentous acts were all of a negative character, there still lay ahead the task (impossible, as it turned out) of creating new institutions in government, church, law, and society. The failure of the victorious forces led by Cromwell and his Independents to create a system acceptable to the "fanatics" on the left—who sought to create a new Zion—and the majority of the English people on the center and right—who preferred monarchy and the old church—proved to be the undoing of the Commonwealth movement. The Restoration of 1660 looks almost inevitable after a study of the preceding fifteen years. England experienced a true revolution, but it was to be an experience that most Englishmen preferred to forget or ignore for the next three hundred years. It was a movement not without its impact on subsequent developments, but the *coup d'état* of 1688 has gone down in history as the Glorious Revolution, while the revolution of 1640–1660 was known as the Puritan Revolution throughout the era when Puritans were called either dissenters or nonconformists and suffered under certain limitations on their political rights. Not until the Victorian era, when constitutional monarchy truly came into its own, were the historians and their public to look with any great interest, much less enthusiasm, at the "Good Old Cause."

The materials included in this collection have been selected and arranged in the hope that the reader will be able to see the development of the revolutionary crisis from its first reform stage in 1640 to the Restoration in 1660. While an essentially chronological order is maintained, all sides in the conflict, as well as all facets of this conflict—political, legal, religious, military, economic, and social—have been included. Considering the vast mass of historical literature and documents available, the task of choosing those few to be included in a collection such as this has been a sobering one. Naturally some of the more well-known items and authors appear, since no such anthology would be complete without them. On the other hand, less well-known documents and authors have also been included in the hope that they will both shed light on the particular problem at hand and add to the reader's own awareness of the rich variety of sources available. As far as possible, whole works have been reproduced, although space limitations frequently demanded that passages be eliminated. Where only part of a long work has been included, I have tried to choose contiguous passages, rather than resort to a scissors-and-paste approach, though even here exceptions had to be made.

The spelling throughout has been modernized. However, the original punctuation has been allowed to stand except where clarity requires modernization.

ENGLAND ON THE EVE OF CIVIL WAR

The two classic descriptions of England in the seventeenth century are those of Sir Thomas Wilson (1601) and Gregory King (1688). Even though Wilson wrote of England thirty-nine years before the convention of the Long Parliament, passages from his *State of England* [1] are included here because the description remains generally valid until 1640, even if in particulars it had become outdated.

James Harrington's *Oceana* (1656) [2] represents both the contemporary and the modern interpretations of the causes of the Revolution. His economic and social interpretation of the breakdown of the pre-Revolutionary fabric of society anticipated by three hundred years the current explanations offered by R. H. Tawney, H. R. Trevor-Roper, et al. The balanced society that we see in Wilson's account was upset, requiring a new constitution to reflect the new economic alignment. Harrington, if he did not give us the last word as to the causes of the Revolution, certainly gave us the first word.

Thomas Hobbes's *Behemoth* (1668) [3], while not so influential for future historiography as the *Oceana*, gives us the Royalist view as to the causes of the conflict. Though not currently as fashionable as Harrington, Hobbes was without doubt the most profound political thinker in seventeenth-century England. It must be noted that the *Behemoth* was burned by the government of Charles II in 1668. Hobbes may have supported the Royalists during the Civil War, but he was no friend of divine right monarchy. He favored the king in 1642 for the same reasons that he supported Cromwell in the 1650s—the well-being of the people depended upon their obedience to the powers that be. The conservatism of the Protectorate and the subsequent Restoration both lend support to the views that Hobbes expressed in *The Leviathan*—the sovereign must be obeyed for the good of the people; there is no justification for rebellion.

1. *THE STATE OF ENGLAND, ANNO DOM. 1601* by *Thomas Wilson*

A learned and skillful Physician, when he desireth to understand perfectly the state and disposition of any body, the first thing he doeth, he will feel the pulse, how it beats, and thereby he findeth the force of life which it holdeth and the vigor of the human which possesseth the same. Thereupon he demandeth of the patient divers questions how the body hath been governed; what diet; what order; what exercise. That known, he beholdeth the outward appearance, he vieweth the face, the body, and each external member. Thirdly he cometh to the inward and unseen parts, and of them he devineth by dreams, delights, cogitations, and sometimes by phantasies which are not always sure.

.   .   .   .

England from the furthest part Southward to Berwick Northward containeth 340 English miles, which are longer than Italian by a 5th part; likewise from the furthest part Eastward to St. Michells Mont in Cornwall Westward it containeth little less, yet not so great as may seem proportionable to this distances of length and breadth for that North and West it holdeth not out in breadth quadrangular but groweth towards the form of a triangle, yet in compass it is found to exceed 800 miles.

Ireland from the South to the North containeth 300 miles Irish, which are somewhat longer than English, as from East to West about 140.

The Islands about England are most of them small, containing some 12, 10 or 8 towns or villages apiece with some castle or fortress, saving 5 of them which are of some good importance viz. Man, Wight, Anglesey, Guernsey, and Jersey; Man is 30 miles in length.

England, for the Commodities it yields, is known to be

inferior to no Country, saving that it wanteth wine and spicery, but to answer that defect it aboundeth in more sorts of other things necessary to life than any other Country, so that it was justly commended by Constantius the father of Constantine the great.

. . . .

But my purpose is not to praise this Country for then I should enter into too large a field, but only to report the benefits of the Country, which is the end of this Treatise.

The Commodities then which this Country aboundeth in and wherewith it helpeth its neighbors are these especially; iron, steel, tin, lead, copper and all other kind of minerals, saving gold and silver, wool, flax, hemp, corn, flesh, fish of all sorts, leather, cloth, salt, butter, cheese, beer, fruits and herbs of all kinds wholesome and medicinable saffron.

The soil of Ireland is fertile and fruitful, but badly manured by reason of the exaction of the Lords and that the Tenants have no certain time in their lands but *ad voluntatem domini* [at the lord's will, or pleasure], so that they regard not either to build houses or till their ground, by which means it groweth weedy yet yieldeth it great store of beasts and pork, excellent horses, and hawks, fish and fowl, in great abundance, some store of sheep bearing a coarse long wool, whereof they make their rugs, and great abundance of wood: there are also mines of iron, lead, and copper and (as some report) gold and silver, but little profit is made of any by reason the people be not industrious to find them out and work them.

In the Islands likewise there is not wanting scarce any of the Commodities before named and that in proportional quantity.

England is divided into 52 provinces which are called Counties or Shires, whereof 12 are in that part of England which is called Wales, whose names to omit prolixity I omit until I come to speak of the Revenue of the Prince because then I must repeat them all.

In these Provinces there are but 25 Cities, 641 Markets and Shire Towns, 186 Castles, 554 Rivers, 900 forests, chases and parks, Parish Churches, 9725 (and bishoprics, 26).

Of the 641 great Towns there are 289 which are not inferior in greatness to most of these Cities, being most walled Towns and every one of them having voice in the Parliament by 2 burgesses which every one doth send thither, and the rest, albeit they be not walled, are some of them greater than many of the Cities in number of people and riches; yea, there are many which go in the number of villages or parishes wherein there are found 3 or 4 thousand communicants, besides the younger sort under 18 years of age; nay, there are some of those Country Towns which, having but one church, are in compass above 40 English miles, all well inhabited and very fruitful ground: I have by mine own experience both in Yorkshire, in the North parts, and in Norfolk, in the South part, proved this, and where the inhabitants of credit there have reported to me that in some of those villages there were 20 gentlemen that might spend some £500, some £400, some £300 sterling yearly, 40 that might dispend betwixt £100 and 100 marks,[1] 50 that might spend £30, £40 and £50, and above 200 that might spend betwixt £20 and 20 marks yearly and all by their lands in that town; this I found at Bristol near Wakefield in Yorkshire, and at Windham in Norfolk, and many other places; this I have set down that thereby the riches and power of the country may be conjectured, which without doubt for the quantity is not equaled in all Christendom.

It is true that in England there is no great reckoning made of Castles and fortresses, for they do willingly let them go to ruin and instead thereof build them stately pleasant houses and palaces. The reasons they allege are these, that if there should be any invasion the enemy should have no holds but such as they must be forced to make themselves, and within that mean time will find means enough to be disturbed therein; and besides they think the courage of the people would be the greater, knowing they have no retiring places, but must needs fight it out at the first brunt; for when there were places of defense it was the cause of a lingering War which was the greatest woe that ever the country endured.

. . . .

[1] The mark equaled 13 shillings, 4 pence.

There are, besides, an infinite number of other Castles which belonging to gentlemen and noblemen as their private houses: and the Queen hath also many other, but to these only she allowed the maintainance of a Captain or Lieutenant or some other officer as Gunner or Porter or Constable, and is at charge to maintain them in reparations because they stand either upon the Sea Coast or on the frontiers of Scotland. Unless it be some few that be inland, unto which in time of civil dissension there was stipend and officers allowed by letters patents from the King, which is still maintained and paid by the Queen, albeit the Castles themselves of these which be inland are suffered to decay, as is great pity to behold.

But those upon the borders of Scotland are well maintained both with soldiers and ammunition, as well for the jealousy of Scotland as also to withstand the incursions of the Scots upon the borders, whom the King himself and the nobility, albeit they were never so assured to England, cannot keep in order, as is found by the continual daily bickerings and robberies which are amongst the borders as well English as Scottish.

Those Castles and forts in the West Country are also well fortified and kept for fear of the Spaniard, the capital enemy of England.

But those toward Ireland, France and the Low Countries, except the Rivers of Thames, are but weakly provided, by reason the former 2 are known not to have any navy able to approach England with any great force, and if they should provide to do it, in the meanwhile there should be time enough also for England to provide for defense, and for the Low Countries England is very confident of their friendship, especially those of the United Provinces their allies, which are only strong in shipping.

And thus the occasion of these Castles and forts and the state of them ministreth knowledge in what terms England standeth with her Neighbor Princes, *viz*. whom she is to fear, hope, war with, hold in league. It being well known what state these princes are in *viz*. Scotland poor but trustless, Spain strong but far off, the Low Countries and Germany assured, Ireland rebellious but unable to hurt, France content yet to live in quiet, and when his humors shall begin to stir, he will first attempt to recover his own in the continent of his own Country, Artois, Burgundy and Navarre, and after which Italy, which will hold him a long while's work.

. . . .

It were too impossible a matter to go about to observe the method in this to tell how many subjects these Kingdoms contain, albeit I could make a reasonable conjecture knowing the number of parishes and, for the most part, how each province is peopled; but it shall not be necessary to rove at this matter as Botero,[2] a stranger, hath done who never came within 1000 miles of these Countries and yet doth take upon him to set down how many souls there be in this Kingdom, as he doth of many others, by hearsay.

But whereas Botero confesseth in his first relation, about 30 years since, that for soldiers England was able to make 2 millions of armed men besides horsemen, I cannot be induced to believe that; but this I know that anno 1588, when the mountain's mouse, the invincible Spanish armada, was so fearfully expected, there was Commission to bring into the field to the musters in every part of the realm all men that were of perfect sense and limb from 16 to 60, except noblemen, gentlemen, clergymen, scholars and lawyers, officers and such as had public charges, leaving of the countrymen only sufficient to till the ground, and then in all those musters there were numbered 300,000, which is half as many more as Botero speaks of, but to say that the half or 3d part of them were fit to be *hommes d'armes*, as he termeth them, I can neither affirm nor believe. So much for the people which make the strength of the Realm; but boys, women, children and impotent and unfit persons for war I leave to their conjectures which can guess according to this proportion. In Ireland I cannot say what number of persons there be, but by report and uncertain conjecture unsure.

. . . .

I could not understand that in this late rebellion the Earl

[2] Giovanni Botero was the author of *The Travellers Breviot, or an Historical Description of the Most Famous Kingdoms*, 1601, which went through seven editions, under various titles.

of Tyrone could with all the rebels of Ireland get together more than twenty thousand, all the Irish being revolted.

. . . .

The Nobility of Ireland be these: the Earl of Tyrone, the Earl of Kildare, the Earl of Ormond, the Earl of Tonmonde [sic], the Earl of Clencarle [sic], the Earl Clanricarde, whereof the 2 latter have the surname of Burgh and are descended of the Lord Burghs of England; there are also divers Barons and chief men there of that name.

. . . .

Their revenues in money are not great at this present, their lands being let out to such as are bound to serve them in war, or in any other service they require, and for such cattle or goods as their Tenants possess their Lords may take as much of it at any time as he pleaseth for his use, and their chief wealth consist in cows.

But the time hath been not long since that the nobility of Ireland have paid yearly to the Kings of England £5,000 sterling toward his wars, or other cause, as it pleased him to imploy it.

And I find that in one Province there was in the time of Henry 8 as many Barons as might dispend £2,000 yearly in money besides all other Commodities. And that the Lord Burgh and the Earl of Kildare were so mighty that they 2 furnished 30,000 men against the Scots invading Ireland, but now through their own rebellion their states are much weakened and very miserable, and the Queen of England is so far from receiving aid out of that Country that it costs her £300,000 yearly to defend it. . . .

It cannot be denied but the Common people [of England] are very rich, albeit they be much decayed from the States they were wont to have, for the gentlemen, which were wont to addict themselves to the wars, are now for the most part grown to become good husbands and know as well how to improve their lands to the uttermost as the farmer or country-man, so that they take their farms into their hands as the leases expire, and either till themselves or else let them out to those who will give most; whereby the yeomanry of England is decayed and become servants to gentlemen, which were wont to be the glory of the Country and good neighborhood and hospitality; notwithstanding there are yet some store of those yeomen left who have long leases of such Lands and Lordships as they hold, yea I know many yeomen in divers Provinces in England which are able yearly to spend betwixt 3 or 5 hundred pound yearly by their Lands and Leases and some twice and some thrice as much; but my young masters the sons of such, not contented with their states of their fathers to be counted yeoman and called John or Robert (such an one), but must skip into his velvet breeches and silken doublet and, getting to be admitted into some Inn of Court or Chancery, must ever after think scorn to be called any other than gentleman; which gentlemen indeed, perceiving them unfit to do them that service that their fathers did, when their leases do expire turn them out of their lands, which was never wont to be done, the farmer accounting his state as good as inheritance in times past, and let them to such as are not by their bad pennyworths able to gentleman it as others have done.

Notwithstanding this that the great yeomanry is decayed, yet by this means the Commonality is increased, 20 now perhaps with their labor and diligence living well and wealthily of that land which our great yeoman held before, who did no other good but maintain beef and brews for such idle persons as would come and eat it, a fine daughter or 2 to be married after with £10,000 to some Covetous Mongrel gentleman. Of these yeomen of the richest sort which are able to lend the Queen money (as they do ordinarily upon her letters called privy seals whensoever she hath any Wars defensive or offensive or any other enterprise) there are accounted to be about 10,000 in Country Villages besides Citizens.

There are, moreover, of yeomen of meaner ability which are called Freeholders, for that they are owners of Lands which hold by no base service of any Lord or superior, such as are able to keep 10 or 11 or 8 or 6 milch kine, 5 or 6 horses to till their ground, besides young beasts and sheep and are accounted to be worth each of them in all their substance and stock betwixt 3 and 5 hundred pounds sterling more or less, of these, I say, there are reckoned to be in

England and Wales about the number of 80,000, as I have seen in sheriffs' books.

The rest are Copyholders and Cottagers, as they call them, who hold some land and tenements of some other Lord which is parcel of the demeisne of his signory or manor at the will of the Lord, and these are some of them men of as great ability as any of the rest; and some poor, and live chiefly upon county labor working by the day for meat and drink and some small wages; these last are they which are thrust out to service in where the richer sort of yeomen and their sons being trained but not sent out of the land, but kept to defend against invasion at home unless they will go voluntary as many do. Notwithstanding, the captain will sometimes press them to the end to get a bribe to release them.

The number of this latter sort is uncertain by cause there is no books or records kept of them, unless it be in private Stewards' hands which is impossible to be gathered altogether, but I can give a reasonable guess by reason of an office which for 7 years together I exercised, wherein I had occasion to take the names of all the inhabitants of 5 shires.

These, by reason of the great privileges they enjoy, every city being, as it were, a Common Wealth among themselves, no other officer of the Queen nor other having authority to intermeddle amongst them, must needs be exceeding well to pass. They are not taxed but by their own officers of their own brotherhood, every art having one or 2 of his own which are continually of the Council of the City in all affairs to see that nothing pass contrary to their profit; besides they are not suffered to be idle in their Cities as they be in other parts of Christendom, but every child of 6 or 7 years old is forced to some art whereby he gaineth his own living and some thing besides to help to enrich his parents or master. I have known in one City *viz.* Norwich where the accounts having been made yearly what children from 6 to 10 years have earned towards their keeping in a year, and it hath been accounted that it hath risen to 12,000 pounds sterling which they have gained, besides other keeping, and that chiefly by knitting of fine jersey stockings, every child being able at or soon after 7 years to earn 4 shillings a week at that trade, which the merchants uttered at London; and some trading therewith France and other parts. And in that City I have known in my time 24 aldermen which were esteemed to be worth £20,000 apiece, some much more, and the better sort of Citizens the half; but if we should speak of London and some other maritime places we should find it much exceeding this rate, it is well known that at this time there are in London some merchants worth £100,000 and he is not accounted rich that cannot reach to £50,000 or near it.

Every City hath a peculiar jurisdiction among themselves granted by the King in divers times, by which jurisdiction, confirmed by letters patents under the great seal of England, they have authority to Judge in all matters Criminal and Civil, that is to say they have *haute*, mean and base justice; but thus, with this restraint that still all Civil causes may be removed from theirs to the higher Courts at Westminster either by a Writ called *Habeas Corpus* before judgment or by a writ of False judgment or Error after judgment.

They have in every City or Corporate Town one chief officer which they call a mayor, who is the Queen's Lieutenant chosen by the greater part of Citizens out of the number of 24 Aldermen which are of their Senate, as it were, for a year only, and his office is to govern the City in good order and to make a law and constitutions for the benefit of the City, which must be confirmed by Common Council, and he is as it were the Chancellor for his time to compromise matters and to mitigate the rigor of the Law.

They have also 2 chief officers called Sheriffs, annual also, which are the judges in all civil causes betwixt citizens or foreign causes brought thither, the one of the Sheriffs is for the City, the other for the Queen. They, or some by their appointment, see all execution done either penal or capital.

Where there is no Mayor, there the City is governed by 2 bailiffs which have equal authority in all causes as Mayor and Sheriffs.

There is no Territory belonging to any City but only the Town and suburbs, neither doth the Queen place any governor in any Town throughout the whole Realm, but the Citizens and townsmen do always elect them and no magistrate endureth above a year at once.

I have seen divers books which have been collected by

Secretaries and Counselors of Estates which did exactly show the several revenues of every nobleman, knights and gentlemen through the realm, and curiously collected by an uncle of mine which not long since was principal Secretary to the Queen: but it were too long in this simple discourse to set down the particularities thereof, but conferring these books together I find great alterations almost every year, so mutable are worldly things and worldly men's affairs; as namely the Earl of Oxford, who in the 1575 was rated at 12,000 a year sterling, within 2 following was vanished and no name of him found, having in that time prodigally spent and consumed all even to the selling of the stones timber and lead of his castles and houses, and yet he liveth and hath the first place amongst Earls, but the Queen is his gracious Mistress and gives him maintainance for his nobility sake, but (to say the truth) out of the Bishopric of Ely, which since his decay could never see other Bishops. And other, the Earl of Arundel, about the same time was reckoned not much inferior to him in state, and before him in dignity, and in one 6 months all was confiscated to the Queen for Treason. The other Earls some daily decay, some increase according to the course of the world, but that which I have noted by perusing many of the said books, and of the latter sort, is that still the total sum groweth much to one reckoning and that is to £100,000 rent yearly, accounting them all in gross to avoid prolixity. If a man would proportion this amongst 19 Earls and a Marquis it would be no great matter, to every one £5,000 rent, but as some exceed that much, so many come short of it.

The 39 Barons and 2 Viscounts do not much exceed that sum, their revenue is reckoned together to amount to £120,000 yearly.

The Bishops' revenues amount to about £22,500 yearly altogether, where of 3 of them, *viz.* Canterbury, Winchester and Ely, receive Rent per Annum betwixt £2,000 and £3,000, the rest betwixt £1,000 and £500 and some less.

The deans are the Chief ecclesiastical persons of every Cathedral Church next unto the Bishops whose command over the prebends and Canons is more than the Bishops, and their Commodities in letting the Church lands and bestowing the places and offices is very great, otherwise their revenue is not much, the best not exceeding £300 yearly, and the rest some 200 some 100 and many less, their whole revenue accounted through England amounted to the sum of £4,500 yearly or thereabouts.

But this must be understood, that the state of the Clergy is not altogether so bare as may perhaps be conjectured by the smallness of their revenue, for that they never raise nor rack their rents nor put out tenants as the Noblemen and gentlemen do to the uttermost penny; but do let their lands as they were let 100 years since, reserving to themselves and their successors some Commodities besides the bare Rent, as corn, muttons, beef, poultry or such like; but to say the Truth, their wings are well clipped of late by Courtiers and noblemen and some quite cut away, both feather, flesh and bone.

These are the States of the Nobility, both Clergy and lay, which are called *nobilitas maior*; there rests to touch those of the meaner nobility, which are termed *nobilitas minor* and are either knights, esquires, gentlemen, lawyers, professors and ministers, archdeacons, prebends, and vicars.

There are accounted to be in England about the number of 500 Knights as I have reckoned them, both by divers commissions of every several Shire remaining in the Chancery office for making of Justices of peace, of which Commission all Knights to be unless they be put by for religion of some particular disfavor. I reckon not among these my Lord of Essex's Knights . . . [but] such as are chief men in their Counties both for living and reputations, though many of them know scarcely what Knighthood means, but are made Knights for the Credit of their County and to induce them to live in a more honorable manner, both for their own Credit and the service of their Prince and Country, than otherwise perhaps they would do; these for the most part are men for living betwixt £1,000 and £2,000 yearly, and many of them equal the best Barons and come not much behind many Earls as I have divers *viz.* Sir John Petre, Sir John Harrington, Sir Nicholas Bacon and others, who are thought to be able to dispend yearly betwixt £5,000 and £7,000 of good land.

Those which we call Esquires are gentlemen whose ancestors are or have been Knights, or else they are the heirs and eldest of their houses and of some competent quantity of revenue fit to be called to office and authority in their County where they live; of these there are estimated to be in England, as I have seen by the book of musters of every several shire, to the number of 16,000 or thereabout, whereof there are of them in Commissions of the peace about 1,400 in every province—in some 40, in some 50, some 30, more or less; these are men in living betwixt £1,000 and £500 rent. Especially about London and the Counties adjoining, where their lands are set to the highest, he is not counted of any great reckoning unless he be betwixt 1,000 marks or £1,000, but Northward and far off a gentleman of good reputation may be content with 300 and 400 yearly. These are the elder brothers.

I cannot speak of the number of younger brothers, albeit I be one of the number myself, but for their estate there is no man hath better cause to know it, nor less cause to praise it; their state is of all stations for gentlemen most miserable, for if our fathers possess £1,000 or £2,000 yearly at his death he cannot give a foot of land to his younger children in inheritance, unless it be by lease for 21 years or for 3 lives, or unless his land be socage tenure whereof there is little, or gavelkind, such as is only in one province, in Kent, or else be purchased by himself and not descended. Then he may demise as much as he thinks good to his younger children, but such a fever hectic hath custom brought in and inured amongst fathers, and such fond desire they have to leave a great show of the stock of their house, though the branches be withered, that they will not do it, but my elder brother forsooth must be my master. He must have all, and all the rest that which the cat left on the malt heap, perhaps some small annuity during his life or what please our elder brother's worship to bestow upon us if we please him, and my mistress his wife. This I must confess doth us good someways, for it makes us industrious to apply ourselves to letters or to arms, whereby many times we become my master elder brothers' masters, or at least their betters in honor and reputation, while he lives at home like a fool and knows the sound of no other bell but his own.

This sort and order of people within these 40 or 50 years, since the practice of civil law hath been as it were wholly banished and abrogated, and since the clergy hath been trodden down by the taking away of church livings, and since the long continuance of peace hath bred an inward canker and rest in men's minds, the people doing nothing but jar and wrangle one with another, these lawyers by the ruins of neighbors' contentions are grown so great, so rich and so proud, that no other sort dare meddle with them; their number is so great now that, to say the truth, they can scarcely live one by another, the practice being drawn into a few hands of those which are most renowned, and all the rest live by pettifogging, seeking means to set their neighbors at variance whereby they may gain on both sides. This is one of the greatest inconveniences in the land, that the number of the Lawyers are so great they undo the country people and buy up all the lands that are to be sold, so that young gentlemen or others newly coming to their livings, some of them prying into his evidence will find the means to set him at variance with some other, or some other with him, by some pretense or quiddity, and when they have half consumed themselves in suit they are fain to sell their land to follow the process and pay their debts, and then that becomes a prey to lawyers.

For the greatness of some of them it is incredible, not to speak of the 12 chief judges and the multitude of sergeants, which are most of them counted men of £20,000 or £30,000 yearly, there is one at this day of a meaner degree, *viz.* the Queen's attorney, who, within this 10 year in my knowledge was not able to dispend above £100 a year and now by his own lands, his coins, and his office, he may dispend betwixt 12 and 14 thousand.

There are in number of Sergeants about 30, Counselors about 2,000, and as many attorneys, besides solicitors and pettifoggers an infinite number, there being no province, city, town, nor scarce village free from them, unless the Isle of Anglesey, which boast they never had lawyers nor foxes.

This State of all others [civil law lawyers] is the weakest, they having no means but by practice in the [Court of] Arches and other the [Arch]bishop of Canterbury's Courts, and some small practice in some other consistories. There are of them some 24 belonging to the Arches which gain well, and every Bishop hath a Chancellor that liveth in some good credit, the rest, God wot, are fain to become power Commissaries and officials of deans and archdeacons, which ride up and down the Country to keep Courts for correcting of bawdy matters etc. and take great pains for small gains.

Unless he chance to prove so rare man of conceit in State matters, and that hath good friends in the Court, and then perhaps he may be called to be a Master of the Requests or Secretary of State *sed non civis homini contingit adire Corinthum* [however, no citizen happens to enter Corinth (or the seat of power)], in my time and my father's and grandfather's there was but one Civilian Secretary of State.

The Queen's revenue is of divers sorts but may be reduced unto two kinds *viz.* ordinary or extraordinary. The Ordinary is that which ariseth of the Crown lands and Commodities and prerogatives of the same whether they be ancient or newly annexed, as by divers Dukedoms, Counties, Baronies, Seigniories, and Lands either for want of heir escheated or otherwise by offense, and this is uncertain and each year augmenteth or diminisheth.

. . . .

The one half only of the aforesaid revenue or there about was wont to be accounted the ancient revenue of the Crown, the rest is augmented in King Henry 8 his time and since by the Abbey and Church Lands and by confiscation and escheats.

Every Bishop, Dean, Archdeacon and spiritual person paid to the Queen in the first 2 years after he is installed in the benefice the full value of one year's profit thereof, according as every living is rated in a book which is called the Queen's book, albeit it be not to the full value as it is now worth perhaps by the 10th part, but as it was let 50 or 60 years since, when that book was made, and the rest of the years as long as he liveth he payeth the 10th part of the value, which was called the 10ths and those 10ths are very certain saving the 2 first years 10ths, if the person comes to his benefice, but if after he be installed in it he die within a month, his executors must pay first fruits. If an other take it and continue no longer, he must do the like, and so if 20 happen in one year; this is no doubt a great matter to the prince, I have in my remembrance known 4 persons die in a year so the Queen hath had 4 times the value of the benefice for that year: so might she do for Bishoprics but that, though they be so old before they be chosen, yet imagining they may live some months after they be installed, the Prince takes the present benefit of the vacation perhaps for half a year, a year, 2 or 3 or 4 or more, as experience tells of some that have been 12 years without a Bishop and at last grew dismembered.

There is besides levied upon the Clergy every year a subsidy which is granted at a Parliament [convocation] for 3 years, and every 3 years there is a new, so they never are without subsidy, this subsidy is perhaps 6 or 4 shillings in the pound of the value of their benefice.

Of all these the Queen receiveth, *communibus annis,* of the Clergy of England for first fruits, tenths and subsidies, as it appeareth by the accounts of every Bishop and Collector of the Spiritualities, to the sum of near a £100,000 sterling.

The Extraordinary revenue of the Crown, which is accounted casual and is some year more some year less, ariseth either (1) of the Wards or (2) of fines for leases of Lands, Woods or houses (3) sale of Woods, coals, minerals and such like (4) Gabelles and Customs (5) taxes and subsidies (6) confiscation of offenders' lands and goods for some capital crime (7) or else upon mulcts, forfeitures and amercements in the Courts of Justice or Exchequer.

The benefit of the Wards is reckoned one year with another to be worth to the Queen betwixt 20 and 30 thousand sterling, albeit the last Treasurer who was also Master of the Wards gained twice as much to him and his besides that which the Queen had, and his son 'tis thought, who hath it now, cometh not behind his father but rather makes much more to the Queen and himself—£30,000.

The fines for leases of Lands, of houses, or sales of Woods etc. have yielded by old books long since betwixt 15 and 20 thousand pounds, now every thing being enhanced it cannot be less than twice as much—£30,000.

The Gabelles, Customs, taxes and subsidies yield ordinarily—£40,000.

The subsidies and taxes being after 2ˢ 8ᵈ the pound of goods and 4ˢ lands.

The punishments pecuniary out of the Courts of Justice though often unjustly, these statutes and faults being punished which the law makers would willing have kept, are accounted to bring ordinarily to the Queen's Coffers—£20,000.

Of the Confiscations of Capital offenders of late there comes no great profit to the Queen, for as they happen nowadays seldom so when they happen (yea and before many times) one impudent courtier or other, for his great service done in standing an hour or 2 in a day bearheaded in the presence chamber, is ready to beg them, so they seldom or never come into the exchequer; but of this kind in the beginning of this Queen's time there was much profit come to the Crown by traitors, rebels, banished persons and voluntary exiles to the value of £50,000 yearly income, but as the Queen then was young and liberal, so she liberally bestowed them upon her servants, but her years hath now brought with it (the inseparable quality thereof) Nearness.

Thus the total sum of the Queen's revenue, besides those casualties whereof is no mention in the exchequer, amounteth to—£348,587.

This sum is raised upon the commodities and ancient benefits belonging to the Crown without ever gifts of friends, pensions of confederates for protection, merchandizing, usury, sale of honors and magistracies, tribute, or imposition of sale of any commodities within the realm, or any such grievous or intolerable taxations as are ordinary in (almost) all other Countries excepting Germany and Scotland; I make no doubt but if the Queen should set such impositions upon her subjects for every kind of thing, as other Princes do, she might well triple her revenue and yet weaken her Estate.

. . . .

The matters belonging to Estate consist either in the political government or administration of Justice.

The policy is either general or particular and again either apparent or secret, thirdly foreign or domestical.

The Laws are municipal and little according with the Civil [Roman] or any other save for the matter of inheritance of land it followeth those of Normandy. The rest of the ancient Laws were made by Edward the Confessor before the conquest and yet not [by] force, but being not very beneficial to the Prince's profit, by little and little they are brought out of use, and new statutes daily made according to every occasion, whereby the laws of England alter like the moon and for the ancient positive law it altered not in word but according to the judges' interpretation.

The Prince hath no authority to make laws nor to dispose of the Crown, that must be done by general consent of all in parliament; yea, the King's eldest son, though the Kingdoms be hereditary, shall not be crowned without the consent of the parliament after the death of his father. His privileges be to make war or peace, to create and choose the principal magistrates and officers throughout the whole kingdom unless in cities and Town, and to determine their offices when he pleases; for no officer of Court or Justice hath his place by inheritance, nor for longer time than *durante beneplacito reginae* [at the queen's pleasure], unless the sheriffs, which are only for a year. To pardon and give life to the condemned or to take away the life or member of any subject at her pleasure, and none other in all the Kingdom hath power of life and member but only the Prince, no not so much as to imprison or otherwise to punish any other, unless it be his servant, without express commission from the Queen.

Policies particular and apparent, some differing from other Countries and some concording, are either for benefit or security.

For benefit are these, and such like to these which follow, whereof I will, to avoid tediousness, touch some of the principal; divers straight Laws for the maintainance of Tillage throughout the land, which otherwise would be converted to sheep pasture, this also increaseth men for defense where as by sheep pasture a whole county may be kept by 2 or 3 shepherds without more men. Two divers other Laws for the preservation of fishing and keeping of 3 days in the week in eating fish, to the end that, there being much abundance of fish the land encompassed round with the sea and plentiful in rivers, the sparing of flesh the said 3 days flesh may also abound as much.

The keeping people from idleness by erecting in every shire houses of correction to set idle people on work, whereby they are forced to earn their livings, and much more, and the restraining of beggars, for if he is able to work he is taken into one of these houses, if not into an hospital, or else hath license given him to beg and crave the devotion of well disposed people by Commissioners which have authority, by appearance of their impotency, so to do.

The keeping low of the Clergy from being over rich, for that order of man have most damnified England by their profuse spending upon their pleasures, and upon idle serving men and other mothworms which depended upon them and eat the fat of the land and were no way profitable; for it is not long since you should not ride nor go through Country or Town but you should meet such troops of this priest's retinue as exceeded 100 or 200 of these caterpillars, neither fit for war nor other service, attending upon this pontifical crew, furnished and appointed in the best manner that might be; but since their wings were clipped shorter they hold opinion that England hath flourished more.

The cause that hath made the yeomanry in England so great I cannot rightly call a policy, because it was no matter invented and set down by authority for the bettering of that state of people, but rather by the subtlety of them and simplicity of gentlemen; for the yeomanry and mean people being servants and vassals to the gents., who are the possessors and lord of the lands and lordships and could not occupy all their lands themselves, but placed farmers therein, at a time when by reason of the great wars money was scarce, and all things else cheap, and so lands let at a small rent, the yeomen and farmers told the gentlemen, their landlords, that they could not be at so great charges to manure and inclose and improve their grounds, and repair and rectify their houses ruined by war, unless they would let them the said land, for some time; and if they would so do, and at a smaller rent, they would pay them some piece of money for a fine, and so much money yearly. The gentlemen, improvi-

dent of what should come after, and gladdened to have
money in hands, did let unto the said farmers all their Lands
and Lordships (saving their dwelling) after the rate aforesaid, some for 30, some 40 and some 50 some 200 years; soon
after the King, by reason of the want of money, altered the
coin and caused that which was before but 6^d to go for 12^d,
and after that again lessened it as much more, so that he
that was wont to pay but 3^d, which though it were all one
in value yet hereby it came to pass that he which paid before
1 pound weight in silver for his farm, paid now but a quarter,
and the yeoman at that time having most money, carrying it
to the Mint, had for every pound 4, paying for the minting,
and the King besides got a great mass of money by his said
mint. This device, and then the price of corn, cattle and all
farmers' Commodities increasing daily in price, and the gentleman who is generally inclined to great and vain expense
had no more than would keep his house and some small rent,
and therefore could not spend away prodigally much of the
wealth of the land because he hath no superfluity, and the
baser sort, which by this means had got the wealth had never
the inclination to spend much, approved the verse to be true
Crescit amor nummi quantum ipsa pecunia crescit [The love
of money grows as money itself grows], and so began England
so rich; but since these long leases are grown to expire, the
gentlemen by this begin to beware how to be so overreached.
Notwithstanding, some report that this was not done without
the policy of the King, who by this means weakened the
ability of his nobility and thereby clipped the wings of their
insolence.

There are divers other policies to enrich the merchants
and artisans by statute and laws made for their benefits, for
which they give the price a great sum of money and yearly
rent and also get them great wealth, whereby to be more
able to contribute to the subsidies, taxes and wars, as to a
certain Company of Merchants to Trade into such a part of
the World and for such and such Commodities, to another
Company another, the 3^d a 3^d, and so many Companies by
license under the Great Seal of England and prohibiting all
others save such a Company or such particular persons,
whereby a few getting the Trade but of some country or com-

modity, which themselves thinks best to sue for, in a short time become very rich. For the benefit of artisans and other Trades there are divers statutes, as the statutes prohibiting any thing wrought in metal to be brought into the Land, whereby the more excelling workmanship of strangers therein may not put English workmen out of request nor take their Trade and benefit from them; and that statute that no stranger, neither master nor apprentice, may be of divers Trades as workers in metal, tanner, boyers[3] and such like, and for fishmongers that no stranger may bring any fish into our coasts, especially Herrings, nor Englishmen buy them out of strangers' ships, that thereby the fishermen may have utterance for their fish, and also for their increase of fishermen, which may after, if occasion serve, be employed in the Queen's ships in time of war; but that confederation of those statutes belongeth rather to Policy which concerns security and defense of the Realm.

They have one policy which all the world cries out of which, notwithstanding, is but new and learned from the Hollanders: *viz.*, to desire to continue in wars with Spain, and Enmity with some other Countries; that having so great store of shipping mariners and force by sea, which otherwise would lie idle and decay, by this in robbing and taking purchase by sea they do greatly enrich the Queen, the Admiral and themselves; for the Queen hath the half, the Admiral the 10th, and themselves the rest; and also do thereby increase both in skill and in number. It is incredible what treasure hath been brought into England by prize and from the Indies within this 12 or 16 years.

By reason there is little store of silver and gold mines in the land, and those which be are not sought for nor tried, therefore as is well known to all that have travelled thither, that it is not lawful for any man to carry any gold or silver out of the realm without special favor and license; and that is obtained by few or none save only 40 shillings, unless some travellers which upon suit may have license to carry so much as will conveniently bear their charges according to their

[3] Boyers were Flemish warships. In another version of Wilson's essay the word "copers" was used in place of "boyers." He probably meant "cooper."

Estates to the places where they go. Now this is a great benefit to the Queen, for the infinite number of strangers, and our own merchants that daily bring in mighty sums of foreign Coin, all which cometh as bullion to the mint to be new minted, whereof the Queen hath the 20th part, besides the officers' fees, and where so much is brought in and little or none carried out in respect there must needs be great store of Treasure, besides the benefit which merchants get for exchanging, which is not a little.

The first and chiefest is that supreme and awful authority which the Prince hath over all subjects great and mean, no man, not the greatest in the whole land, having more authority than the meanest but as he deriveth it from the Prince by Commission, and thereby none able to make a head but where the Prince's name goeth, nor daring to resist the Prince's Commandment, the Constitution of the law having bred such a natural obedience in all; unless some upon presumption of her favor borroweth a little, which he will surely pay clearly for if he have any secret enemies to urge against him, and to make the Queen look through a pair of spectacles and make the fault seem greater than it is, as hath been lately approved in the actions of some of the greatest.

There are some good Laws made to avoid emulation amongst noblemen and gentlemen and also factions which are too tedious to repeat.

The main point is the weakening of the domestic enemies, for whereas the land is divided into 4 sorts of persons *viz.* (1) religious Protestants, (2) politic Protestants, (3) religious Papists, (4) politic Papists, the first whereof were only found to be sure to the state, the other 3 dangerous, they have for the diminishing and weakening of these 3 latter made laws that every man that hath voice in the Parliament or any state of possession in the land shall take his corporal oath for the maintainance of the religion now established, and never consent to the altering thereof, nor admitting of any successor which shall incline to the contrary; now where the politic Protestant did favor the Papist for fear of alteration of this religion as one that places his *summum bonum* in this life, and therefore to it only hath regard, and whereas the politic Papist in like sort hoped for the alteration of this religion, by this means both the fear and hope is so cut of that the number of these 2 sorts are much diminished, and daily doth decrease. For the last sort they have bereaved them of a great part of their living, the Queen taking their Lands and letting them to whom she pleased, thereby to take from them the power and command of their men and tenants, and besides leaveth them neither arms offensive nor defensive that can do any great hurt, and for their persons confineth them to certain places which they must not pass without license, to avoid conventicles and devising amongst themselves, and these that have no lands nor will yield to become confirmable they are either imprisoned or banished.

There is no person neither stranger nor subject that may depart out of the realm without license of the Queen or the Privy Council or the Warden of the Cinq ports, nor enter without being examined by Commissioners for that purpose in every port Town, whereby few dangerous persons for practice against the Country can depart, and for the rest it skilleth not; besides all the letters that are carried out are opened and read, unless they be such as they suspect not; and such as are brought in or sealed up by the officers of the post, and sent by the Lord Warden by another trusty messenger, because there have been found letters of practice and Treason which have been brought by bad persons directed in the back side to privy Counselors, which letters notwithstanding were to be delivered to Papists and other bad members.

They suffer very few to be acquainted with matters of state for fear of divulging it, whereby their practices are subject to be revealed, and therefore they will suffer few to rise to places of reputation that are skillful or studious of matters of policy, but hold them low and far off so that the greatest politicians that rule most will not have about them other than base penclerks, that can do nothing but write as they are bidden, or some mechanical dunce that cannot conceive his Master's drifts and policies, for if they have Lynx's eyes they must look into their actions. This was first brought by the old Treasurer [Lord Burghley] of whom it was written that he was like an aged tree that lets none grow which near him planted be, and it is well followed by his son at this day and by other that are *eiusdem farinae* [of the same kind].

In all great offices and places of charge they do always place 2 persons of contrary factions and that are bred of such causes, or grown to such greatness, as they are ever irreconcilable, to the end, each having his enemy's eye to overlook him, it may make him look more warily to his charge, and that if any body should incline to any unfaithfulness in such charges of importance as concern the public safety, it might be spied before it be brought to any dangerous head; which cannot be done all at once without many precedent actions conducing thereunto, whereof some must needs be perceived by a watchful enemy, than which nothing is more vigilant and piercing. This is seen always in the Tower, the place of most trust, where the Lieutenant and Steward, Master of the Ordinance and Lieutenant of the same, have been ever in my remembrance vowed enemies, and this is too apparent in the Deputies of Ireland and Governor of Munster at this time and heretofore.

They are persuaded, according to the opinion of the Lacedemonians, that fortifying of towns doth more hurt than good to their preservation, in that it makes the people either cowardly or revolting, and besides if the Enemy land and gain them, nothing more damageable; it is true that before these new devices of artillery and such like of that kind, sanpices, petards, rams and such like, there were many strong Towns in England after the manner of strength we accounted in those days, but since no force is found able to withstand the subtlety of man's invention they are not of the opinion that walls and fortifications can help them, but that the best fortification is on the fortitude and faithfulness of subjects' hearts.

2. *OCEANA by James Harrington*

Henceforth the country-lives, and great tables of the nobility, which no longer nourished veins that would bleed for them, were fruitless and loathsome till they changed the air, and of princes became courtiers; where their revenues, never to have been exhausted by beef and mutton, were found narrow, whence followed racking of rents, and at length sale of lands: the riddance through the statute of alienations being rendered far more quick and facile than formerly it had been through the new invention of entails.

To this it happened, that Coraunus [Henry VIII] the successor of that king, dissolving the abbeys, brought with the declining state of the nobility so vast a prey to the industry of the people, that the balance of the commonwealth was too apparently in the popular party, to be unseen by the wise council of queen Parthenia [Elizabeth], who converting her reign through the perpetual lovetricks that passed between her and her people into a kind of romance, wholly neglected the nobility. And by these degrees came the house of commons to raise that head, which since has been so high and formidable to their princes, that they have looked pale upon those assemblies. Nor was there any thing now wanting to the destruction of the throne, but that the people, not apt to see their own strength, should be put to feel it; when a prince, [Charles I] as stiff in disputes as the nerve of monarchy was grown slack, received that unhappy encouragement from his clergy which became his utter ruin, while trusting more to their logic than the rough philosophy of his parliament, it came to an irreparable breach; for the house of peers, which alone had stood in this gap, now sinking down between the king and the commons, showed that Crassus was dead, and the *isthmus* broken.[1] But a monarchy divested of its nobility, has no refuge under heaven but an army. Wherefore the dissolution of this government caused the war, not the war the dissolution of this government.

Of the king's success with his arms it is not necessary to give any further account, than that they proved as ineffectual as his nobility; but without a nobility or an army (as has been shown) there can be no monarchy. Wherefore what is there in nature that can arise out of these ashes, but a popular government, or a new monarchy to be erected by the victorious army?

To erect a monarchy, be it never so new, unless like

[1] Harrington is referring to Marcus Licinius Crassus, one of the first triumvirate with Caesar and Pompey. Here he represents the House of Lords, who in turn provide the link (*isthmus*) between king and Commons.

[Hobbes's] Leviathan you can hang it, as the country-fellow speaks, by geometry, (for what else is it to say, that every other man must give up his will to the will of this one man without any other foundation?) it must stand upon old principles, that is, upon a nobility or an army planted on a due balance of dominion. *Aut viam inveniam aut faciam* [either find a way or make a way], was an adage of Caesar; and there is no standing for a monarchy unless it finds this balance, or makes it. If it finds it, the work's done to its hand: for, where there is inequality of estates, there must be inequality of power; and where there is inequality of power, there can be no commonwealth. To make it, the sword must extirpate out of dominion all other roots of power, and plant an army upon that ground. An army may be planted nationally or provincially. To plant it nationally, it must be in one of the four ways mentioned, that is, either monarchically in part, as the *Roman beneficiarii*; or monarchically, in the whole, as the *Turkish timariots*;[2] aristocratically, that is, by earls and barons, as the *Neustrians* were planted by Turbo [William the Conqueror]; or democratically, that is, by equal lots, as the Israelitish army in the land of *Canaan* by Joshua. In every one of these ways there must not only be confiscations, but confiscations to such a proportion as may answer to the work intended.

To conclude, *Oceana*, or any other nation of no greater extent, must have a competent nobility, or is altogether incapable of monarchy: for where there is equality of estates, there must be equality of power: and where there is equality of power, there can be no monarchy.

To come then to the generation of the commonwealth; it has been shown how through the ways and means used by Panurgus [Henry VII] to abase the nobility, and so to mend that flaw which we have asserted to be incurable in this kind of constitution, he suffered the balance to fall into the power of the people, and so broke the government: but the balance being in the people, the commonwealth (though they do not see it) is already in the nature of them. There wants nothing else but time (which is slow and dangerous) or art (which

[2] Timariots were holders of military fiefs in Turkey.

would be more quick and secure) for the bringing of those native arms (wherewithal they are found already) to resist they know not how every thing that opposes them, to such maturity as may fix them upon their own strength and bottom.

But whereas this art is prudence; and that part of prudence which regards the present work, is nothing else but the skill of raising such superstructures of government, as are natural to the known foundations: they never mind the foundation, but through certain animosities (wherewith by striving one against another they are infected) or through freaks, by which, not regarding the course of things, nor how they conduce to their purpose, they are given to building in the air, come to be divided and subdivided into endless parties and factions, both civil and ecclesiastical: which briefly to open, I shall first speak of the people in general, and then of their divisions.

A People (says Machiavelli) that is corrupt, is not capable of a commonwealth. But in showing what a corrupt people is, he has either involved himself, or me; nor can I otherwise come out of the labyrinth, than by saying, the balance altering a people, as to the foregoing government, must of necessity be corrupt: but corruption in this sense signifies no more than that the corruption of one government (as in natural bodies) is the generation of another. Wherefore if the balance alters from monarchy, the corruption of the people in this case is that which makes them capable of a commonwealth. But whereas I am not ignorant, that the corruption which he means is in manners, this also is from the balance. For the balance leading from monarchical into popular, abates the luxury of the nobility, and, enriching the people, brings the government from a more private to a more public interest; which coming nearer, as has been shown, to justice and right reason, the people upon a like alteration is so far from such a corruption of manners, as should render them incapable of a commonwealth, that of necessity they must thereby contract such a reformation of manners as will bear no other kind of government. On the other side, where the balance changes from popular to oligarchical or monarchical, the public interest, with the reason and justice included in the same, becomes more private; luxury is introduced in the room of temperance, and servitude in that of freedom; which causes such a corruption of manners both in the nobility and people, as, by the example of *Rome* in the time of the *Triumvirs*, is more at large discovered by the author to have been altogether incapable of a commonwealth.

But the balance of *Oceana* changing quite contrary to that of *Rome*, the manners of the people were not thereby corrupted, but on the contrary adapted to a commonwealth. For differences of opinion in a people not rightly informed of their balance, or a division into parties (while there is not any common ligament of power sufficient to reconcile or hold them) is no sufficient proof of corruption. Nevertheless, seeing this must needs be matter of scandal and danger, it will not be amiss, in showing what were the parties, to show what were their errors.

The parties into which this nation was divided, were temporal, or spiritual: and the temporal parties were especially two, the one *royalists*, the other *republicans*: each of which asserted their different causes, either out of prudence or ignorance, out of interest or conscience.

For prudence, either that of the ancients is inferior to the modern (which we have hitherto been setting face to face, that any one may judge) or that of the royalist must be inferior to that of the commonwealthsman. And for interest, taking the commonwealthsman to have really intended the public (for otherwise he is a hypocrite and the worst of men) that of the royalist must of necessity have been more private. Wherefore the whole dispute will come upon matter of conscience: and this, whether it be urged by the right of kings, the obligation of former laws, or of the oath of allegiance, is absolved by the balance.

For if the right of kings were as immediately derived from the breath of God as the life of man, yet this excludes not death and dissolution. But, that the dissolution of the late monarchy was as natural as the death of a man, has been already shown. Wherefore it remains with the royalists to discover by what reason or experience it is possible for a monarchy to stand upon a popular balance; or, the balance being popular, as well the oath of allegiance, as all other monarchical laws, imply an impossibility, and are therefore void.

To the commonwealthsman I have no more to say, but that if he excludes any party, he is not truly such; nor shall ever found a commonwealth upon the natural principle of the same, which is justice. And the royalist for having not opposed a commonwealth in *Oceana* (where the laws were so ambiguous that they might be eternally disputed, and never reconciled) can neither be justly for that cause excluded from his full and equal share in the government; nor prudently, for this reason, that a commonwealth consisting of a party will be in perpetual labor of her own destruction: whence it was that the *Romans* having conquered the *Albans,* incorporated them with equal right into the commonwealth. And if the royalists be *flesh of your flesh,* and nearer of blood than were the *Albans* to the *Romans,* you being also both Christians, the argument's the stronger. Nevertheless there is no reason that a commonwealth should any more favor a party remaining in fixed opposition against it, than Brutus did his own sons. But if it fixes them upon that opposition, it is its own fault, not theirs; and this is done by excluding them. Men that have equal possessions, and the same security for their estates and their liberties that you have, have the same cause with you to defend both: but if you will be trampling, they fight for liberty, though for monarchy; and you for tyranny, though under the name of a commonwealth: the nature of orders in a government rightly instituted being void of all jealousy, because, let the parties which it embraces be what they will, its orders are such as they neither would resist if they could, nor could if they would, as has been partly already shown, and will appear more at large by the following model.

The parties that are spiritual are of more kinds than I need mention; some for a national religion, and others for liberty of conscience, with such animosity on both sides, as if these two could not consist together, and of which I have already sufficiently spoken, to show, that indeed the one cannot well subsist without the other. But they of all the rest are the most dangerous, who, holding that the saints must govern, go about to reduce the commonwealth to a party, as well for

the reasons already shown, as that their pretences are against
Scripture, where the saints are commanded to submit to the
higher powers, and to be subject to the ordinance of man.
And that men, pretending under the notion of saints or
religion to civil power, have hitherto never failed to dishonor
that profession, the world is full of examples, whereof I shall
confine myself at present only to a couple, the one of old,
the other of new *Rome*.

In old *Rome* the patricians or nobility pretending to be
the godly party, were questioned by the people for ingrossing
all the magistracies of that commonwealth, and had nothing
to say why they did so, but that magistracy required a kind
of holiness which was not in the people: at which the people
were filled with such indignation as had come to cutting of
throats, if the nobility had not immediately laid by the inso-
lency of that plea; which nevertheless when they had done,
the people for a long time after continued to elect no other
but patrician magistrates.

The example of new *Rome* in the rise and practise of the
hierarchy (too well known to require any further illustration)
is far more immodest.

This has been the course of nature: and when it has pleased
or shall please God to introduce any thing that is above the
course of nature, he will, as he has always done, confirm it
by miracle; for so in his prophecy of the reign of Christ
upon earth, he expressly promises: seeing that *the souls of
them that were beheaded for* Jesus, *shall be seen to live and
reign with him*; which will be an object of sense, the rather,
because the rest of the dead are not to live again till the
thousand years be finished. And it is not lawful for men to
persuade us that a thing already is, though there be no such
object of our sense, which God has told us shall not be till
it be an object of our sense.

The saintship of a people as to government, consists in the
election of magistrates fearing God, and hating covetousness,
and not in their confining themselves, or being confined to
men of this or that party or profession. It consists in making
the most prudent and religious choice they can; yet not in
trusting to men, but, next God, to their own orders. *Give us
good men, and they will make us good laws*, is the maxim

of a demagog, and is (through the alteration which is commonly perceivable in men, when they have power to work their own wills) exceeding fallible. But *give us good orders, and they will make us good men*, is the maxim of a legislator, and the most infallible in the politics.

3. BEHEMOTH *by Thomas Hobbes*

A. If those soldiers had been, as they and all other of his subjects ought to have been, at his Majesty's command, the peace and happiness of the three kingdoms had continued as it was left by King James. But the people were corrupted generally, and disobedient persons esteemed the best patriots.

B. But sure there were men enough, besides those that were ill-affected, to have made an army sufficient to have kept the people from uniting into a body able to oppose him [the King].

A. Truly, I think, if the King had had money, he might have had soldiers enough in England. For there were very few of the common people that cared much for either of the causes, but would have taken any side for pay or plunder. But the King's treasury was very low, and his enemies, that pretended the people's ease from taxes, and other specious things, had the command of the purses of the city of London, and of most cities and corporate towns in England, and of many particular persons besides.

B. But how came the people to be so corrupted? And what kind of people were they that did so seduce them?

A. The seducers were of divers sorts. One sort were ministers; ministers, as they called themselves, of Christ; and sometimes, in their sermons to the people, God's ambassadors; pretending to have a right from God to govern every one his parish, and their assembly the whole nation.

Secondly, there were a very great number, though not comparable to the other, which notwithstanding that the Pope's power in England, both temporal and ecclesiastical, had been by Act of Parliament abolished, did still retain a belief that we ought to be governed by the Pope, whom they pretended to be the vicar of Christ, and, in the right of Christ, to be the governor of all Christian people. And these were known by the name of Papists; as the ministers I mentioned before, were commonly called Presbyterians.

Thirdly, there were not a few, who in the beginning of the troubles were not discovered, but shortly after declared themselves for a liberty in religion, and those of different opinions one from another. Some of them, because they would have all congregations free and independent upon one another, were called Independents. Others that held baptism to infants, and such as understood not into what they are baptized, to be ineffectual, were called therefore Anabaptists. Others that held that Christ's kingdom was at this time to begin upon the earth, were called Fifth-monarchy-men; besides divers other sects, as Quakers, Adamites, &c., whose names and peculiar doctrines I do not well remember. And these were the enemies which arose against his Majesty from the private interpretation of the Scripture, exposed to every man's scanning in his mother-tongue.

Fourthly, there were an exceeding great number of men of the better sort, that had been so educated, as that in their youth having read the books written by famous men of the ancient Grecian and Roman commonwealths concerning their polity and great actions; in which books the popular government was extolled by that glorious name of liberty, and monarchy disgraced by the name of tyranny; they became thereby in love with their forms of government. And out of these men were chosen the greatest part of the House of Commons, or if they were not the greatest part, yet by advantage of their eloquence, were always able to sway the rest.

Fifthly, the city of London and other great towns of trade, having in admiration the prosperity of the Low Countries after they had revolted from their monarch, the King of Spain, were inclined to think that the like change of government here, would to them produce the like prosperity.

Sixthly, there were a very great number that had either wasted their fortunes, or thought them too mean for the good parts they thought were in themselves; and more there were, that had able bodies, but saw no means how honestly to get their bread. These longed for a war, and hoped to maintain themselves hereafter by the lucky choosing of a party to side with, and consequently did for the most part serve under them that had greatest plenty of money.

Lastly, the people in general were so ignorant of their duty, as that not one perhaps of ten thousand knew what right any man had to command him, or what necessity there was of King or Commonwealth, for which he was to part with his money against his will; but thought himself to be so much master of whatsoever he possessed, that it could not be taken from him upon any pretence of common safety without his own consent. King, they thought, was but a title of the highest honour, which gentleman, knight, baron, earl, duke, were but steps to ascend to, with the help of riches; they had no rule of equity, but precedents and custom; and he was thought wisest and fittest to be chosen for a Parliament, that was most averse to the granting of subsidies or other public payments.

B. In such a constitution of people, methinks, the King is already ousted of his government, so as they need not have taken arms for it. For I cannot imagine how the King should come by any means to resist them.

A. There was indeed very great difficulty in the business. But of that point you will be better informed in the pursuit of this narration.

SEEDS OF CONFLICT

A. POLITICAL

Even though from Harrington to the present there has
been the belief that the Revolution was caused by the
changes in the economic and social balance of society, it is
still a fact that those who participated in these events in the
Long Parliament and in the service of the king and the
church thought they were in the throes of a constitutional
and religious conflict. In this section we first look at the
political or constitutional conflict and then at the religious.

The debates in the Long Parliament do not reveal any
significant defense of the king or of his views on divine right
monarchy. Therefore, the following selections are limited to
the views of the opposition. Before the outbreak of war this
opposition included future Royalists as well as Parliamentarians. Defense of monarchy would wait until after the war
began, by which time the Royalists would be fighting for a
reformed monarchy, not that espoused by James I in his
True Law of Free Monarchy.

The sudden dissolution of the Short Parliament in May
1640 forced the king to resort once again to extraordinary
devices to secure funds. But these were not sufficient to fi-
nance the army needed to repel the Scots who invaded
northern England in the summer. The opposition in the
Short Parliament demanded a new parliament and twelve
peers led by Essex, Bedford, Brooke, Saye and Sele, and Warwick sent a petition to the king calling for a new parliament
[3]. During the first week of the Long Parliament, before
any specific actions were taken, Pym made a speech that

summed up the grievances of most members and the country [2].

John Milton's *Tenure of Kings and Magistrates* [1] was written on the eve of the king's trial and published soon after, and was intended as a justification for that trial. It is presented here, out of order chronologically, since it does represent, philosophically, the antithesis of divine right monarchy. While no one in 1640 spoke the words that Milton later used, *The Tenure of Kings* does reflect the logical conclusion to which the claims to parliamentary sovereignty pointed.

The *Grand Remonstrance* [4] and *The Nineteen Propositions* [5] are the two most significant documents of the Long Parliament. They give in concrete terms the parliamentary position at the point where verbal warfare was turned into a clash of arms. In turn they served the king's interest by providing a reason for the conservatives and many of the moderates to wash their hands of the "extremists" and rally to the king. Through these two documents Pym provided Charles with a party.

1. THE TENURE OF KINGS by John Milton

No man who knows ought, can be so stupid to deny that all men naturally were born free, being the image and resemblance of God himself, and were by privilege above all the creatures, born to command and not to obey: and that they lived so. 'Till from the root of *Adam's* transgression, falling among themselves to do wrong and violence, and foreseeing that such courses must needs tend to the destruction of them all, they agreed by common league to bind each other from mutual injury, and jointly to defend themselves against any that gave disturbance or opposition to such agreement. Hence came Cities, Towns and Commonwealths. And because no faith in all was found sufficiently binding, they saw it needful to ordain some authority, that might restrain by force and punishment what was violated against peace and common right. This authority and power of self-defense and preservation being originally and naturally in every one

of them, and unitedly in them all, for ease, for order, and
lest each man should be his own partial Judge, they communicated and derived either to one, whom for the eminence
of his wisdom and integrity they chose above the rest, or to
more than one whom they thought of equal deserving: the
first was called a King; the other Magistrates. Not to be their
Lords and Masters (though afterward those names in some
places were given voluntarily to such as had been Authors
of inestimable good to the people) but to be their Deputies
and Commissioners, to execute, by virtue of their entrusted
power, that justice which else every man by the bond of
nature and of Covenant must have executed for himself, and
for one another. And to him that shall consider well why
among free Persons, one man by civil right should bear authority and jurisdiction over another, no other end or reason
can be imaginable. These for a while governed well, and with
much equity decided all things at their own arbitrement:
till the temptation of such a power left absolute in their
hands perverted them at length to injustice and partiality.
Then did they who now by trial had found the danger and
inconveniences of committing arbitrary power to any, invent
Laws either framed, or consented to by all, that should confine and limit the authority of whom they chose to govern
them: that so man, of whose failing they had proof, might
no more rule over them, but law and reason abstracted as
much as might be from personal errors and frailties. While
as the Magistrate was set above the people, so the Law was
set above the Magistrate. When this would not serve, but
that the Law was either not executed, or misapplied, they
were constrained from that time, the only remedy left them,
to put conditions and take Oaths from all Kings and Magistrates at their first instalment to do impartial justice by Law:
who upon those terms, and no other, received Allegiance from
the people, that is to say, bond or Covenant to obey them
in execution of those Laws which they the people had themselves made, or assented to. And this ofttimes with express
warning, that if the King or Magistrate proved unfaithful to
his trust, the people would be disengaged. They added also
Counselors and Parliaments, nor to be only at his beck, but
with him or without him, at set times, or at all times, when

any danger threatened to have care of the public safety. Therefore saith *Claudius Seysell* a French Statesman, *The Parliament was set as a bridle to the King;* which I instance rather, not because our English Lawyers have not said the same long before, but because that French Monarchy is granted by all to be a far more absolute than ours. That this and the rest of what hath hitherto been spoken is most true, might be copiously made appear throughout all Stories Heathen and Christian; even of those Nations where Kings and Emperors have sought means to abolish all ancient memory of the People's right by their encroachments and usurpations. But I spare long insertions, appealing to the known constitutions of both the latest Christian Empires in Europe, the Greek and German, besides the French, Italian, Aragonian, English, and not least the Scottish Histories: not forgetting this only by the way, that *William* the Norman though a Conqueror, and not unsworn at his Coronation, was compelled the second time to take oath at St. *Albans,* ere the people would be brought to yield obedience.

It being thus manifest that the power of Kings and Magistrates is nothing else, but what is only derivative, transferred and committed to them in trust from the People, to the Common good of them all, in whom the power yet remains fundamentally, and cannot be taken from them, without a violation of their natural birthright, and seeing that from hence *Aristotle* and the best of Political writers have defined a King, him who governs to the good and profit of his People, and not for his own ends, it follows from necessary causes, that the Titles of Sovereign Lord, natural Lord, and the like, are either arrogancies, or flatteries, not admitted by Emperors and Kings of best note, and disliked by the Church both of Jews, *Isai.* 26. 13. and ancient Christians, as appears by *Tertullian* and others. Although generally the people of Asia, and with them the Jews also, especially since the time they chose a King against the advice and counsel of God, are noted by wise Authors much inclinable to slavery.

· · · ·

We may pass therefore hence to Christian times. And first our Savior himself, how much he favored Tyrants, and how

much intended they should be found or honored among
Christians, declares his mind not obscurely; accounting their
absolute authority no better than Gentilism, yea though they
flourished it over with the splendid name of Benefactors;
charging those that would be his Disciples to usurp no such
dominion; but that they who were to be of most authority
among them, should esteem themselves Ministers and Servants to the public. *Matt.* 20. 25. *The Princes of the Gentiles
exercise Lordship over them,* and *Mark* 10. 42. *They that
seem to rule,* saith he, either slighting or accounting them
no lawful rulers, *but ye shall not be so, but the greatest
among you shall be your Servant.* And although he himself
were the meekest, and came on earth to be so, yet to a Tyrant
we hear him not vouchsafe an humble word: but *Tell that
Fox, Luke.* 13. So far we ought to be from thinking that
Christ and his Gospel should be made a Sanctuary for Tyrants from justice, to whom his Law before never gave such
protection. And wherefore did his Mother the Virgin *Mary*
give such praise to God in her prophetic song, that he had
now by the coming of Christ *Cut down Dynasties or proud
Monarchs from the throne,* if the Church, when God manifests his power in them to do so, should rather choose all
misery and vassalage to serve them, and let them still sit on
their potent seats to be adored for doing mischief. Surely it
is not for nothing that tyrants by a kind of natural instinct
both hate and fear none more than the true Church and
Saints of God, as the most dangerous enemies and subverters
of Monarchy, though indeed of tyranny; hath not this been
the perpetual cry of Courtiers, and Court Prelates? whereof
no likelier cause can be alleged, but that they well discerned
the mind and principles of most devout and zealous men,
and indeed the very discipline of Church, tending to the
dissolution of all tyranny. No marvel then if since the faith
of Christ received, in purer or impurer times, to depose a
King and put him to death for Tyranny, hath been accounted
so just and requisite, that neighbor Kings have both upheld
and taken part with subjects in the action. And *Ludovicus
Pius,* himself an Emperor, and Son of *Charles* the great,
being made Judge, *Du Haillan* is my author, between *Mile-
gast* King of the *Vultzes* and his Subjects who had deposed

him, gave his verdict for the Subjects, and for him whom they had chosen in his room. Note here that the right of electing whom they please is, by the impartial testimony of an Emperor, in the people. For, said he, *A just Prince ought to be preferred before an unjust, and the end of government before the prerogative.* And *Constantinus Leo,* another Emperor, in the *Byzantine* Laws saith, *that the end of a King is for the general good, which he not performing is but the counterfeit of a King.* And to prove that some of our own Monarchs have acknowledged that their high office exempted them not from punishment, they had the Sword of St. *Edward* borne before them by an officer who was called Earl of the Palace, even at the times of their highest pomp and solemnities, to mind them, saith *Matthew Paris,* the best of our Historians, that if they erred, the Sword had power to restrain them. And what restraint the Sword comes to at length, having both edge and point, if any *Skeptic* will doubt, let him feel. It is also affirmed from diligent search made in our ancient books of Law, that the Peers and Barons of England had a legal right to judge the King: which was the cause most likely, for it could be no slight cause, that they were called his Peers, or equals. This however may stand immovable, so long as man hath to deal with no better than man; that if our Law judge all men to the lowest by their Peers, it should in all equity ascend also, and judge the highest. And so much I find both in our own and foreign Story, that Dukes, Earls, and Marqueses were at first not hereditary, not empty and vain titles, but names of trust and office, and with the office ceasing, as induces me to be of opinion, that every worthy man in Parliament, for the word Baron imports no more, might for the public good be thought a fit Peer and judge of the King; without regard had to petty caveats, and circumstances, the chief impediment in high affairs, and ever stood upon most by circumstantial men. Whence doubtless our Ancestors who were not ignorant with what rights either Nature or ancient Constitution had endowed them, when Oaths both at Coronation, and renewed in Parliament would not serve, thought it no way illegal to depose and put to death their tyrannous Kings. Insomuch that the Parliament drew up a charge against *Richard the second,* and the

Commons requested to have judgment decreed against him, that the realm might not be endangered. And *Peter Martyr* a Divine of foremost rank, on the third of *Judges* approves their doings. Sir *Thomas Smith*[1] also a Protestant and a Statesman, in his *Commonwealth of England*, putting the question whether it be lawful to rise against a Tyrant, answers that the vulgar judge of it according to the event, and the learned according to the purpose of them that do it. But far before these days, *Gildas*[2] the most ancient of all our Historians, speaking of those times wherein the Roman Empire decaying quitted and relinquished what right they had by Conquest to this Island, and resigned it all into the peoples' hands, testifies that the people thus re-invested with their own original right, about the year 446, both elected them Kings, whom they thought best (the first Christian British Kings that ever reigned here since the Romans) and by the same right, when they apprehended cause, usually deposed and put them to death. This is the most fundamental and ancient tenure that any King of *England* can produce or pretend to; in comparison of which, all other titles and pleas are but of yesterday. If any object that *Gildas* condemns the Britons for so doing, the answer is as ready; that he condemns them no more for so doing than he did before for choosing such, for saith he, *They anointed them Kings, not of God, but such as were more bloody than the rest*. Next he condemns them not at all for deposing or putting them to death, but for doing it over hastily, without trial or well examining the cause, and for electing others worse in their room. Thus we have here both domestic and most ancient examples that the people of Britain have deposed and put to death their Kings in those primitive Christian times. And to couple reason with example, if the Church in all ages, Primitive, Romish, or Protestant, held it ever no less their duty than the power of their Keys, though without ex-

[1] Secretary of State under Elizabeth I. His *Commonwealth of England* was the best and most influential treatise on English government in the sixteenth century.

[2] Gildas' (516?–570?) *History* and *Letters* are among the most useful literary sources for our knowledge of early Anglo-Saxon England.

press warrant of Scripture, to bring indifferently both King and Peasant under the utmost rigor of their Canons and Censures Ecclesiastical, even to the smiting him with a final excommunion, if he persist impenitent, what hinders but that the temporal Law both may and ought, though without a special Text or precedent, extend with like indifference the civil Sword, to the cutting off without exemption him that capitally offends. Seeing that justice and Religion are from the same God, and works of justice ofttimes more acceptable.

. . . .

There is nothing that so actually makes a King of *England*, as rightful possession and Supremacy *in all causes both civil and Ecclesiastical:* and nothing that so actually makes a Subject of *England*, as those two Oaths of Allegiance and Supremacy observed *without equivocating, or any mental reservation.* Out of doubt then when the King shall command things already constituted in Church, or State, obedience is the true essence of a subject, either to do, if it be lawful, or if he hold the thing unlawful, to submit to that penalty which the Law imposes, so long as he intends to remain a Subject. Therefore when the people or any part of them shall rise against the King and his authority executing the Law in any thing established civil or Ecclesiastical, I do not say it is rebellion, if the thing commanded though established be unlawful, and that they sought first all due means of redress (and no man is further bound to Law) but I say it is an absolute renouncing both of Supremacy and Allegiance, which in one word is an actual and total deposing of the King, and the setting up of another supreme authority over them.

2. MASTER PYM'S SPEECH IN PARLIAMENT, 1640

The distempers of this Kingdom are well known, they need not repetition. For though we have good Laws, yet they want their execution; or if they are executed, it is in a wrong sense. I shall endeavor to apply a remedy to the breaches that are made, and to that end, I shall discover first the quality of the disease.

First, There is a design to alter Law and Religion: the parties that effect this, are Papists, who are obliged by a maxim in their doctrine, that they are not only bound to maintain their Religion, but also to extirpate all others.

The second is their Hierarchy which cannot amount to the height they aim at, without a breach of our Law. To which their Religion necessarily joins, that if the one stands, the other must fall.

Thirdly, Agents and Pensioners to foreign States, who see we cannot comply to them, if we maintain our Religion established, which is contrary to theirs, here they intend chiefly the Spanish white gold works which are of most effect.

Fourthly, Favorites, such as for promotion prize not conscience, and such are our Judges spiritual, and temporal; such are also some of our Councilors of State. All these, though severed, yet in their contrivements they aim at one end, and to this they walk on four feet.

First, Discountenancing of Preachers, and virtuous men, they persecute under the law of purity.

Secondly, Countenancing of Preachers of contrary dispositions.

Thirdly, The negotiating with the faction of *Rome* by Preaching, and to instructions to Preach of the absolute Monarchy of Kings.

Here follow several Heads.

First, The political interpretation of the Law to serve their turns, and thus to impose taxes with a color of Law; a Judge said it when a *habeas corpus* was paid for.

Secondly, By keeping the King in continual want, that he may seek to their counsels for relief; to this purpose, to keep the Parliaments in distaste, that their counsels may be taken. The King by them is brought to this, as a woman that used her self to poison could not live with good meat. Search the Chronicles, and we see no King that ever used Parliaments, was brought to this want.

Thirdly, Arbitrary proceedings in Courts of Justice; we have all Law left to the conscience of a single man. All Courts are now Courts of conscience [equity], without conscience.

Fourthly, Plotters to enforce a war between *Scotland,* and

us; that when we had well wearied one another, we might be both brought to what scorn they pleased; The partition wall is only unity.

Fifthly, the sudden dissolving of Parliaments, and punishing of Parliament men, all to affright us from speaking what we think. One was committed for not delivering up the Petitions of the House; then a declaration which slandered our Proceedings, as full of lies, as leaves, who would have the first ground to be our example. And Papists are under appearance to the King his best Subjects, for they contribute money to the War, which the Protestants will not do.

Sixthly, Another is military, by getting places of importance into the Papists' hands, as who are Commanders in the last Army but they? none more strong in Arms, than they, to whom their Armor is delivered contrary to the Statute. Their endeavor is to bring in strangers to be Billeted upon us; we have had no account of the Spanish Navy, and now our fear is from *Ireland.*

Lastly, the next is Papistical that proceeds of Agents here in *London,* by whose desires many Monasteries and Nunneries here in *London* were erected.

3. *PETITION OF TWELVE PEERS FOR THE SUM-MONING OF A NEW PARLIAMENT* [28 *August* 1640]

To the King's Most Excellent Majesty.

The humble Petition of your Majesty's most loyal and obedient subjects, whose names are here underwritten in behalf of themselves and divers others.

Most Gracious Sovereign,

The sense of that duty and service which we owe to your Sacred Majesty, and our earnest affection to the good and welfare of this your realm of England, have moved us in all humility to beseech your Royal Majesty to give us leave to offer unto your princely wisdom the apprehension which we and other your faithful subjects have conceived of the great distempers and dangers now threatening the Church and

State and your Royal person, and the fittest means by which they may be removed and prevented.

The evils and dangers whereof your Majesty may be pleased to take notice are these:

That your Majesty's sacred person is exposed to hazard and danger in the present expedition against the Scottish army, and by occasion of this war your revenue is much wasted, your subjects burdened with coat-and-conduct-money, billeting of soldiers, and other military charges, and divers rapines and disorders committed in several parts in this your realm, by the soldiers raised for that service, and your whole kingdom become full of fear and discontents.

The sundry innovations in matters of religion, the oath and canons lately imposed upon the clergy and other your Majesty's subjects.

The great increase of Popery, and employing of Popish Recusants, and others ill-affected to the religion by law established in places of power and trust, especially in commanding of men and arms both in the field and in sundry counties of this your realm, whereas by the laws they are not permitted to have arms in their own houses.

The great mischiefs which may fall upon this kingdom if the intentions which have been credibly reported, of bringing in Irish and foreign forces, shall take effect.

The urging of ship-money, and prosecution of some sheriffs in the Star Chamber for not levying of it.

The heavy charges of merchandise to the discouragement of trade, the multitude of monopolies, and other patents, whereby the commodities and manufactures of the kingdom are much burthened, to the great and universal grievance of your people.

The great grief of your subjects by the long intermission of Parliaments, in the late and former dissolving of such as have been called, without the hoped effects which otherwise they might have procured.

For remedy whereof, and prevention of the dangers that may ensue to your royal person and to the whole state, they do in all humility and faithfulness beseech your most Excellent Majesty that you would be pleased to summon a Parliament within some short and convenient time, whereby the causes of these and other great grievances which your people lie under may be taken away, and the authors and counsellors of them may be there brought to such legal trial and condign punishment as the nature of the several offenses shall require, and that the present war may be composed by your Majesty's wisdom without bloodshed, in such manner as may conduce to the honor and safety of your Majesty's person, the comforts of your people, and the uniting of both of your realms against the common enemies of the reformed religion. And your Majesty's petitioners shall ever pray, &c.

Rutland.	Bolingbroke.
Fra. Bedford.	Mulgrave.
W. Hertford.	W. Saye and Sele.
Rob. Essex.	Rob. Brooke.
Exeter.	E. Mandeville.
Warwick.	Ed. Howard (of Escrick).

4. THE GRAND REMONSTRANCE, WITH THE PETITION ACCOMPANYING IT
[*Presented to the King, 1 December 1641*]

The Petition of the House of Commons, which accompanied the Remonstrance of the state of the kingdom, when it was presented to His Majesty at Hampton Court, December 1, 1641.

Most Gracious Sovereign,

Your Majesty's most humble and faithful subjects the Commons in this present Parliament assembled, do with much thankfulness and joy acknowledge the great mercy and favor of God, in giving your Majesty a safe and peaceable return out of Scotland into your kingdom of England, where the pressing dangers and distempers of the State have caused us with much earnestness to desire the comfort of your gracious presence, and likewise the unity and justice of your royal authority, to give more life and power to the dutiful and loyal counsels and endeavors of your Parliament, for the prevention of that eminent ruin and destruction wherein your kingdoms of England and Scotland are threatened. The duty which we owe to your Majesty and our country, cannot but make us very sensible and apprehensive, that the multiplicity, sharpness and malignity of those evils under which we have now many years suffered, are fomented and cherished by a corrupt and ill-affected party; who amongst other their mischievous devices for the alteration of religion and government, have sought by many false scandals and imputations, cunningly insinuated and dispersed amongst the people, to blemish and disgrace our proceedings in this Parliament, and to get themselves a party and faction amongst your subjects, for the better strengthening themselves in their wicked courses, and hindering those provisions and remedies which might, by the wisdom of your Majesty and counsel of your Parliament, be opposed against them.

For preventing whereof, and the better information of your Majesty, your Peers and all other your loyal subjects, we have been necessitated to make a declaration of the state of the kingdom, both before and since the assembly of this Parliament, unto this time, which we do humbly present to your Majesty, without the least intention to lay any blemish upon your royal person, but only to represent how your royal authority and trust have been abused, to the great prejudice and danger of your Majesty, and of all your good subjects.

And because we have reason to believe that those malignant parties, whose proceedings evidently appear to be mainly for the advantage and increase of Popery, is composed, set up, and acted by the subtile practice of the Jesuits and other engineers and factors for Rome, and to the great danger of this kingdom, and most grievous affliction of your loyal subjects, have so far prevailed as to corrupt divers of your Bishops and others in prime places of the Church, and also to bring divers of these instruments to be of your Privy Council, and other employments of trust and nearness about your Majesty, the Prince, and the rest of your royal children.

And by this means have had such an operation in your counsel and the most important affairs and proceedings of your government, that a most dangerous division and chargeable preparation for war betwixt your kingdoms of England

and Scotland, the increase of jealousies betwixt your Majesty and your most obedient subjects, the violent distraction and interruption of this Parliament, the insurrection of the Papists in your kingdom of Ireland, and bloody massacre of your people, have been not only endeavored and attempted, but in a great measure compassed and effected.

For preventing the final accomplishment whereof, your poor subjects are enforced to engage their persons and estates to the maintaining of a very expensive and dangerous war, notwithstanding they have already since the beginning of this Parliament undergone the charge of £150,000 sterling, or thereabouts, for the necessary support and supply of your Majesty in these present and perilous designs. And because all our most faithful endeavors and engagements will be ineffectual for the peace, safety and preservation of your Majesty and your people, if some present, real and effectual course be not taken for suppressing this wicked and malignant party:—

We, your most humble and obedient subjects, do with all faithfulness and humility beseech your Majesty:—

1. That you will be graciously pleased to concur with the humble desires of your people in a parliamentary way, for the preserving the peace and safety of the kingdom from the malicious designs of the Popish party:—

For depriving the Bishops of their votes in Parliament, and abridging their immoderate power usurped over the Clergy, and other your good subjects, which they have perniciously abused to the hazard of religion, and great prejudice and oppression to the laws of the kingdom, and just liberty of your people:—

For the taking away such oppressions in religion, Church government and discipline, as have been brought in and fomented by them:—

For uniting all such your loyal subjects together as join in the same fundamental truths against the Papists, by removing some oppressive and unnecessary ceremonies by which divers weak consciences have been scrupled, and seem to be divided from the rest, and for the due execution of those good laws which have been made for securing the liberty of your subjects.

2. That your Majesty will likewise be pleased to remove from your council all such as persist to favor and promote any of those pressures and corruptions wherewith your people have been grieved; and that for the future your Majesty will vouchsafe to employ such persons in your great and public affairs, and to take such to be near you in places of trust, as your Parliament may have cause to confide in; that in your princely goodness to your people you will reject and refuse all mediation and solicitation to the contrary, how powerful and near soever.

3. That you will be pleased to forbear to alienate any of the forfeited and escheated lands in Ireland which shall accrue to your Crown by reason of this rebellion, that out of them the Crown may be the better supported, and some satisfaction made to your subjects of this kingdom for the great expenses they are like to undergo [in] this war.

Which humble desires of ours being graciously fulfilled by your Majesty, we will, by the blessing and favor of God, most cheerfully undergo the hazard and expenses of this war, and apply ourselves to such other courses and counsels as may support your real estate with honor and plenty at home, with power and reputation abroad, and by our loyal affections, obedience and service, lay a sure and lasting foundation of the greatness and prosperity of your Majesty, and your royal posterity in future times.

THE GRAND REMONSTRANCE

The Commons in this present Parliament assembled, having with much earnestness and faithfulness of affection and zeal to the public good of this kingdom, and His Majesty's honor and service, for the space of twelve months wrestled with great dangers and fears, the pressing miseries and calamities, the various distempers and disorders which had not only assaulted, but even overwhelmed and extinguished the liberty, peace and prosperity of this kingdom, the comfort and hopes of all His Majesty's good subjects, and exceedingly weakened and undermined the foundation and strength of his own royal throne, do yet find an abounding malignity and opposition in those parties and factions who have been the cause of those evils, and do still labor to cast aspersions upon that which hath been done, and to raise many difficulties for the hindrance of that which remains yet undone, and to foment jealousies between the King and Parliament, that so they may deprive him and his people of the fruit of his own gracious intentions, and their humble desires of procuring the public peace, safety and happiness of this realm.

For the preventing of those miserable effects which such malicious endeavors may produce, we have thought good to declare the root and the growth of these mischievous designs: the maturity and ripeness to which they have attained before the beginning of the Parliament: the effectual means which have been used for the extirpation of those dangerous evils, and the progress which hath therein been made by His Majesty's goodness and the wisdom of the Parliament: the ways of obstruction and opposition by which that progress hath been interrupted: the courses to be taken for the removing those obstacles, and for the accomplishing of our most dutiful and faithful intentions and endeavors of restoring and establishing the ancient honor, greatness and security of this Crown and nation.

The root of all this mischief we find to be a malignant and pernicious design of subverting the fundamental laws and principles of government, upon which the religion and justice of this kingdom are firmly established. The actors and promoters hereof have been:

1. The Jesuited Papists, who hate the laws, as the obstacles of that change and subversion of religion which they so much long for.

2. The Bishops, and the corrupt part of the Clergy, who cherish formality and superstition as the natural effects and more probable supports of their own ecclesiastical tyranny and usurpation.

3. Such Councillors and Courtiers as for private ends have engaged themselves to further the interests of some foreign princes or states to the prejudice of His Majesty and the State at home.

The common principles by which they molded and governed all their particular counsels and actions were these:

First, to maintain continual differences and discontents

between the King and the people, upon questions of prerogative and liberty, that so they might have the advantage of siding with him, and under the notions of men addicted to his service, gain to themselves and their parties the places of greatest trust and power in the kingdom.

A second, to suppress the purity and power of religion and such persons as were best affected to it, as being contrary to their own ends, and the greatest impediment to that change which they thought to introduce.

A third, to conjoin those parties of the kingdom which were most propitious to their own ends, and to divide those who were most opposite, which consisted in many particular observations.

To cherish the Arminian part in those points wherein they agree with the Papists, to multiply and enlarge the difference between the common Protestants and those whom they call Puritans, to introduce and countenance such opinions and ceremonies as are fittest for accommodation with Popery, to increase and maintain ignorance, looseness and profaneness in the people; that of those three parties, Papists, Arminians and Libertines, they might compose a body fit to act such counsels and resolutions as were most conducible to their own ends.

A fourth, to disaffect the King to Parliaments by slander and false imputations, and by putting him upon other ways of supply, which in show and appearance were fuller of advantage than the ordinary course of subsidies, though in truth they brought more loss than gain both to the King and people, and have caused the great distractions under which we both suffer.

As in all compounded bodies the operations are qualified according to the predominant element, so in this mixed party, the Jesuited counsels, being most active and prevailing, may easily be discovered to have had the greatest sway in all their determinations, and if they be not prevented, are likely to devour the rest, or to turn them into their own nature.

In the beginning of His Majesty's reign the party began to revive and flourish again, having been somewhat damped by the breach with Spain in the last year of King James, and by His Majesty's marriage with France; the interests and counsels of that State being not so contrary to the good of religion and the prosperity of this kingdom as those of Spain; and the Papists of England, having been ever more addicted to Spain than France, yet they still retained a purpose and resolution to weaken the Protestant parties in all parts, and even in France, whereby to make way for the change of religion which they intended at home.

1. The first effect and evidence of their recovery and strength was the dissolution of the Parliament at Oxford, after there had been given two subsidies to His Majesty, and before they received relief in any one grievance many other more miserable effects followed.

2. The loss of the Rochelle fleet, by the help of our shipping, set forth and delivered over to the French in opposition to the advice of Parliament, which left that town without defense by sea, and made way, not only to the loss of that important place, but likewise to the loss of all the strength and security of the Protestant religion in France.

3. The diverting of His Majesty's course of wars from the West Indies, which was the most facile and hopeful way for this kingdom to prevail against the Spaniard, to an expenseful and successless attempt upon Cadiz, which was so ordered as if it had rather been intended to make us weary of war than to prosper in it.

4. The precipitate breach with France, by taking their ships to a great value without making recompense to the English, whose goods were thereupon imbarred and confiscated in that kingdom.

5. The peace with Spain without consent of Parliament, contrary to the promise of King James to both Houses, whereby the Palatine's cause was deserted and left to chargeable and hopeless treaties, which for the most part were managed by those who might justly be suspected to be no friends to that cause.

6. The charging of the kingdom with billeted soldiers in all parts of it, and the concomitant design of German horse, that the land might either submit with fear or be enforced with rigor to such arbitrary contributions as should be required of them.

7. The dissolving of the Parliament in the second year of His Majesty's reign, after a declaration of their intent to grant five subsidies.

8. The exacting of the like proportion of five subsidies, after the Parliament dissolved, by commission of loan, and divers gentlemen and others imprisoned for not yielding to pay that loan, whereby many of them contracted such sicknesses as cost them their lives.

9. Great sums of money required and raised by privy seals.

10. An unjust and pernicious attempt to extort great payments from the subject by way of excise, and a commission issued under the seal to that purpose.

11. The Petition of Right, which was granted in full Parliament, blasted, with an illegal declaration to make it destructive to itself, to the power of Parliament, to the liberty of the subject, and to that purpose printed with it, and the Petition made of no use but to show the bold and presumptuous injustice of such ministers as durst break the laws and suppress the liberties of the kingdom, after they had been so solemnly and evidently declared.

12. Another Parliament dissolved 4 Car., [1629] the privilege of Parliament broken, by imprisoning divers members of the House, detaining them close prisoners for many months together, without the liberty of using books, pen, ink or paper; denying them all the comforts of life, all means of preservation of health, not permitting their wives to come unto them even in the time of their sickness.

13. And for the completing of that cruelty, after years spent in such miserable durance, depriving them of the necessary means of spiritual consolation, not suffering them to go abroad to enjoy God's ordinances in God's House, or God's ministers to come to them to minister comfort to them in their private chambers.

14. And to keep them still in this oppressed condition, not admitting them to be bailed according to law, yet vexing them with informations in inferior courts, sentencing and fining some of them for matters done in Parliament; and extorting the payments of those fines from them, enforcing others to put in security of good behavior before they could be released.

15. The imprisonment of the rest, which refused to be bound, still continued, which might have been perpetual if necessity had not the last year brought another Parliament to relieve them, of whom one died[1] by the cruelty and harshness of his imprisonment, which would admit of no relaxation, notwithstanding the imminent danger of his life did sufficiently appear by the declaration of his physician, and his release, or at least his refreshment, was sought by many humble petitions, and his blood still cries either for vengeance or repentance of those Ministers of State, who have at once obstructed the course both of His Majesty's justice and mercy.

16. Upon the dissolution of both these Parliaments, untrue and scandalous declarations were published to asperse their proceedings, and some of their members unjustly; to make them odious, and color the violence which was used against them; proclamations set out to the same purpose; and to the great dejecting of the hearts of the people, forbidding them even to speak of Parliaments.

17. After the breach of the Parliament in the fourth of His Majesty, injustice, oppression and violence broke in upon us without any restraint or moderation, and yet the first project was the great sums exacted through the whole kingdom for default of knighthood, which seemed to have some color and shadow of a law, yet if it be rightly examined by that obsolete law which was pretended for it, it will be found to be against all the rules of justice, both in respect of the persons charged, the proportion of the fines demanded, and the absurd and unreasonable manner of their proceedings.

18. Tonnage and Poundage hath been received without color or pretense of law; many other heavy impositions continued against law, and some so unreasonable that the sum of the charge exceeds the value of the goods.

19. The Book of Rates[2] lately enhanced to a high propor-

[1] Sir John Eliot.
[2] "The Book of Rates was issued from time to time by the king to state the value of goods according to the current prices of the day. This was necessary because poundage was laid on goods by the £1 value, not on their weight or measure. Most writers confuse

tion, and such merchants that would not submit to their illegal and unreasonable payments, were vexed and oppressed above measure; and the ordinary course of justice, the common birthright of the subject of England, wholly obstructed unto them.

20. And although all this was taken upon pretense of guarding the seas, yet a new unheard-of tax of ship-money was devised, and upon the same pretense, by both which there was charged upon the subject near £700,000 some years, and yet the merchants have been left so naked to the violence of the Turkish pirates, that many great ships of value and thousands of His Majesty's subjects have been taken by them, and do still remain in miserable slavery.

21. The enlargements of forests, contrary to *Carta de Foresta*, and the composition thereupon.

22. The exactions of coat and conduct money and divers other military charges.

23. The taking away the arms of trained bands of divers counties.

24. The desperate design of engrossing all the gunpowder into one hand, keeping it in the Tower of London, and setting so high a rate upon it that the poorer sort were not able to buy it, nor could any have it without license, thereby to leave the several parts of the kingdom destitute of their necessary defense, and by selling so dear that which was sold to make an unlawful advantage of it, to the great charge and detriment of the subject.

25. The general destruction of the King's timber, especially that in the Forest of Deane, sold to Papists, which was the best storehouse of this kingdom for the maintenance of our shipping.

26. The taking away of men's right, under the color of the King's title to land, between high and low water marks.

27. The monopolies of soap, salt, wine, leather, sea-coal, and in a manner of all things of most common and necessary use.

28. The restraint of the liberties of the subjects in their habitation, trades and other interests.

29. Their vexation and oppression by purveyors, clerks of the market and saltpeter men.

30. The sale of pretended nuisances, as building in and about London.

31. Conversion of arable into pasture, continuance of pasture, under the name of depopulation, have driven many millions out of the subjects' purses, without any considerable profit to His Majesty.

32. Large quantities of common and several grounds hath been taken from the subject by color of the Statute of Improvement, and by abuse of the Commission of Sewers, without their consent, and against it.

33. And not only private interest, but also public faith, have been broken in seizing of the money and bullion in the mint, and the whole kingdom like to be robbed at once in that abominable project of brass money.

34. Great numbers of His Majesty's subjects for refusing those unlawful charges, have been vexed with long and expensive suits, some fined and censured, others committed to long and hard imprisonments and confinements, to the loss of health in many, of life in some, and others have had their houses broken up, their goods seized, some have been restrained from their lawful callings.

35. Ships have been interrupted in their voyages, surprised at sea in a hostile manner by projectors, as by a common enemy.

36. Merchants prohibited to unlade their goods in such ports as were for their own advantage, and forced to bring them to those places which were much for the advantage of the monopolisers and projectors.

37. The Court of Star Chamber hath abounded in extravagant censures, not only for the maintenance and improvement of monopolies and their unlawful taxes, but for divers other causes where there hath been no offense, or very small; whereby His Majesty's subjects have been oppressed by grievous fines, imprisonments, stigmatisings, mutilations, whippings, pillories, gags, confinements, banishments; after so rigid a manner as hath not only deprived men of the

society of their friends, exercise of their professions, comfort of books, use of paper or ink, but even violated that near union which God hath established between men and their wives, by forced and constrained separation, whereby they have been bereaved of the comfort and conversation one of another for many years together, without hope of relief, if God had not by His overruling providence given some interruption to the prevailing power, and counsel of those who were the authors and promoters of such peremptory and heady courses.

38. Judges have been put out of their places for refusing to do against their oaths and consciences; others have been so awed that they durst not do their duties and the better to hold a rod over them, the clause *Quam diu se bene gesserit* [during good behavior] was left out of their patents, and a new clause *Durante bene placito* [at the (King's) pleasure] inserted.

39. Lawyers have been checked for being faithful to their clients; solicitors and attorneys have been threatened, and some punished, for following lawful suits. And by this means all the approaches to justice were interrupted and forecluded.

40. New oaths have been forced upon the subject against law.

41. New judicatories erected without law. The Council Table have by their orders offered to bind the subjects in their freeholds, estates, suits and actions.

42. The pretended Court of the Earl Marshal was arbitrary and illegal in its being and proceedings.

43. The Chancery, Exchequer Chamber, Court of Wards, and other English Courts, have been grievous in exceeding their jurisdiction.

44. The estate of many families weakened, and some ruined by excessive fines, exacted from them for compositions of wardships.

45. All leases of above a hundred years made to draw on wardship contrary to law.

46. Undue proceedings used in the finding of offices to make the jury find for the King.

47. The Common Law Courts, feeling all men more inclined to seek justice there, where it may be fitted to their

own desire, are known frequently to forsake the rules of the Common Law, and straying beyond their bounds, under pretense of equity, to do injustice.

48. Titles of honor, judicial places, sergeantships at law, and other offices have been sold for great sums of money, whereby the common justice of the kingdom hath been much endangered, not only by opening a way of employment in places of great trust, and advantage to men of weak parts, but also by giving occasion to bribery, extortion, partiality, it seldom happening that places ill-gotten are well used.

49. Commissions have been granted for examining the excess of fees, and when great exactions have been discovered, compositions have been made with delinquents, not only for the time past, but likewise for immunity and security in offending for the time to come, which under color of remedy hath but confirmed and increased the grievance to the subject.

50. The usual course of pricking Sheriffs not observed, but many times Sheriffs made in an extraordinary way, sometimes as a punishment and charge unto them; sometimes such were pricked out as would be instruments to execute whatsoever they would have to be done.

51. The Bishops and the rest of the Clergy did triumph in the suspensions, excommunications, deprivations, and degradations of divers painful, learned and pious ministers, in the vexation and grievous oppression of great numbers of His Majesty's good subjects.

52. The High Commission grew to such excess of sharpness and severity as was not much less than the Romish Inquisition, and yet in many cases by the Archbishop's power was made much more heavy, being assisted and strengthened by authority of the Council Table.

53. The Bishops and their Courts were as eager in the country; although their jurisdiction could not reach so high in rigor and extremity of punishment, yet were they no less grievous in respect of the generality and multiplicity of vexations, which lighting upon the meaner sort of tradesmen and artificers did impoverish many thousands.

54. And so afflict and trouble others, that great numbers to avoid their miseries departed out of the kingdom, some

into New England and other parts of America, others into Holland.

55. Where they have transported their manufactures of cloth, which is not only a loss by diminishing the present stock of the kingdom, but a great mischief by impairing and endangering the loss of that particular trade of clothing, which hath been a plentiful fountain of wealth and honor to this nation.

56. Those were fittest for ecclesiastical preferment, and soonest obtained it, who were most officious in promoting superstition, most virulent in railing against godliness and honesty.

57. The most public and solemn sermons before His Majesty were either to advance prerogative above law, and decry the property of the subject, or full of such kind of invectives.

58. Whereby they might make those odious who sought to maintain the religion, laws and liberties of the kingdom, and such men were sure to be weeded out of the commission of the peace, and out of all other employments of power in the government of the country.

59. Many noble personages were councillors in name, but the power and authority remained in a few of such as were most addicted to this party, whose resolutions and determinations were brought to the table for countenance and execution, and not for debate and deliberation, and no man could offer to oppose them without disgrace and hazard to himself.

60. Nay, all those that did not wholly concur and actively contribute to the furtherance of their designs, though otherwise persons of never so great honor and abilities, were so far from being employed in any place of trust and power, that they were neglected, discountenanced, and upon all occasions injured and oppressed.

61. This faction was grown to that height and entireness of power, that now they began to think of finishing their work, which consisted of these three parts.

62. I. The government must be set free from all restraint of laws concerning our persons and estates.

63. II. There must be a conjunction between Papists and

Protestants in doctrine, discipline and ceremonies; only it must not yet be called Popery.

64. III. The Puritans, under which name they include all those that desire to preserve the laws and liberties of the kingdom, and to maintain religion in the power of it, must be either rooted out of the kingdom with force, or driven out with fear.

65. For the effecting of this it was thought necessary to reduce Scotland to such Popish superstitions and innovations as might make them apt to join with England in that great change which was intended.

66. Whereupon new canons and a new liturgy were pressed upon them, and when they refused to admit of them, an army was raised to force them to it, towards which the Clergy and the Papists were very forward in their contribution.

67. The Scots likewise raised an army for their defense.

68. And when both armies were come together, and ready for a bloody encounter, His Majesty's own gracious disposition, and the counsel of the English nobility and dutiful submission of the Scots, did so far prevail against the evil counsel of others, that a pacification was made, and His Majesty returned with peace and much honor to London.

69. The unexpected reconciliation was most acceptable to all the kingdom, except to the malignant party; whereof the Archbishop and the Earl of Strafford being heads, they and their faction began to inveigh against the peace, and to aggravate the proceedings of the states, which so incensed His Majesty, that he forthwith prepared again for war.

70. And such was their confidence, that having corrupted and distempered the whole frame and government of the kingdom, they did now hope to corrupt that which was the only means to restore all to a right frame and temper again.

71. To which end they persuaded His Majesty to call a Parliament, not to seek counsel and advice of them, but to draw countenance and supply from them, and to engage the whole kingdom in their quarrel.

72. And in the meantime continued all their unjust levies of money, resolving either to make the Parliament pliant to their will, and to establish mischief by a law, or else to break it, and with more color to go on by violence to take what

they could not obtain by consent. The ground alleged for the justification of this war was this,

73. That the undutiful demands of the Parliaments in Scotland was a sufficient reason for His Majesty to take arms against them, without hearing the reason of those demands, and thereupon a new army was prepared against them, their ships were seized in all ports both of England and Ireland, and at sea, their petitions rejected, their commissioners refused audience.

74. This whole kingdom most miserably distempered with levies of men and money, and imprisonments of those who denied to submit to those levies.

75. The Earl of Strafford passed into Ireland, caused the Parliament there to declare against the Scots, to give four subsidies towards that war, and to engage themselves, their lives and fortunes, for the prosecution of it, and gave directions for an army of eight thousand foot and one thousand horse to be levied there, which were for the most part Papists.

76. The Parliament met upon the 13th of April, 1640. The Earl of Strafford and Archbishop of Canterbury, with their party, so prevailed with His Majesty, that the House of Commons was pressed to yield a supply for maintenance of the war with Scotland, before they had provided any relief for the great and pressing grievances of the people, which being against the fundamental privilege and proceeding of Parliament, was yet in humble respect to His Majesty, so far admitted as that they agreed to take the matter of supply into consideration, and two several days it was debated.

77. Twelve subsidies were demanded for the release of ship-money alone, a third day was appointed for conclusion, when the heads of that party began to fear the people might close with the King, in satisfying his desires of money; but that withal they were like to blast their malicious designs against Scotland, finding them very much indisposed to give any countenance to that war.

78. Thereupon they wickedly advised the King to break off the Parliament and to return to the ways of confusion, in which their own evil intentions were most likely to prosper and succeed.

79. After the Parliament ended the 5th of May, 1640,

this party grew so bold as to counsel the King to supply himself out of his subjects' estates by his own power, at his own will, without their consent.

80. The very next day some members of both Houses had their studies and cabinets, yea, their pockets searched: another of them not long after was committed close prisoner for not delivering some petitions which he received by authority of that House.

81. And if harsher courses were intended (as was reported) it is very probable that the sickness of the Earl of Strafford, and the tumultuous rising in Southwark and about Lambeth were the causes that such violent intentions were not brought into execution.

82. A false and scandalous Declaration against the House of Commons was published in His Majesty's name, which yet wrought little effect with the people, but only to manifest the impudence of those who were authors of it.

83. A forced loan of money was attempted in the City of London.

84. The Lord Mayor and Aldermen in their several wards, enjoined to bring in a list of the names of such persons as they judged fit to lend, and of the sums they should lend. And such Aldermen as refused to do so were committed to prison.

85. The Archbishop and the other Bishops and Clergy continued the Convocation, and by a new commission turned it into a provincial Synod, in which, by an unheard-of presumption, they made canons that contain in them many matters contrary to the King's prerogative, to the fundamental laws and statutes of the realm, to the right of Parliaments, to the property and liberty of the subject, and matters tending to sedition and of dangerous consequence, thereby establishing their own usurpations, justifying their altar-worship, and those other superstitious innovations which they formerly introduced without warrant of law.

86. They imposed a new oath upon divers of His Majesty's subjects, both ecclesiastical and lay, for maintenance of their own tyranny, and laid a great tax on the Clergy, for supply of His Majesty, and generally they showed themselves very affectionate to the war with Scotland, which was by some of

them styled *Bellum Episcopale*, and a prayer composed and enjoined to be read in all churches, calling the Scots rebels, to put the two nations in blood and make them irreconcilable.

87. All those pretended canons and constitutions were armed with the several censures of suspension, excommunication, deprivation, by which they would have thrust out all the good ministers, and most of the well-affected people of the kingdom, and left an easy passage to their own design of reconciliation with Rome.

88. The Popish party enjoyed such exemptions from penal laws as amounted to a toleration, besides many other encouragements and Court favors.

89. They had a Secretary of State, Sir Francis Windebank, a powerful agent for speeding all their desires.

90. A Pope's Nuncio residing here, to act and govern them according to such influences as he received from Rome, and to intercede for them with the most powerful concurrence of the foreign Princes of that religion.

91. By his authority the Papists of all sorts, nobility, gentry, and clergy, were convocated after the manner of a Parliament.

92. New jurisdictions were erected of Romish Archbishops, taxes levied, another state molded within this state, independent in government, contrary in interest and affection, secretly corrupting the ignorant or negligent professors of our religion, and closely uniting and combining themselves against such as were found in this posture, waiting for an opportunity by force to destroy those whom they could not hope to seduce.

93. For the effecting whereof they were strengthened with arms and munitions, encouraged by superstitious prayers, enjoined by the Nuncio to be weekly made for the prosperity of some great design.

94. And such power had they at Court, that secretly a commission was issued out, or intended to be issued to some great men of that profession, for the levying of soldiers, and to command and employ them according to private instructions, which we doubt were framed for the advantage of those who were the contrivers of them.

95. His Majesty's treasure was consumed, his revenue anticipated.

96. His servants and officers compelled to lend great sums of money.

97. Multitudes were called to the Council Table, who were tired with long attendances there for refusing illegal payments.

98. The prisons were filled with their commitments; many of the Sheriffs summoned into the Star Chamber, and some imprisoned for not being quick enough in levying the ship-money; the people languished under grief and fear, no visible hope being left but in desperation.

99. The nobility began to weary of their silence and patience, and sensible of the duty and trust which belongs to them: and thereupon some of the most ancient of them did petition His Majesty at such a time, when evil counsels were so strong, that they had occasion to expect more hazard to themselves, than redress of those public evils for which they interceded.

100. Whilst the kingdom was in this agitation and distemper, the Scots, restrained in their trades, impoverished by the loss of many of their ships, bereaved of all possibility of satisfying His Majesty by any naked supplication, entered with a powerful army into the kingdom, and without any hostile act or spoil in the country they passed, more than forcing a passage over the Tyne at Newburn, near Newcastle, possessed themselves of Newcastle, and had a fair opportunity to press on further upon the King's army.

101. But duty and reverence to His Majesty, and brotherly love to the English nation, made them stay there, whereby the King had leisure to entertain better counsels.

102. Wherein God so blessed and directed him that he summoned the Great Council of Peers to meet at York upon the 24th of September, and there declared a Parliament to begin the 3rd of November then following.

103. The Scots, the first day of the Great Council, presented an humble Petition to His Majesty, whereupon the Treaty was appointed at Ripon.

104. A present cessation of arms agreed upon, and the

full conclusion of all differences referred to the wisdom and care of the Parliament.

105. As our first meeting, all oppositions seemed to vanish, the mischiefs were so evident which those evil counsellors produced, that no man durst stand up to defend them: yet the work itself afforded difficulty enough.

106. The multiplied evils and corruption of fifteen years, strengthened by custom and authority, and the concurrent interest of many powerful delinquents, were now to be brought to judgment and reformation.

107. The King's household was to be provided for:—they had brought him to that want, that he could not supply his ordinary and necessary expenses without the assistance of his people.

108. Two armies were to be paid, which amounted very near to £80,000 a month.

109. The people were to be tenderly charged, having been formerly exhausted with many burdensome projects.

110. The difficulties seemed to be insuperable, which by the Divine Providence we have overcome. The contrarieties incompatible, which yet in a great measure we have reconciled.

111. Six subsidies have been granted and a Bill of poll-money, which if it be duly levied, may equal six subsidies more, in all £600,000.

112. Besides we have contracted a debt to the Scots of £220,000, yet God hath so blessed the endeavors of this Parliament, that the kingdom is a great gainer by all these charges.

113. The ship-money is abolished, which cost the kingdom about £200,000 a year.

114. The coat and conduct-money, and other military charges are taken away, which in many countries amounted to little less than the ship-money.

115. The monopolies are all suppressed, whereof some few did prejudice the subject, above £1,000,000 yearly.

116. The soap £100,000.

117. The wine £300,000.

118. The leather must needs exceed both, and salt could be no less than that.

119. Besides the inferior monopolies, which, if they could be exactly computed, would make up a great sum.

120. That which is more beneficial than all this is, that the root of these evils is taken away, which was the arbitrary power pretended to be in His Majesty of taxing the subject, or charging their estates without consent in Parliament, which is now declared to be against law by the judgment of both Houses, and likewise by an Act of Parliament.

121. Another step of great advantage is this, the living grievances, the evil counsellors and actors of these mischiefs have been so quelled.

122. By the justice done upon the Earl of Strafford, the flight of the Lord Finch and Secretary Windebank,

123. The accusation and imprisonment of the Archbishop of Canterbury, of Judge Berkeley,[3] and

124. The impeachment of divers other Bishops and Judges, that it is like not only to be an ease to the present times, but a preservation to the future.

125. The discontinuance of Parliaments is prevented by the Bill for a triennial Parliament, and the abrupt dissolution of this Parliament by another Bill, by which it is provided it shall not be dissolved or adjourned without the consent of both Houses.

126. Which two laws well considered may be thought more advantageous than all the former, because they secure a full operation of the present remedy, and afford a perpetual spring of remedies for the future.

127. The Star Chamber.

128. The High Commission.

129. The Courts of the President and Council in the North were so many forges of misery, oppression and violence, and are all taken away, whereby men are more secured in their persons, liberties and estates, than they could be by any law or example for the regulation of those Courts or terror of the Judges.

130. The immoderate power of the Council Table, and the excessive abuse of that power is so ordered and re-

[3] Sir Robert Berkeley (1584–1656). Justice of the Court of King's Bench supporting the royal prerogative, he denied that *"lex is rex"* [law is king]; rather *"rex is lex"* [the king is the law].

strained, that we may well hope that no such things as were frequently done by them, to the prejudice of the public liberty, will appear in future times but only in stories, to give us and our posterity more occasion to praise God for His Majesty's goodness, and the faithful endeavors of this Parliament.

131. The canons and power of canon-making are blasted by the votes of both Houses.

132. The exorbitant power of Bishops and their courts are much abated, by some provisions in the Bill against the High Commission Court, the authors of the many innovations in doctrine and ceremonies.

133. The ministers that have been scandalous in their lives, have been so terrified in just complaints and accusations, that we may well hope they will be more modest for the time to come; either inwardly convicted by the sight of their own folly, or outwardly restrained by the fear of punishment.

134. The forests are by a good law reduced to their right bounds.

135. The encroachments and oppressions of the Stannary Courts,[4] the extortions of the clerk of the market.

136. And the compulsion of the subject to receive the Order of Knighthood against his will, paying of fines for not receiving it, and the vexatious proceedings thereupon for levying of those fines, are by other beneficial laws reformed and prevented.

137. Many excellent laws and provisions are in preparation for removing the inordinate power, vexation and usurpation of Bishops, for reforming the pride and idleness of many of the clergy, for easing the people of unnecessary ceremonies in religion, for censuring and removing unworthy and unprofitable ministers, and for maintaining godly and diligent preachers through the kingdom.

138. Other things of main importance for the good of this kingdom are in proposition, though little could hitherto be done in regard of the many other more pressing businesses,

[4] The Stannary Courts had jurisdiction over cases concerned with the tin mines in Cornwall and Devonshire.

which yet before the end of this Session we hope may receive some progress and perfection.

139. The establishing and ordering the King's revenue, that so the abuse of officers and superfluity of expenses may be cut off, and the necessary disbursements for His Majesty's honor, the defense and government of the kingdom, may be more certainly provided for.

140. The regulating of courts of justice, and abridging both the delays and charges of law-suits.

141. The settling of some good courses for preventing the exportation of gold and silver, and the inequality of exchanges between us and other nations, for the advancing of native commodities, increase of our manufactures, and well balancing of trade, whereby the stock of the kingdom may be increased, or at least kept from impairing, as through neglect hereof it hath done for many years last past.

142. Improving the herring-fishing upon our coasts, which will be of mighty use in the employment of the poor, and a plentiful nursery of mariners for enabling the kingdom in any great action.

143. The oppositions, obstructions and the difficulties wherewith we have been encountered, and which still lie in our way with some strength and much obstinacy, are these; the malignant party whom we have formerly described to be the actors and promoters of all our misery, they have taken heart again.

144. They have been able to prefer some of their own factors and agents to degrees of honor, to places of trust and employment, even during the Parliament.

145. They have endeavored to work in His Majesty ill impressions and opinions of our proceedings, as if we had altogether done our own work, and not his; and had obtained from him many things very prejudicial to the Crown, both in respect of prerogative and profit.

146. To wipe out this slander we think good only to say thus much: that all that we have done is for His Majesty, his greatness, honor and support, when we yield to give £25,000 a month for the relief of the Northern Counties; this was given to the King, for he was bound to protect his subjects.

147. They were His Majesty's evil counsellors, and their ill instruments that were actors in those grievances which brought in the Scots.

148. And if His Majesty please to force those who were the authors of this war to make satisfaction, as he might justly and easily do, it seems very reasonable that the people might well be excused from taking upon them this burden, being altogether innocent and free from being any cause of it.

149. When we undertook the charge of the army, which cost above £50,000 a month, was not this given to the King? Was it not His Majesty's army? Were not all the commanders under contract with His Majesty, at higher rates and greater wages than ordinary?

150. And have we not taken upon us to discharge all the brotherly assistance of £300,000, which we gave the Scots? Was it not toward repair of those damages and losses which they received from the King's ships and from his ministers?

151. These three particulars amount to above £1,100,000.

152. Besides, His Majesty hath received by impositions upon merchandise at least £400,000.

153. So that His Majesty hath had out of the subjects' purse since the Parliament began, £1,500,000, and yet these men can be so impudent as to tell His Majesty that we have done nothing for him.

154. As to the second branch of this slander, we acknowledge with much thankfulness that His Majesty hath passed more good Bills to the advantage of the subjects than have been in many ages.

155. But withal we cannot forget that these venomous councils did manifest themselves in some endeavors to hinder these good acts.

156. And for both Houses of Parliament we may with truth and modesty say thus much: that we have ever been careful not to desire anything that should weaken the Crown either in just profit or useful power.

157. The triennial Parliament for the matter of it, doth not extend to so much as by law we ought to have required (there being two statutes still in force for a Parliament to be once a year), and for the manner of it, it is in the King's

power that it shall never take effect, if he by a timely summons shall prevent any other way of assembling.

158. In the Bill for continuance of this present Parliament, there seems to be some restraint of the royal power in dissolving of Parliaments, not to take it out of the Crown, but to suspend the execution of it for this time and occasion only: which was so necessary for the King's own security and the public peace, that without it we could not have undertaken any of these great charges, but must have left both the armies to disorder and confusion, and the whole kingdom to blood and rapine.

159. The Star Chamber was much more fruitful in oppression than in profit, the great fines being for the most part given away, and the rest stalled[5] at long times.

160. The fines of the High Commission were in themselves unjust, and seldom or never came into the King's purse. These four Bills are particularly and more specially instanced.

161. In the rest there will not be found so much as a shadow of prejudice to the Crown.

162. They have sought to diminish our reputation with the people, and to bring them out of love with Parliaments.

163. The aspersions which they have attempted this way have been such as these:

164. That we have spent much time and done little, especially in those grievances which concern religion.

165. That the Parliament is a burden to the kingdom by the abundance of protections which hinder justice and trade; and by many subsidies granted much more heavy than any formerly endured.

166. To which there is a ready answer; if the time spent in this Parliament be considered in relation backward to the long growth and deep root of those grievances, which we have removed, to the powerful supports of those delinquents, which we have pursued, to the great necessities and other charges of the commonwealth for which we have provided.

167. Or if it be considered in relation forward to many advantages, which not only the present but future ages are like to reap by the good laws and other proceedings in this

[5] To be paid by installments.

Parliament, we doubt not but it will be thought by all indifferent judgments, that our time hath been much better employed than in a far greater proportion of time in many former Parliaments put together; and the charges which have been laid upon the subject, and the other inconveniences which they have borne, will seem very light in respect of the benefit they have and may receive.

168. And for the matter of protections, the Parliament is so sensible of it that therein they intended to give them whatsoever ease may stand with honor and justice, and are in a way of passing a Bill to give them satisfaction.

169. They have sought by many subtle practices to cause jealousies and divisions betwixt us and our brethren of Scotland, by slandering their proceedings and intentions towards us, and by secret endeavors to instigate and incense them and us one against another.

170. They have had such a party of Bishops and Popish lords in the House of Peers, as hath caused much opposition and delay in the prosecution of delinquents, hindered the proceedings of divers good Bills passed in the Commons' House, concerning the reformation of sundry great abuses and corruptions both in Church and State.

171. They have labored to seduce and corrupt some of the Commons' House to draw them into conspiracies and combinations against the liberty of the Parliament.

172. And by their instruments and agents they have attempted to disaffect and discontent His Majesty's army, and to engage it for the maintenance of their wicked and traitorous designs; the keeping up of Bishops in votes and functions, and by force to compel the Parliament to order, limit and dispose their proceedings in such manner as might best concur with the intentions of this dangerous and potent faction.

173. And when one mischievous design and attempt of theirs to bring on the army against the Parliament and the City of London hath been discovered and prevented;

174. They presently undertook another of the same damnable nature, with this addition to it, to endeavor to make the Scottish army neutral, whilst the English army, which they had labored to corrupt and envenom against us by their false and slanderous suggestions, should execute their malice

to the subversion of our religion and the dissolution of our government.

175. Thus they have been continually practicing to disturb the peace, and plotting the destruction even of all the King's dominions; and have employed their emissaries and agents in them, all for the promoting their devilish designs, which the vigilancy of those who were well affected hath still discovered and defeated before they were ripe for execution in England and Scotland.

176. Only in Ireland, which was farther off, they have had time and opportunity to mold and prepare their work, and had brought it to that perfection that they had possessed themselves of that whole kingdom, totally subverted the government of it, routed out religion, and destroyed all the Protestants whom the conscience of their duty to God, their King and country, would not have permitted to join with them, if by God's wonderful providence their main enterprise upon the city and castle of Dublin had not been detected and prevented upon the very eve before it should have been executed.

177. Notwithstanding they have in other parts of that kingdom broken out into open rebellion, surprising towns and castles, committed murders, rapes and other villainies, and shaken off all bonds of obedience to His Majesty and the laws of the realm.

178. And in general have kindled such a fire, as nothing but God's infinite blessing upon the wisdom and endeavors of this State will be able to quench it.

179. And certainly had not God in His great mercy unto this land discovered and confounded their former designs, we had been the prologue to this tragedy in Ireland, and had by this been made the lamentable spectacle of misery and confusion.

180. And now what hope have we but in God, when as the only means of our subsistence and power of reformation is under Him in the Parliament?

181. But what can we the Commons, without the conjunction of the House of Lords, and what conjunction can we expect there, when the Bishops and recusant lords are so numerous and prevalent that they are able to cross and

interrupt our best endeavors for reformation, and by that means give advantage to this malignant party to traduce our proceedings?

182. They infuse into the people that we mean to abolish all Church government, and leave every man to his own fancy for the service and worship of God, absolving him of that obedience which he owes under God unto His Majesty, whom we know to be entrusted with the ecclesiastical law as well as with the temporal, to regulate all the members of the Church of England, by such rules of order and discipline as are established by Parliament, which is his great council, in all affairs both in Church and State.

183. We confess our intention is, and our endeavors have been, to reduce within bounds that exorbitant power which the prelates have assumed unto themselves, so contrary both to the Word of God and to the laws of the land, to which end we passed the Bill for the removing them from their temporal power and employments, that so the better they might with meekness apply themselves to the discharge of their functions, which Bill themselves opposed, and were the principal instruments of crossing it.

184. And we do here declare that it is far from our purpose or desire to let loose the golden reins of discipline and government in the Church, to leave private persons or particular congregations to take up what form of Divine Service they please, for we hold it requisite that there should be throughout the whole realm a conformity to that order which the laws enjoin according to the Word of God. And we desire to unburden the consciences of men of needless and superstitious ceremonies, suppress innovations, and take away the monuments of idolatry.

185. And the better to effect the intended reformation, we desire there may be a general synod of the most grave, pious, learned and judicious divines of this island; assisted with some from foreign parts, professing the same religion with us, who may consider of all things necessary for the peace and good government of the Church, and represent the results of their consultations unto the Parliament, to be there allowed of and confirmed, and receive the stamp of authority,

thereby to find passage and obedience throughout the kingdom.

186. They have maliciously charged us that we intend to destroy and discourage learning, whereas it is our chiefest care and desire to advance it, and to provide a competent maintenance for conscionable and preaching ministers throughout the kingdom, which will be a great encouragement to scholars, and a certain means whereby the want, meanness and ignorance, to which a great part of the clergy is now subject, will be prevented.

187. And we intended likewise to reform and purge the fountains of learning, the two Universities, that the streams flowing from thence may be clear and pure, and an honor and comfort to the whole land.

188. They have strained to blast our proceedings in Parliament, by wresting the interpretations of our orders from their genuine intention.

189. They tell the people that our meddling with the power of episcopacy hath caused sectaries and conventicles, when idolatrous and Popish ceremonies, introduced into the Church by the command of the Bishops, have not only debarred the people from thence, but expelled them from the kingdom.

190. Thus with Elijah, we are called by this malignant party the troublers of the State, and still, while we endeavor to reform their abuses, they make us the authors of those mischiefs we study to prevent.

191. For the perfecting of the work begun, and removing all future impediments, we conceive these courses will be very effectual, seeing the religion of the Papists hath such principles as do certainly tend to the destruction and extirpation of all Protestants, when they shall have opportunity to effect it.

192. It is necessary in the first place to keep them in such condition as that they may not be able to do us any hurt, and for avoiding of such connivance and favor as hath heretofore been shown unto them.

193. That His Majesty be pleased to grant a standing Commission to some choice men named in Parliament, who may take notice of their increase, their counsels and proceed-

ings, and use all due means by execution of the laws to prevent all mischievous designs against the peace and safety of this kingdom.

194. Thus some good course be taken to discover the counterfeit and false conformity of Papists to the Church, by color whereof persons very much disaffected to the true religion have been admitted into place of greatest authority and trust in the kingdom.

195. For the better preservation of the laws and liberties of the kingdom, that all illegal grievances and exactions be presented and punished at the sessions and assizes.

196. And that Judges and Justices be very careful to give this in charge to the grand jury, and both the Sheriff and Justices to be sworn to the due execution of the Petition of Right and other laws.

197. That His Majesty be humbly petitioned by both Houses to employ such councillors, ambassadors and other ministers, in managing his business at home and abroad as the Parliament may have cause to confide in, without which we cannot give His Majesty such supplies for support of his own estate, nor such assistance to the Protestant party beyond the sea, as is desired.

198. It may often fall out that the Commons may have just cause to take exceptions at some men for being councillors, and yet not charge those men with crimes, for there be grounds of diffidence which lie not in proof.

199. There are others, which though they may be proved, yet are not legally criminal.

200. To be a known favorer of Papists, or to have been very forward in defending or countenancing some great offenders questioned in Parliament; or to speak contemptuously of either Houses of Parliament or Parliamentary proceedings.

201. Or such as are factors or agents for any foreign prince of another religion; such are justly suspected to get councillors' places, or any other of trust concerning public employment for money; for all these and divers others we may have great reason to be earnest with His Majesty, not to put his great affairs into such hands, though we may be unwilling

to proceed against them in any legal way of charge or impeachment.

202. That all Councillors of State may be sworn to observe those laws which concern the subject in his liberty, that they may likewise take an oath not to receive or give reward or pension from any foreign prince, but such as they shall within some reasonable time discover to the Lords of His Majesty's Council.

203. And although they should wickedly forswear themselves, yet it may herein do good to make them known to be false and perjured to those who employ them, and thereby bring them into as little credit with them as with us.

204. That His Majesty may have cause to be in love with good counsel and good men, by showing him in an humble and dutiful manner how full of advantage it would be to himself, to see his own estate settled in a plentiful condition to support his honor; to see his people united in ways of duty to him, and endeavors of the public good; to see happiness, wealth, peace and safety derived to his own kingdom, and procured to his allies by the influence of his own power and government.

5. THE NINETEEN PROPOSITIONS SENT BY THE TWO HOUSES OF PARLIAMENT TO THE KING AT YORK [1 June 1642]

Your Majesty's most humble and faithful subjects, the Lords and Commons in Parliament, having nothing in their thoughts and desires more precious and of higher esteem (next to the honor and immediate service of God) than the just and faithful performance of their duty to your Majesty and this kingdom: and being very sensible of the great distractions and distempers, and of the imminent dangers and calamities which those distractions and distempers are like to bring upon your Majesty and your subjects; all which have proceeded from the subtile insinuations, mischievous practices and evil counsels of men disaffected to God's true religion, your Majesty's honor and safety, and the public peace and prosperity of your people, after a serious observation of the causes of those mischiefs, do in all humility and sincerity present to your Majesty their most dutiful petition and advice, that out of your princely wisdom for the establishing your own honor and safety, and gracious tenderness of the welfare and security of your subjects and dominions, you will be pleased to grant and accept these their humble desires and propositions, as the most necessary effectual means, through God's blessing, of removing those jealousies and differences which have unhappily fallen betwixt you and your people, and procuring both your Majesty and them a constant course of honor, peace, and happiness.

THE NINETEEN PROPOSITIONS

1. That the Lords and others of your Majesty's Privy Council, and such great officers and Ministers of State, either at home or beyond the seas, may be put from your Privy Council, and from those offices and employments, excepting such as shall be approved of by both Houses of Parliament; and that the persons put into the places and employments of those that are removed may be approved of by both Houses of Parliament; and that the Privy Councillors shall take an oath for the due execution of their places, in such form as shall be agreed upon by both Houses of Parliament.

2. That the great affairs of the kingdom may not be concluded or transacted by the advice of private men, or by any unknown or unsworn councillors, but that such matters as concern the public, and are proper for the High Court of Parliament, which is your Majesty's great and supreme council, may be debated, resolved and transacted only in Parliament, and not elsewhere: and such as shall presume to do anything to the contrary shall be reserved to the censure and judgment of Parliament: and such other matters of state as are proper for your Majesty's Privy Council shall be debated and concluded by such of the nobility and others as shall from time to time be chosen for that place, by approbation of both Houses of Parliament: and that no public act concerning the affairs of the kingdom, which are proper for your Privy Council, may be esteemed of any validity, as proceeding from the royal authority, unless it be done by the advice

and consent of the major part of your Council, attested under their hands: and that your Council may be limited to a certain number, not exceeding five and twenty, nor under fifteen: and if any councillor's place happen to be void in the interval of Parliament, it shall not be supplied without the assent of the major part of the Council, which choice shall be confirmed at the next sitting of Parliament, or else to be void.

3. That the Lord High Steward of England, Lord High Constable, Lord Chancellor, or Lord Keeper of the Great Seal, Lord Treasurer, Lord Privy Seal, Earl Marshall, Lord Admiral, Warden of the Cinque Ports, Chief Governor of Ireland, Chancellor of the Exchequer, Master of the Wards, Secretaries of State, two Chief Justices and Chief Baron, may always be chosen with the approbation of both Houses of Parliament; and in the intervals of Parliament, by assent of the major part of the Council, in such manner as is before expressed in the choice of councillors.

4. That he, or they unto whom the government and education of the King's children shall be committed, shall be approved of by both Houses of Parliament; and in the intervals of Parliament, by the assent of the major part of the Council, in such manner as is before expressed in the choice of councillors; and that all such servants as are now about them, against whom both Houses shall have any just exceptions, shall be removed.

5. That no marriage shall be concluded or treated for any of the King's children, with any foreign prince, or other person whatsoever, abroad or at home, without the consent of Parliament, under the penalty of a premunire, upon such as shall conclude or treat of any marriage as aforesaid; and that the said penalty shall not be pardoned or dispensed with but by the consent of both Houses of Parliament.

6. That the laws in force against Jesuits, priests, and Popish recusants, be strictly put in execution, without any toleration or dispensation to the contrary; and that some more effectual course may be enacted, by authority of Parliament, to disable them from making any disturbance in the State, or eluding the law by trusts or otherwise.

7. That the votes of Popish lords in the House of Peers may be taken away, so long as they continue Papists: and that your Majesty will consent to such a Bill as shall be drawn for the education of the children of Papists by Protestants in the Protestant religion.

8. That your Majesty will be pleased to consent that such a reformation be made of the Church government and liturgy, as both Houses of Parliament shall advise; wherein they intend to have consultations with divines, as is expressed in their declaration to that purpose; and that your Majesty will contribute your best assistance to them, for the raising of a sufficient maintenance for preaching ministers throughout the kingdom; and that your Majesty will be pleased to give your consent to laws for the taking away of innovations and superstition, and of pluralities, and against scandalous ministers.

9. That your Majesty will be pleased to rest satisfied with that course that the Lords and Commons have appointed for ordering of the militia, until the same shall be further settled by a Bill; and that your Majesty will recall your Declarations and Proclamations against the Ordinance made by the Lords and Commons concerning it.

10. That such members of either House of Parliament as have, during the present Parliament, been put out of any place and office, may either be restored to that place and office, or otherwise have satisfaction for the same, upon the petition of that House whereof he or they are members.

11. That all Privy Councillors and Judges may take an oath, the form whereof to be agreed on and settled by Act of Parliament, for the maintaining of the Petition of Right and of certain statutes made by the Parliament, which shall be mentioned by both Houses of Parliament: and that an enquiry of all the breaches and violations of those laws may be given in charge by the Justices of the King's Bench every Term, and by the Judges of Assize in their circuits, and Justices of the Peace at the sessions, to be presented and punished according to law.

12. That all the Judges, and all the officers placed by approbation of both Houses of Parliament, may hold their

places *quam diu bene se gesserint* [during good behavior].

13. That the justice of Parliament may pass upon all delinquents, whether they be within the kingdom or fled out of it; and that all persons cited by either House of Parliament may appear and abide the censure of Parliament.

14. That the general pardon offered by your Majesty may be granted, with such exceptions as shall be advised by both Houses of Parliament.

15. That the forts and castles of this kingdom may be put under the command and custody of such persons as your Majesty shall appoint, with the approbation of your Parliament: and in the intervals of Parliament, with approbation of the major part of the Council, in such manner as is before expressed in the choice of councillors.

16. That the extraordinary guards and military forces now attending your Majesty, may be removed and discharged; and that for the future you will raise no such guards or extraordinary forces, but according to the law, in case of actual rebellion or invasion.

17. That your Majesty will be pleased to enter into a more strict alliance with the States of the United Provinces, and other neighboring princes and states of the Protestant religion, for the defense and maintenance thereof, against all designs and attempts of the Pope and his adherents to subvert and suppress it; whereby your Majesty will obtain a great access of strength and reputation, and your subjects be much encouraged and enabled, in a Parliamentary way, for your aid and assistance, in restoring your royal sister and her princely issue to those dignities and dominions which belong unto them, and relieving the other Protestant princes who have suffered in the same cause.

18. That your Majesty will be pleased, by Act of Parliament, to clear the Lord Kimbolton and the five members of the House of Commons,[1] in such manner that future Par-

[1] These are the five members of the House of Commons (John Pym, John Hampden, Denzil Holles, Sir Arthur Hesilrige, and William Strode) whom Charles I attempted to arrest on January 4, 1642. One of the peers was included on the king's list of traitors— Lord Montague of Kimbolton, later Earl of Manchester, and General in the Parliamentary Army.

liaments may be secured from the consequence of that evil precedent.

19. That your Majesty will be graciously pleased to pass a Bill for restraining peers made hereafter, from sitting or voting in Parliament, unless they be admitted thereunto with the consent of both Houses of Parliament.

And these our humble desires being granted by your Majesty, we shall forthwith apply ourselves to regulate your present revenue in such sort as may be for your best advantage; and likewise to settle such an ordinary and constant increase of it, as shall be sufficient to support your royal dignity in honor and plenty, beyond the proportion of any former grants of the subjects of this kingdom to your Majesty's royal predecessors. We shall likewise put the town of Hull into such hands as your Majesty shall appoint, with the consent and approbation of Parliament, and deliver up a just account of all the magazine, and cheerfully employ the uttermost of our power and endeavors in the real expression and performance of our most dutiful and loyal affections, to the preserving and maintaining the royal honor, greatness and safety of your Majesty and your posterity.

B. RELIGIOUS

As with the political and constitutional conflicts, so with the religious: most of the interesting and significant literature represents the views of the Puritan opposition. Just as few openly defended divine right monarchy in the Long Parliament, so few rallied to the support of Archbishop Laud and his church. Not until the triumph of Puritanism and its denial of religious freedom to the Anglicans would there be any profound defense of the Anglican Church. Since Anglicanism and Puritanism were essentially in agreement on doctrinal matters, the issues that divided them were those of church government and forms of ritual.

In 1637 Laud appeared in Star Chamber at the trial of

Bastwick, Burton, and Prynne and gave a speech in defense of the episcopacy [1]. He clearly showed the union between the institutions of monarchy and episcopacy, which, conversely, helps us to understand the basis for unity between the Puritan clergy and the supporters of parliamentary government. William Prynne's *Anti-Arminianism* [2] was published several years before Laud's speech and shows the extent to which there was thought to be a doctrinal difference between Laudianism (Arminianism), with an emphasis on free will, and Calvinistic predestination. Actually Laud had little interest in dogma. His Arminianism was grounded less in doctrinal free will than in a general predilection for retaining as much of the old Catholic ritual and clericalism as was compatible with England's independence from Rome. Just as Charles I's principles of government had few supporters in 1640, so Laud's rule of the church had driven great numbers of Anglicans into the arms of the Puritans. Not until after his fall would there be many laymen who would stand up and be counted for Anglicanism.

A *Glimpse of Sion's Glory* [3] is one of the best of the early pieces of millenarian utopianism. It not only represents a strong underlying element in much seventeenth-century Puritan thought, but it anticipates the Levellers and Diggers in the secular arena and the Fifth Monarchy Men in the religious.

"The Root and Branch Petition" [5] followed soon after the release from prison of Burton and Prynne and was supported by the London mob. It did show that even if episcopacy still had life in it, Laudianism was finished. "The Solemn League and Covenant" [6] was the death blow to Anglicanism. The Scots demanded that England adopt the Presbyterian system as the price of their support against the king. While this agreement was entered into for political and military reasons—all Puritans not being Presbyterians—it was undoubtedly true that parliament was agreed that bishops would be no more.

The alliance between parliament and the Presbyterians was later to prove very embarrassing for both sides. The latter proved to be no more interested in real religious freedom

than the Anglicans had been. As the New Model Army began
to scent victory, some of the Presbyterian clergy published "A
Letter of the Ministers against Toleration." It was in answer
to this "Letter" that William Walwyn wrote "Toleration
Justified [4]." It demonstrates that in 1646 those who were
to be the Levellers were still close to Cromwell and his Independents.

1. LAUD'S SPEECH AT THE CENSURE

In the meantime I shall remember what an ancient, under
the name of S. Hierom, tells me, *Indignum est et præpos-
terum*, 'Tis unworthy in itself, and preposterous in demeanor,
for a man to be ashamed for doing good, because other men
glory in speaking ill.

And I can say it clearly and truly, as in the presence of
God, I have done nothing, as a prelate, to the uttermost of
what I am conscious, but with a single heart, and with a sincere intention for the good government and honor of the
Church, and the maintenance of the orthodox truth and religion of Christ, professed, established, and maintained in this
Church of England.

For my care of this Church, the reducing of it into order,
the upholding of the external worship of God in it, and the
settling of it to the rules of its first reformation, are the
causes (and the sole causes, whatever are pretended) of all
this malicious storm, which hath lowered so black upon me,
and some of my brethren. And in the meantime, they which
are the only, or the chief innovators of the Christian world,
having nothing to say, accuse us of innovation; they themselves and their complices in the meantime being the greatest innovators that the Christian world hath almost ever
known. I deny not but others have spread more dangerous
errors in the Church of Christ; but no men, in any age of it,
have been more guilty of innovation than they, while themselves cry out against it. *Quis tulerit Gracchos?* [Who could
endure the Gracchi (complaining of sedition)?]

And I said well, *Quis tulerit Gracchos?* For 'tis most apparent to any man that will not wink, that the intention of these men, and their abettors, was and is to raise a sedition, being as great incendiaries in the State (where they get power) as they have ever been in the Church; Novatian himself hardly greater.

Our main crime is (would they all speak out, as some of them do), that we are bishops; were we not so, some of us might be as passable as other men.

And a great trouble 'tis to them, that we maintain that our calling of bishops is *jure divino*, by divine right: of this I have said enough, and in this place, in Leighton's case, nor will I repeat. Only this I will say, and abide by it, that the calling of bishops is *jure divino*, by divine right, though not all adjuncts to their calling. And this I say in as direct opposition to the Church of Rome, as to the Puritan humor.

And I say further, that from the Apostles' times, in all ages, in all places, the Church of Christ was governed by bishops: and lay-elders never heard of, till Calvin's new-fangled device at Geneva.

Now this is made by these men, as if it were *contra Regem*, against the King, in right or in power.

But that's a mere ignorant shift; for our being bishops *jure divino*, by divine right, takes nothing from the King's right or power over us. For though our office be from God and Christ immediately, yet may we not exercise that power, either of order or jurisdiction, but as God hath appointed us, that is, not in his Majesty's or any Christian king's kingdoms, but by and under the power of the King given us so to do.

And were this a good argument against us, as bishops, it must needs be good against priests and ministers too; for themselves grant that their calling is *jure divino*, by divine right; and yet I hope they will not say, that to be priests and ministers is against the King, or any his royal prerogatives.

Next, suppose our calling, as bishops, could not be made good *jure divino*, by divine right, yet *jure ecclesiastico*, by ecclesiastical right, it cannot be denied. And here in England the bishops are confirmed, both in their power and means, by Act of Parliament. So that here we stand in as good case as the present laws of the realm can make us. And so we must stand till the laws shall be repealed by the same power that made them.

Now then, suppose we had no other string to hold by, (I say suppose this, but I grant it not,) yet no man can libel against our calling, (as these men do,) be it in pulpit, print, or otherwise, but he libels against the King and the State, by whose laws we are established. Therefore, all these libels, so far forth as they are against our calling, are against the King and the law, and can have no other purpose than to stir up sedition among the people.

If these men had any other intention, or if they had any Christian or charitable desire to reform anything amiss, why did they not modestly petition his Majesty about it, that in his princely wisdom he might set all things right, in a just and orderly manner? But this was neither their intention nor way. For one clamors out of his pulpit, and all of them from the press, and in a most virulent and unchristian manner set themselves to make a heat among the people; and so by mutiny to effect that which by law they cannot; and by most false and unjust calumnies to defame both our callings and persons. But for my part, as I pity their rage, so I heartily pray God to forgive their malice.

No nation hath ever appeared more jealous of religion than the people of England have ever been. And their zeal to God's glory hath been, and at this day is a great honor to them. But this zeal of theirs hath not been at all times and in all persons alike guided by knowledge. Now zeal, as it is of excellent use, where it sees its way, so it is very dangerous company where it goes on in the dark: and these men, knowing the disposition of the people, have labored nothing more than to misinform their knowledge, and misguide their zeal, and so to fire that into a sedition, in hope that they whom they causelessly hate might miscarry in it.

For the main scope of these libels is to kindle a jealousy in men's minds that there are some great plots in hand, dangerous plots (so says Mr. Burton expressly) to change the orthodox religion established in England, and to bring in, I know not what, Romish superstition in the room of it. As if the external decent worship of God could not be upheld in this kingdom, without bringing in of Popery.

2. *William Prynne, ANTI-ARMINIANISM* (1630)

The Anti-Arminian orthodox assertions, now in controversy (which I shall here evince to be the ancient, the undoubted, the established doctrine of the Church of England) contract themselves into these seven dogmatical conclusions:

1. That God from all eternity hath, by his immutable purpose and decree, predestinated unto life, not all men, not any indefinite or undetermined, but only a certain select number of particular men (commonly called the Elect, invisible true Church of Christ), which number can neither be augmented nor diminished; others hath he eternally and perpetually reprobated unto death.

2. That the only moving or efficient cause of election, of predestination unto life, is the mere good pleasure, love, free grace, and mercy of God; not the preconsideration of any foreseen faith, perseverance, good works, good will, good endeavors, or any other pre-required quality or condition whatsoever, in the persons elected.

3. That though sin be the only cause of damnation, yet the sole, the primary cause of reprobation or non-election (that is, why God doth not elect those men that perish, or why he doth pass by this man rather than another, as he rejected Esau when he elected Jacob) is the mere free will and pleasure of God, not the prevision, the pre-consideration of any actual sin, infidelity, or final impenitency in the persons rejected.

4. That there is not any such free will, any such universal or sufficient grace communicated unto all men, whereby they may repent, believe, or be saved if they will themselves.

5. That Christ Jesus died sufficiently for all men (his death being of sufficient intrinsical merit in itself, though not in God's intention, or his Spirit's application, to redeem and save even all mankind), but primarily, really, and effectually for none but the Elect, for whom alone he hath actually impetrated, effectually obtained remission of sins, and life eternal.

6. That the Elect do always constantly obey, neither do

they, or can they, finally or totally resist the inward powerful and effectual call or working of God's Spirit in their hearts, in the very act of their conversion: neither is it in their own power to convert or not convert themselves, at that very instant time when they were converted.

7. That true justifying, saving faith is proper and peculiar to the Elect alone, who after they are once truly regenerated and engrafted into Christ by faith, do always constantly persevere unto the end; and though they sometimes fall through infirmity into grievous sins, yet they never fall totally nor finally from the habits, seeds, and state of grace.

3. [Hanserd Knollys], A GLIMPSE OF SION'S GLORY (1641)

Rev. 19. 6: *And I heard as it were the voice of a great multitude, and as the voice of many waters, and as the voice of mighty thunderings, saying: Hallelujah, for the Lord God Omnipotent reigneth.*

At the pouring forth of the first vial, there was a voice saying: *Babylon is fallen, it is fallen.* At the pouring forth of the sixth, John hears a voice as the voice of many waters, and as the voice of thunderings, saying: *Hallelujah, the Lord God Omnipotent reigneth,* immediately following the other. Babylon's falling is Sion's raising. Babylon's destruction is Jerusalem's salvation. The fourth vial was poured upon the sun, which is yet doing, namely upon the Emperor and that house of Austria, and will be till that house be destroyed. . . . This is the work that is in hand. As soon as ever this is done, that Antichrist is down, Babylon fallen, then comes in Jesus Christ reigning gloriously; then comes in this *Hallelujah, the Lord God Omnipotent reigneth.* . . . It is the work of the day to cry down Babylon, that it may fall more and more; and it is the work of the day to give God no rest till he sets up Jerusalem as the praise of the whole world. Blessed is he that dasheth the brats of Babylon against the stones. Blessed is he that hath any hand in pulling down Babylon. And beautiful likewise are the feet of them that bring glad tidings unto Jerusalem, unto Zion, saying, *The Lord God*

Omnipotent reigneth. This is the work of this exercise: to show unto you how, upon the destruction of Babylon, Christ shall reign gloriously, and how we are to further it. . . .

From whence came this hallelujah? *I heard as it were the voice of a great multitude, and as the voice of many waters.* By waters we are to understand people: the voice of many waters, of many people. . . .

The voice, of Jesus Christ reigning in his Church, comes first from the multitude, the common people. The voice is heard from them first, before it is heard from any others. God uses the common people and the multitude to proclaim that the Lord God Omnipotent reigneth. As when Christ came at first the poor receive[d] the Gospel—not many wise, not many noble, not many rich, but the poor—so in the reformation of religion, after Antichrist began to be discovered, it was the common people that first came to look after Christ. . . . The business, brethren, concerning the Scots, it is a business in the issue whereof we hope there will be great things. Where began it? At the very feet, at the very soles of the feet. You that are of the meaner rank, common people, be not discouraged; for God intends to make use of the common people in the great work of proclaiming the kingdom of his Son: *The Lord God Omnipotent reigneth.* The voice that will come of Christ's reigning is like to begin from those that are the multitude, that are so contemptible, especially in the eyes and account of Antichrist's spirits and the prelacy: the vulgar multitude, the common people—what more condemned in their mouths than they? . . .

Though the voice of Christ's reign came first from the multitude; yet it comes but in a confused manner, as the noise of many waters. Though the multitude may begin a thing, and their intention may be good in it, yet it is not for them to bring it to perfection: that which they do commonly is mixed with much confusion and a great deal of disorder. . . . The people had a hint of something: Down with Antichrist, down with popery. Not understanding distinctly what they did, their voice was but as the voice of many waters. Therefore it follows: *and as the voice of mighty thunderings.* . . . After the beginning of this confused noise among the multitude, God moves the hearts of great ones, of noble, of

learned ones; and they come in to the work, and their voice
is as the voice of mighty thundering, a voice that strikes terror, and hath a majesty in it to prevail. . . . This is the work
of the day, for us to lift up our voice to heaven, that it might
be mighty to bring forth more and more the voice of our
Parliament as a voice of thunder, a terrible voice to the Anti-
christian party, that they may say, *The Lord God Omnipotent reigneth.* And let us not be discouraged, for our prayers,
though they be poor and mean, and scattered, they may
further the voice of thunderings. . . .

Though Christ's kingdom be for a while darkened, Christ
shall reign gloriously. That is implied. It is revealed to John
as a great wonder, as a glorious thing. Why, did not Christ
reign before? Yes, but not in that manner that now he is to
reign: the kingdom of Christ hath been exceedingly darkened
in the world: though it now begins to appear a little more
brightly, it hath been exceedingly darkened. . . .

It may be, it is to be a stumbling block to wicked and
ungodly men in his just judgment, that they should see and
not understand. And it was upon this ground that God suffered his kingdom to be darkened hitherto, that Antichrist
might prevail: because of much glory that he is intending
to bring out of the prevailing of Antichrist in the world,
therefore in his providence he hath so permitted it as that
the kingdom of his Son for many years should be darkened.
And (my brethren) if the kingdom of Christ had been kept
in congregations in that way that we and some other churches
are in, it had been impossible that Antichrist should have
got head. But God in his providence, because he would permit Antichrist to rise and to rule for a long time—and he had
many things to bring out of the kingdom of Antichrist, to
work for his glory—therefore God hath left this truth to be so
dark: the setting up of Christ in his kingly office. Thirdly,
because God would exercise the faith and other graces of his
Spirit in his children, that they might believe in, and love
Jesus Christ for his spiritual beauty, though there appears
nothing but spiritual beauty, though no outward beauty, no
outward kingdom doth appear, but he be as a spiritual king
only. . . . And the less Christ doth reign outwardly in the
world, the less glorious his kingdom doth appear outwardly,

the more let us labor to bring our hearts under his spiritual reign. . . . For yet the voice is not heard much, that the Lord God Omnipotent reigneth, abroad in the world, though lately some noise we have heard. But blessed be God, in our congregations amongst us we may hear that the Lord God Omnipotent reigneth. It is through our wretched wickedness if his kingly power be not fully set up amongst us in all his ordinances. And that we should have an opportunity to set up his kingly power amongst us here, while it is so much opposed and so little known in the world, it is a great mercy. . . .

But though it be dark for a while, certainly he shall reign, and the voice will be glorious and distinct one day, saying, *Hallelujah, the Lord God Omnipotent reigneth*. He shall reign first personally; secondly, in his Saints.

First, personally. We will not fully determine of the manner of his personal reigning. But thus far we may see there is . . . a probability, in his person, God and Man, he shall reign upon the earth, here in this world, before that great and solemn day. There are divers scriptures that have somewhat of this in them. We cannot give the distinct voice of those scriptures, but many of God's Saints, they do hear something, and when a thing grows nearer and nearer God will reveal it more distinct. Zech. 12. 10: *They shall look upon him whom they have pierced, and shall mourn for him as one mourneth for his only son*. It is usually understood either of a spiritual looking by the eye of faith or beholding Christ at the day of judgment. But why should we take it for a spiritual looking, and looking at the day of judgment? That [the] place doth not hold out; that is not the thing intended. They shall mourn every one apart: this is not like the setting forth of the mourning at the day of judgment. And take but this one rule: that all texts are to be understood literally, except they make against some other scriptures, or except the very coherence and dependence of the scripture shows it otherwise, or it makes against the analogy of faith. Now there is nothing against this, but it may be so. A second scripture that seems to hold out somewhat is that in the 26th of Matthew, 29: *I will not henceforth drink of the fruit of the vine, until that day when I drink it new with you in my*

Father's kingdom. It is true, this is likewise interpreted in a mystical sense; but there is no reason why we may not take it literally. Not in the kingdom of his Father in heaven; but in that kingdom that he shall come in here, to drink the fruit of the vine, to have communion with his Saints in this world. 2 Thess. 2. 8: *Antichrist shall be destroyed by the brightness of Christ's coming, the brightness of his personal coming.* And that place (Rev. 20) where it is said, *The Saints shall reign with him a thousand years,* which cannot be meant reigning with him in heaven. It is made as a proper peculiar benefit unto such as had refused Antichrist's government, especially to the Christian Church. It is likely divers of the prophets and patriarchs may come in, but especially it belongs to the Christian Church. Now the reigning with Christ a thousand years is not meant reigning with him in heaven. For after these thousand years there shall be many enemies raised against the Church; Gog and Magog shall gather themselves together. If it were meant of heaven, that could not be; and therefore it must be meant of Jesus Christ coming and reigning here gloriously for a thousand years. And although this may seem to be strange, yet heretofore it hath not been accounted so. It hath been a truth received in the primitive times. Justin Martyr, that lived presently after John, he spake of this as a thing that all Christians acknowledged; and likewise Lactantius hath such expressions in divers places of his seventh book. . . .

God intends to honor Christ and the Saints before the world. . . . And God is pleased to raise the hearts of his people to expect it; and those that are most humble, most godly, most gracious, most spiritual, searching into the scriptures, have their hearts most raised in expectation of this. And it is not like, that that work of the Spirit of theirs shall be in vain. But God is beginning to clear it up more and more. God is beginning to stir in the world, and to do great things in the world, the issue whereof (I hope) will come to that we speak of. . . .

The first thing wherein the happiness of the Church consists is this: that it shall be delivered from all the enemies of it, and from all molesting troubles, and so be in a most blessed safety and security. The God of peace shall tread down Satan shortly, and all that are of Satan. Christ is described in this Rev. 19, with his garment dyed in blood, when he doth appear to come and take the kingdom. And he appeared with many crowns on his head; that notes his many victories, and his name was King of Kings and Lord of Lords. And the Saints appeared triumphing with him, clothed with white linen and set upon white horses. Is that a clothing for soldiers? Yes, for the army of Christ, that rather comes to triumph than for to fight. Christ fighteth and vanquisheth all these enemies; and they come triumphing in white. . . . And this city that is described in the Revelation shall have the gates always open, in regard of the security that is there—no danger at all of any enemy.

Secondly, there shall be a wonderful confluence of people to this church: both Jew and Gentile shall join together to flow to the beautifulness of the Lord. Dan. 2. 35: Christ is compared to the stone that shall break the image and shall become a mountain, and fill the whole heaven. Isa. 60. [8]: *They shall come as doves to the windows.* And when John came to measure the city, the Church, it was a great and mighty city.

Thirdly, because where there is much confluence, there useth to be a contraction of much filthiness; therefore, in the third place, it shall be most pure—a pure church, yea, in great part, if not altogether; nay, we may almost affirm, altogether to be delivered from hypocrites. *Without there shall be dogs, and whosoever shall work or make a lie.* Not without, in hell; but without the church. Hypocrites shall be discovered and cast out from the church. Though many get into the church now; then the righteous nation shall enter in. In the 44th of Ezekiel, 9, there is a description of the Church under the Gospel; and he shows that none uncircumcised in heart shall enter in there. But the fulfilling of the prophecies of those chapters in the latter end of Ezekiel will not be till this time; and then no uncircumcised in heart shall enter. Rev. 21. 27: *There shall in no wise enter into it anything that defileth, &c. . . .* It is a most pure church, and therefore is described: the walls to be precious stones, the city to be as clear as glass, and the pavement to be pure gold.

Fourthly, there shall be abundance of glorious prophecies fulfilled, and glorious promises accomplished. When you read the Prophets, you have prophecies of many glorious things; and the knowledge of this truth will help to understand those prophecies. . . .

Fifthly, abundance of hidden mysteries of godliness will be cleared then, that now are exceeding dark. . . . Rev. 11. 19: *There was seen the Ark of the Testament;* whereas the Ark stood before in the Holy of Holies that was shut up, that none was to come into it but the High Priest. But now it is opened to all. In the Ark were the secrets, a type of the secrets that shall be opened at this time, that were shut up before. Glorious truths shall be revealed, and above all the mystery of the Gospel and the righteousness of faith shall be discovered. Before, what a little of the mystery of the Gospel and the righteousness of faith was discovered! But this will grow brighter and brighter till that time, which is the great design of God for his glory to all eternity.

Sixthly, the gift of the Saints shall be abundantly raised. He that is weak shall be as David; and he that is strong, as the Angel of the Lord (Zech. 12. 8). And then shall be accomplished that promise that *God will pour his Spirit on them; and their young men shall see visions, and their old men shall dream dreams.* It was fulfilled in part upon the Apostles, but the full is not till that time knowledge shall be increased.

Seventhly, the graces of the Saints shall be wonderfully enlarged, even in a manner glorified; though not so full as afterwards in the highest heaven, but mightily raised. The Saints shall be all clothed in white linen, which is the righteousness of the Saints; that is, the righteousness they have by Christ, whereby they shall be righteous before God, and holy before men. Holiness shall be written upon their pots, and upon their bridles: upon every thing their graces shall shine forth exceedingly to the glory of God. . . .

The people of God have been, and are, a despised people. But their reproach shall be for ever taken away, and they shall not be ashamed of religion, for it shall be glorified before the sons of men. . . . There are notable texts of scripture to show the great honor that shall be in the ways of religion. Isa. 49. 23: *Kings shall be thy nursing fathers, and queens thy nursing mothers; they shall bow down to thee, and lick up the dust of thy feet.* What a high expression is this for the honor of godliness! . . . The second place is in Zech. 12. 5: *The governors of Judah shall say in their hearts: The inhabitants of Jerusalem shall be my strength in the Lord of Hosts, their God.* We know that now in many places the governors of Judah, the great ones of the country, their spirits have been set against the Saints of God. We know what reproachful names they have put upon them, and how they have discountenanced them. Though the governors of Judah have counted them factious, and schismatics, and Puritans, there is a time coming when the governors of Judah shall be convinced of the excellency of God's people, so convinced as to say in their hearts that the inhabitants of Jerusalem, that is, the Saints of God gathered together in a church, are the best commonwealth's men: not seditious men, not factious, not disturbers of the state. . . . This shall be when the Lord God Omnipotent reigneth in his Church. And through God's mercy we see light peeping out this way. . . .

In the ninth place, the presence of Jesus Christ and of God shall be exceeding glorious in the Church: then the name of it shall be called Jehovah Shammah, *The Lord is there.* They shall follow the Lamb wheresoever he goeth; they shall see the King in his beauty and glory. And such a presence of Christ will be there as it is questionable whether there shall be need of ordinances, at least in that way that now there is. And therefore some interpret that place so: *They shall be all taught of God, and shall not need to teach one another.* . . . The presence of Christ shall be there and supply all kind of ordinances. . . .

In the tenth place, . . . many of the worthies of God, that have lived in former times, shall rise again. . . .

The eleventh is this: there shall be most blessed union of all the churches of the world. . . . Blessed will the time be when all dissensions shall be taken away; and when there shall be a perfect union of all, and not any distinction of Calvinists or Lutherans, or the like, but all shall come and serve God and be called by one name.

The twelfth is the resurrection of the creatures of the world: and so in that regard there shall be abundance of outward glory and prosperity. . . . When the fulness of the glory of the adoption of the sons of God shall come, the creatures shall be delivered to them. The whole world is purchased by Christ, and purchased for the Saints, that is Christ's aim. *All is yours,* says the Apostle, *the whole world;* and therefore (Rev. 21. 7) it is said, *The Saints shall inherit all things.* You see that the Saints have little now in the world; now they are the poorest and the meanest of all; but then when the adoption of the sons of God shall come in the fulness of it, the world shall be theirs; for the world is purchased for them by Jesus Christ. *Not only heaven shall be your kingdom, but this world bodily.* . . .

But you will say, Are these things true? To that we answer: For the truth of them I will go no further than this chapter, verse 9, *These are the true sayings of God.* . . .

But how can they be? Zech. 8. 9: *If it be marvellous in your eyes, should it also be marvellous in my eyes? saith the Lord of Hosts.* . . . It is God Omnipotent that shall do these things, by that power, *whereby he is able to subdue all things unto himself.* Mountains shall be made plain, and he shall come skipping over mountains and over difficulties. Nothing shall hinder him. . . .

But when shall these things be? Truly, brethren, we hope it is not long before they shall be; and the nearer the time comes, the more clearly these things shall be revealed. . . . No place in scripture gives us so much light to know when this shall be as Dan. 12. 11. *And from the time that the daily sacrifices shall be taken away, and the abomination that maketh desolate set up, there shall be a thousand, two hundred and ninety days.* What is the meaning of this? The light that I have from this, I acknowledge to be from that worthy instrument of God, Mr. Brightman.[1] A day is usually taken for a year, and so many days as were set, so many years it should be. All the question is about the beginning of the time. This abomination of desolation was in Julian's time, in

[1] Thomas Brightman published *Apocalypsis Apocalypseos* in 1609. This was one of several works which documented the final victory of God's elect.

360, because then Julian would set up the Temple again (that was destroyed), in despite of the Christians, and would set up the Jewish religion again. That was the abomination of desolation, says he; and the whole Jewish religion was not consumed till that time. Now reckon so many years according to the number of the days, it comes to 1650; and it is now 1641, and that place for the abomination of desolation is like to be it as any that can be named. But it is said, *Blessed is he that comes to another number:* 1335 days; that is 45 years more added. That is, says he, in 1650 they shall begin; but it shall be 45 years before it comes to full head, and blessed is he that comes to this day. And he hath hit right in other things, as never the like, in making Sardis to be the church of Germany, and foretold from thence how things would fall out, and we see now are. Now we have also a voice from the multitude as from the waters, and it begins to come from the thunderings. . . .

If God hath such an intention to glorify his Church, and that in this world, oh, let every one say to his own heart: What manner of persons ought we to be? . . . Because you are beginning this despised work, gathering a church together, which way God will honor. Certainly, the communion of Saints, and independency of congregations, God will honor. And this work is a foundation of abundance of glory that God shall have, and will continue till the coming of Christ. And blessed are they that are now content to keep the word of God's patience. And do you keep the word of God's patience though you suffer for it, as you now do. . . . Take heed that you lose not this opportunity; certainly if there should fall out any just cause amongst you of scandal in regard of divisions, or any other way, you may do more hurt to hinder this glorious work than all the persecutors could do. For you will persuade the consciences of men that this is not the way of Christ—persecutors cannot do so—so that the governors of Judah will not say, *Our strength is in the inhabitants of Jerusalem, those that profess themselves to be the people of Jerusalem.*

4. TOLERATION JUSTIFIED by William Walwyn (1646)

That the ministers [Presbyterian] know that the Independent Government for the General is resolved upon by the Independents, though they have not yet modelized every particular, which is a work of time, as the framing of the Presbyterian Government was. The Independents however have divers reasons for dissenting from the Presbyterian way, which they have given in already. And though they have not concluded every particular of their own, but are still upon the search, and enquiry; yet it is seasonable however to move for toleration, for that the ground of moving is not because they are Independents, but because every man ought to be free in the worship and service of God, compulsion being the way to increase, not the number of Converts, but of Hypocrites.

5. THE ROOT AND BRANCH PETITION
[11 December 1640]

The humble Petition of many of His Majesty's subjects in and about the City of London, and several Counties of the Kingdom,

Showeth,

That whereas the government of archbishops and lord bishops, deans and archdeacons, &c., with their courts and ministrations in them, have proved prejudicial and very dangerous both to the Church and Commonwealth, they themselves having formerly held that they have their jurisdiction or authority of human authority, till of these later times, being further pressed about the unlawfulness, that they have claimed their calling immediately from the Lord Jesus Christ, which is against the laws of this kingdom, and derogatory to His Majesty and his state royal. And whereas the said government is found by woeful experience to be a main cause and occasion of many foul evils, pressures and grievances of a very high nature unto His Majesty's subjects in their own consciences, liberties and estates, as in a schedule of particulars hereunto annexed may in part appear:

We therefore most humbly pray, and beseech this honorable assembly, the premises considered, that the said government, with all its dependencies, roots and branches, may be abolished, and all laws in their behalf made void, and the government according to God's Word may be rightly placed amongst us: and we your humble suppliants, as in duty we are bound, will daily pray for His Majesty's long and happy reign over us, and for the prosperous success of this high and honorable Court of Parliament.

> A *Particular of the manifold evils, pressures, and grievances caused, practiced and occasioned by the Prelates and their dependents.*

1. The subjecting and enthralling all ministers under them and their authority, and so by degrees exempting them from the temporal power; whence follows,

2. The faint-heartedness of ministers to preach the truth of God, lest they should displease the prelates; as namely, the doctrine of predestination, of free grace, of perseverance, of original sin remaining after baptism, of the sabbath, the doctrine against universal grace, election for faith foreseen, free-will against antichrist, non-residents, human inventions in God's worship; all which are generally withheld from the people's knowledge, because not relishing to the bishops.

3. The encouragement of ministers to despise the temporal magistracy, the nobles and gentry of the land; to abuse the subjects, and live contentiously with their neighbors, knowing that they, being the bishops' creatures, shall be supported.

4. The restraint of many godly and able men from the ministry, and thrusting out of many congregations their faithful, diligent, and powerful ministers, who lived peaceably with them, and did them good, only because they cannot in conscience submit unto and maintain the bishops' needless devices; nay, sometimes for no other cause but for their zeal in preaching, or great auditories.

5. The suppressing of that godly design set on foot by certain saints, and sugared with many great gifts by sundry

well-affected persons for the buying of impropriations, and placing of able ministers in them, maintaining of lectures, and founding of free schools, which the prelates could not endure, lest it should darken their glories, and draw the ministers from their dependence upon them.

6. The great increase of idle, lewd and dissolute, ignorant and erroneous men in the ministry, which swarm like the locusts of Egypt over the whole kingdom; and will they but wear a canonical coat, a surplice, a hood, bow at the name of Jesus, and be zealous of superstitious. ceremonies, they may live as they list, confront whom they please, preach and vent what errors they will, and neglect preaching at their pleasures without control.

7. The discouragement of many from bringing up their children in learning; the many schisms, errors, and strange opinions which are in the Church; great corruptions which are in the Universities; the gross and lamentable ignorance almost everywhere among the people; the want of preaching ministers in very many places both of England and Wales; the loathing of the ministry, and the general defection to all manner of profaneness.

8. The swarming of lascivious, idle, and unprofitable books and pamphlets, play-books and ballads; as namely, Ovid's 'Fits of Love,' 'The Parliament of Women,' which came out at the dissolving of the last Parliament; Barns's 'Poems,' Parker's 'Ballads,' in disgrace of religion, to the increase of all vice, and withdrawing of people from reading, studying, and hearing the Word of God, and other good books.

9. The hindering of godly books to be printed, the blotting out or perverting those which they suffer, all or most of that which strikes either at Popery or Arminianism; the adding of what or where pleaseth them, and the restraint of reprinting books formerly licensed, without relicensing.

10. The publishing and venting of Popish, Arminian, and other dangerous books and tenets; as namely, 'That the Church of Rome is a true Church, and in the worst times never erred in fundamentals'; 'that the subjects have no propriety in their estates, but that the King may take from them what he pleaseth'; 'that all is the King's, and that he is bound

by no law'; and many other, from the former whereof hath sprung,

11. The growth of Popery and increase of Papists, Priests and Jesuits in sundry places, but especially about London since the Reformation; the frequent venting of crucifixes and Popish pictures both engraven and printed, and the placing of such in Bibles.

12. The multitude of monopolies and patents, drawing with them innumerable perjuries; the large increase of customs and impositions upon commodities, the ship-money, and many other great burthens upon the Commonwealth, under which all groan.

13. Moreover, the offices and jurisdictions of archbishops, lord bishops, deans, archdeacons, being the same way of Church government, which is in the Romish Church, and which was in England in the time of Popery, little change thereof being made (except only the head from whence it was derived), the same arguments supporting the Pope which do uphold the prelates, and overthrowing the prelates, which do pull down the Pope; and other Reformed Churches, having upon their rejection of the Pope cast the prelates out also as members of the beast. Hence it is that the prelates here in England, by themselves or their disciples, plead and maintain that the Pope is not Antichrist, and that the Church of Rome is a true Church, hath not erred in fundamental points, and that salvation is attainable in that religion, and therefore have restrained to pray for the conversion of our Sovereign Lady the Queen. Hence also hath come,

14. The great conformity and likeness both continued and increased of our Church to the Church of Rome, in vestures, postures, ceremonies and administrations, namely as the bishops' rochets and the lawn-sleeves, the four-cornered cap, the cope and surplice, the tippet, the hood, and the canonical coat; the pulpits, clothed, especially now of late, with the Jesuits' badge upon them every way.

15. The standing up at *Gloria Patri* and at the reading of the Gospel, praying towards the East, the bowing at the name of Jesus, the bowing to the altar towards the East, cross in baptism, the kneeling at the Communion.

16. The turning of the Communion-table altar-wise, set-

ting images, crucifixes, and conceits over them, and tapers and books upon them, and bowing or adoring to or before them; the reading of the second service at the altar, and forcing people to come up thither to receive, or else denying the sacrament to them; terming the altar to be the mercy-seat, or the place of God Almighty in the church, which is a plain device to usher in the Mass.

17. The christening and consecrating of churches and chapels, the consecrating fonts, tables, pulpits, chalices, churchyards, and many other things, and putting holiness in them; yea, reconsecrating upon pretended pollution, as though everything were unclean without their consecrating; and for want of this sundry churches have been interdicted, and kept from use as polluted.

18. The Liturgy for the most part is framed out of the Romish Breviary, Rituals, Mass-book, also the Book of Ordination for archbishops and ministers framed out of the Roman Pontifical.

19. The multitude of canons formerly made, wherein among other things excommunication, *ipso facto*, is denounced for speaking of a word against the devices above-said, or subscription thereunto, though no law enjoined a restraint from the ministry without subscription, and appeal is denied to any that should refuse subscription or unlawful conformity, though he be never so much wronged by the inferior judges. Also the canons made in the late Sacred Synod, as they call it, wherein are many strange and dangerous devices to undermine the Gospel and the subjects' liberties, to propagate Popery, to spoil God's people, ensnare ministers, and other students, and so to draw all into an absolute subjection and thralldom to them and their government, spoiling both the King and the Parliament of their power.

20. The countenancing plurality of benefices, prohibiting of marriages without their license, at certain times almost half the year, and licensing of marriages without banns asking.

21. Profanation of the Lord's Day, pleading for it, and enjoining ministers to read a Declaration set forth (as it is thought) by their procurement for tolerating of sports upon

that day, suspending and depriving many godly ministers for not reading the same only out of conscience, because it was against the law of God so to do, and no law of the land to enjoin it.

22. The pressing of the strict observation of the saints' days, whereby great sums of money are drawn out of men's purses for working on them; a very high burthen on most people, who getting their living on their daily employments, must either omit them, and be idle, or part with their money, whereby many poor families are undone, or brought behind-hand; yet many churchwardens are sued, or threatened to be sued by their troublesome ministers, as perjured persons, for not presenting their parishioners who failed in observing holy-days.

23. The great increase and frequency of whoredoms and adulteries, occasioned by the prelates' corrupt administration of justice in such cases, who taking upon them the punishment of it, do turn all into monies for the filling of their purses; and lest their officers should defraud them of their gain, they have in their late canon, instead of remedying these vices, decreed that the commutation of penance shall not be without the bishops' privity.

24. The general abuse of that great ordinance of excommunication, which God hath left in His Church as the last and greatest punishment which the Church can inflict upon obstinate and great offenders; and the prelates and their officers, who of right have nothing to do with it, do daily excommunicate men, either for doing that which is lawful, or for vain, idle, and trivial matters, as working, or opening a shop on a holy-day, for not appearing at every beck upon their summons, not paying a fee, or the like; yea, they have made it, as they do all other things, a hook or instrument wherewith to empty men's purses, and to advance their own greatness; and so that sacred ordinance of God, by their perverting of it, becomes contemptible to all men, and is seldom or never used against notorious offenders, who for the most part are their favorites.

25. Yea further, the pride and ambition of the prelates being boundless, unwilling to be subject either to man or laws, they claim their office and jurisdiction to be *Jure Divino*,

exercise ecclesiastical authority in their own names and rights, and under their own seals, and take upon them temporal dignities, places and offices in the Commonwealth, that they may sway both swords.

26. Whence follows the taking Commissions in their own Courts and Consistories, and where else they sit in matters determinable of right at Common Law, the putting of ministers upon parishes, without the patron's and people's consent.

27. The imposing of oaths of various and trivial articles yearly upon churchwardens and sidesmen, which they cannot take without perjury, unless they fall at jars continually with their ministers and neighbors, and wholly neglect their own calling.

28. The excercising of the oath *ex officio*, and other proceedings by way of inquisition, reaching even to men's thoughts, the apprehending and detaining of men by pursuivants, the frequent suspending and depriving of ministers, fining and imprisoning of all sorts of people, breaking up of men's houses and studies, taking away men's books, letters, and other writings, seizing upon their estates, removing them from their callings, separating between them and their wives against both their wills, the rejecting of prohibitions with threatenings, and the doing of many other outrages, to the utter infringing the laws of the realm and the subjects' liberties, and ruining of them and their families; and of later time the judges of the land are so awed with the power and greatness of the prelates, and other ways promoted, that neither prohibition, *Habeas Corpus*, nor any other lawful remedy can be had, or take place, for the distressed subjects in most cases; only Papists, Jesuits, Priests, and such others as propagate Popery or Arminianism, are countenanced, spared, and have much liberty; and from hence followed amongst others these dangerous consequences.

1. The general hope and expectation of the Romish party, that their superstitious religion will ere long be fully planted in this kingdom again, and so they are encouraged to persist therein, and to practice the same openly in divers places, to the high dishonor of God, and contrary to the laws of the realm.

2. The discouragement and destruction of all good subjects, of whom are multitudes, both clothiers, merchants and others, who being deprived of their ministers, and overburthened with these pressures, have departed the kingdom to Holland, and other parts, and have drawn with them a great manufacture of cloth and trading out of the land into other places where they reside, whereby wool, the great staple of the kingdom, is become of small value, and vends not; trading is decayed, many poor people want work, seamen lose employment, and the whole land is much impoverished, to the great dishonor of this kingdom and blemishment to the government thereof.

3. The present wars and commotions happened between His Majesty and his subjects of Scotland, wherein His Majesty and all his kingdoms are endangered, and suffer greatly, and are like to become a prey to the common enemy in case the wars go on, which we exceedingly fear will not only go on, but also increase to an utter ruin of all, unless the prelates with their dependences be removed out of England, and also they and their practices, who, as we under your Honor's favors, do verily believe and conceive have occasioned the quarrel.

All which we humbly refer to the consideration of this Honorable Assembly, desiring the Lord of heaven to direct you in the right way to redress all these evils.

6. THE SOLEMN LEAGUE AND COVENANT
[*House of Commons, 25 September 1643*]

A solemn league and covenant for Reformation and Defense of Religion, the honor and happiness of the King, and the peace and safety of the three kingdoms of England, Scotland and Ireland.

We noblemen, barons, knights, gentlemen, citizens, burgesses, ministers of the Gospel, and commons of all sorts in the kingdoms of England, Scotland and Ireland, by the providence of God living under one King, and being of one reformed religion; having before our eyes the glory of God, and the advancement of the kingdom of our Lord and Savior Jesus

Christ, the honor and happiness of the King's Majesty and his posterity, and the true public liberty, safety and peace of the kingdoms, wherein every one's private condition is included; and calling to mind the treacherous and bloody plots, conspiracies, attempts and practices of the enemies of God against the true religion and professors thereof in all places, especially in these three kingdoms, ever since the reformation of religion; and how much their rage, power and presumption are of late, and at this time increased and exercised, whereof the deplorable estate of the Church and kingdom of Ireland, the distressed estate of the Church and kingdom of England, and the dangerous estate of the Church and kingdom of Scotland, are present and public testimonies: we have (now at last) after other means of supplication, remonstrance, protestations and sufferings, for the preservation of ourselves and our religion from utter ruin and destruction, according to the commendable practice of these kingdoms in former times, and the example of God's people in other nations, after mature deliberation, resolved and determined to enter into a mutual and solemn league and covenant, wherein we all subscribe, and each one of us for himself, with our hands lifted up to the most high God, do swear,

I

That we shall sincerely, really and constantly, through the grace of God, endeavor in our several places and callings, the preservation of the reformed religion in the Church of Scotland, in doctrine, worship, discipline and government, against our common enemies; the reformation of religion in the kingdoms of England and Ireland, in doctrine, worship, discipline and government, according to the Word of God, and the example of the best reformed Churches; and we shall endeavor to bring the Churches of God in the three kingdoms to the nearest conjunction and uniformity in religion, confession of faith, form of Church government, directory for worship and catechising, that we, and our posterity after us, may, as brethren, live in faith and love, and the Lord may delight to dwell in the midst of us.

II

That we shall in like manner, without respect of persons, endeavor the extirpation of Popery, prelacy (that is, Church government by Archbishops, Bishops, their Chancellors and Commissaries, Deans, Deans and Chapters, Archdeacons, and all other ecclesiastical officers depending on that hierarchy), superstition, heresy, schism, profaneness, and whatsoever shall be found to be contrary to sound doctrine and the power of godliness, lest we partake in other men's sins, and thereby be in danger to receive of their plagues; and that the Lord may be one, and His name one in the three kingdoms.

III

We shall with the same sincerity, reality and constancy, in our several vocations, endeavor with our estates and lives mutually to preserve the rights and privileges of the Parliaments, and the liberties of the kingdoms, and to preserve and defend the King's Majesty's person and authority, in the preservation and defense of the true religion and liberties of the kingdoms, that the world may bear witness with our consciences of our loyalty, and that we have no thoughts or intentions to diminish His Majesty's just power and greatness.

IV

We shall also with all faithfulness endeavor the discovery of all such as have been or shall be incendiaries, malignants or evil instruments, by hindering the reformation of religion, dividing the King from his people, or one of the kingdoms from another, or making any faction or parties amongst the people, contrary to the league and covenant, that they may be brought to public trial and receive condign punishment, as the degree of their offenses shall require or deserve, or the supreme judicatories of both kingdoms respectively, or others having power from them for that effect, shall judge convenient.

V

And whereas the happiness of a blessed peace between these kingdoms, denied in former times to our progenitors, is by the good providence of God granted to us, and hath been lately concluded and settled by both Parliaments: we shall each one of us, according to our places and interest, endeavor that they may remain conjoined in a firm peace and union to all posterity, and that justice may be done upon the willful opposers thereof, in manner expressed in the precedent articles.

VI

We shall also, according to our places and callings, in this common cause of religion, liberty and peace of the kingdom, assist and defend all those that enter into this league and covenant, in the maintaining and pursuing thereof; and shall not suffer ourselves, directly or indirectly, by whatsoever combination, persuasion or terror, to be divided and withdrawn from this blessed union and conjunction, whether to make defection to the contrary part, or give ourselves to a detestable indifferency or neutrality in this cause, which so much concerneth the glory of God, the good of the kingdoms, and the honor of the King; but shall all the days of our lives zealously and constantly continue therein, against all opposition, and promote the same according to our power, against all lets and impediments whatsoever; and what we are not able ourselves to suppress or overcome we shall reveal and make known, that it may be timely prevented or removed: all which we shall do as in the sight of God.

And because these kingdoms are guilty of many sins and provocations against God, and His Son Jesus Christ, as is too manifest by our present distresses and dangers, the fruits thereof: we profess and declare, before God and the world, our unfeigned desire to be humbled for our own sins, and for the sins of these kingdoms; especially that we have not as we ought valued the inestimable benefit of the Gospel; that we have not labored for the purity and power thereof; and that we have not endeavored to receive Christ in our hearts, nor to walk worthy of Him in our lives, which are the causes of other sins and transgressions so much abounding amongst us; and our true and unfeigned purpose, desire and endeavor, for ourselves and all others under our power and charge, both in public and in private, in all duties we owe to God and man, to amend our lives, and each one to go before another in the example of a real reformation, that the Lord may turn away His wrath and heavy indignation, and establish these Churches and kingdoms in truth and peace. And this covenant we make in the presence of Almighty God, the Searcher of all hearts, with a true intention to perform the same, as we shall answer at that Great Day when the secrets of all hearts shall be disclosed: most humbly beseeching the Lord to strengthen us by His Holy Spirit for this end, and to bless our desires and proceedings with such success as may be a deliverance and safety to His people, and encouragement to the Christian Churches groaning under or in danger of the yoke of Antichristian tyranny, to join in the same or like association and covenant, to the glory of God, the enlargement of the kingdom of Jesus Christ, and the peace and tranquillity of Christian kingdoms and commonwealths.

THE RIVAL ARMIES

Traditionally the history books have made much of the supposed natural superiority of the Cavalier or Royalist army over the Parliamentary army at the commencement of hostilities. The following selection from the Royalist Clarendon [1], stresses, perhaps with the advantage of hindsight, the difficulties Charles had in preparing his disparate forces for battle. He records the great advantages in men, money, organization, and compulsion which were at the service of parliament, years before the creation of the New Model Army.

Yet it is true that not until after "The Self-Denying Ordinance" [2] and the creation of the New Model Army in 1645 was victory won by parliament. This New Model, some of whose exploits Cromwell described in a letter to the Speaker of the House of Commons [3], was surely one of the most remarkable military forces in European history. It was, in microcosm, the embodiment of all the contending factions —religious, political, social—that were contenders for the fruits of victory in parliament and society at large. The Council of the Army, representing the officers, and the Council of Agitators, representing the ordinary ranks, were both to give birth to constitutional schemes upon which the new English society would be based. (These constitutions will be found in Chapter VI.)

The officers by and large favored a limited monarchy, which meant an accommodation with the defeated king, and Presbyterianism, as provided in "The Solemn League and Covenant." While it is difficult to generalize about the common soldiers (many of whom seemed to want little more than a down payment on their back pay), the Agitators whom they chose to represent them were invariably Levellers, Diggers, Fifth Monarchy Men, or members of one or other of the many sects that were now emerging. In *The Case of the Army Truly Stated* [4], issued 1647, we have a long and detailed statement of their grievances, both as soldiers and as ordinary citizens. It is at least implied that the common soldiers and citizens would not feel that their victory was complete unless a truly representative parliament was assigned supreme political power and that all representative congregations had religious autonomy.

For the next six years the struggle for power in England was between these two fundamental points of view—limited monarchy, an hierarchical church, and an hierarchical society versus a republic, independent congregations, and social egalitarianism. Oliver Cromwell's great personal power was due to his remarkable ability to combine within himself a little from each side and to play the role of balancer.

1. *Clarendon, LIFE and HISTORY OF THE REBELLION*

A. ROYALISTS

372. This great conflux of men of all conditions and qualities and humors could not continue long together at York without some impatience and commotion; and most men wondered that there appeared no provision to be made towards a war, which they saw would be inevitable, and, when the levies of soldiers under the earl of Essex were hastened with so much vigor, that the King should have no other preparation towards an army than a single troop of guards, made up of gentlemen volunteers, who all men foresaw would quit the troop when there should be an army: and many do yet believe that the King too long deferred his recourse to arms, and that if he had raised forces upon his first repulse at Hull his service would have been very much advanced, and that the Parliament would not have been able to have drawn an army together. And so they reproach the councils which were then about the King, as they were censured by many at that time: but neither they then nor these now do understand the

true reason thereof. The King had not at that time one barrel of powder nor one musket, nor any other provision necessary for an army, and, which was worse, was not sure of any port to which they might be securely assigned; nor had he money for the support of his own table for the term of one month. He expected with impatience the arrival of all these by the care and activity of the Queen, who was then in Holland, and by the sale of her own as well as of the crown jewels, and by the friendship of Harry, Prince of Orange,[1] did all she could to provide all that was necessary; and the King had newly directed her to send all to Newcastle, which was but then secured to him by the diligence of that earl. In the mean time, both the King himself and they who best knew the state of his affairs, seemed to be without any thoughts of making war, and to hope that the Parliament would at last incline to some accommodation; for which both his majesty and those persons were exposed to a thousand reproaches.

373. The Queen had many difficulties to contend with; for though the Prince of Orange had a very signal affection for the King's service, and did all he could to dispose the States to concern themselves in his majesty's quarrel, yet his authority and interest was much diminished with the vigor of his body and mind, and the States of Holland were so far from being inclined to the King that they did him all the mischieve they could. They had before assisted the rebellion in Scotland, with giving them credit for arms and ammunition before they had money to buy any; and they did afterwards several ways discover their affections to the Parliament, which had so many spies there that the Queen could do nothing they had not present notice of; so that it was no easy matter for the Queen to provide arms and ammunition but the Parliament had present notice of it, and of the ways which were thought upon to transport them to the King: and then their fleet, under the command of the earl of Warwick, lay ready to obstruct and intercept that communication, nor was any remedy in view to remove this mischieve; inso-

[1] Frederick Henry, Prince of Orange, Stadtholder of the United Provinces (Netherlands).

much as it was no easy thing for the King to send to, or to receive letters from, the Queen.

374. There was a small ship of 28 or 30 guns, that was part of the fleet that wafted her majesty into Holland from Dover, which was called the Providence, under the command of captain Straughan, when the fleet was commanded by sir John Pennington, and before the earl of Warwick was superinduced into that charge against the King's will. That ship, the captain whereof was known to be faithful to his majesty, was by the Queen detained and kept in Holland from the time of her majesty's arrival, under several pretenses, of which the captain made use when he afterwards received orders from the earl of Warwick to repair to the fleet in the Downs, until, after many promises and excuses, it was at last discerned that he had other business and commands; and so was watched by the other ships as an enemy. This vessel the Queen resolved to send to the King, principally to inform his majesty of the straits she was in, of the provisions she had made; and to return with such particular advice and directions from his majesty that she might take further resolutions. And because the vessel was light, and drew not much water, and so could run into any creek or open road or harbor, and from thence easily send an express to the King, there was put into it about two hundred barrels of powder, and two or three thousand arms, with seven or eight field-pieces; which they knew would be very welcome to the King, and serve for a beginning and countenance to draw forces together. The captain was no sooner put to sea but notice was sent to the fleet in the Downs; who immediately sent three or four ships to the north, which easily got the Providence in view before it could reach that coast, and chased it with all their sails till they saw it enter into the river of Humber; when, looking upon it as their own, they made less haste to follow it, being content to drive it before them into their own port of Hull, there being as they thought no other way to escape them, until they plainly saw the ship entering into a narrow creek out of the Humber, which declined Hull and led into the country some miles above it; which was a place well known to the captain, and designed by him from the beginning. It was in vain for them then to hasten their pur-

suit; for they quickly found that their great ships could not enter into that passage, and that the river was too shallow to follow him; and so, with shame and anger, they gave over the chase, whilst the captain continued his course, and, having never thought of saving the ship, run it on shore near Burlington, and with all expedition gave notice to the King of his arrival; who immediately caused the persons of quality in the parts adjacent to draw the train-bands of the country together, to secure the incursions from Hull; and by this means the arms, ammunition, and artillery were quickly brought to York.

375. The King was well content that it should be generally believed that this small ship (the size whereof was known to few), had brought a greater quantity and proportion of provisions for the war than in truth it had; and therefore, though it had brought no money, which he expected, he forthwith granted commissions to raise regiments of horse and foot to such persons of quality and interest as were able to comply with their obligations. He declared the earl of Lindsey, Lord High Chamberlain of England, his general of the army; a person of great honor and courage and generally beloved, who had many years before had good command in Holland and Germany, and had been admiral at sea in several expeditions. Sir Jacob Ashly was declared major general of the foot, a command he was very equal to, and had exercised before, and executed after with great approbation. The generalship of the horse his majesty reserved for his nephew prince Rupert, who was daily expected, and arrived soon after: and all levies were hastened with as much expedition as was possible in so great a scarcity and notorious want of money; of which no more need be said, after it is remembered that all the lords and council about the King, with several other persons of quality, voluntarily made a subscription for the payment of so many horse for three months, in which time they would needs believe that the war should be at an end; every one paying down what the three months' pay would amount to into the hands of a treasurer appointed to receive it; and this money was presently paid for the making those levies of horse which were designed, and which could not have been made but by those moneys.

425. Towards such as any ways (though under the obligation of oaths or offices) opposed or discountenanced what they went about, they proceeded with the most extravagant severity that had been ever heard of; of which I shall only mention two instances. The first, of the lord mayor of London, sir Richard Gurny, a citizen of great wealth, reputation, and integrity; whom the Lords had, upon the complaint of the House of Commons, before their sending the last petition to the King (of which his majesty gave them a touch in his answer), committed to the Tower of London, for causing the King's proclamation against the militia, by virtue of his majesty's writ to him directed and according to the known duty of his place, to be publicly proclaimed. And shortly after, that they might have a man more compliant with their designs to govern the city, notwithstanding that he insisted upon his innocence, [and] made it appear that he was obliged by the laws of the land, the customs of the city, and the constitution of his office and his oath, to do whatsoever he had done, he was by their lordships, in the presence of the Commons, adjudged to be put out of his office of lord mayor of London; to be utterly incapable of bearing office in city or kingdom; incapable of all honor or dignity; and to be imprisoned during the pleasure of the two Houses of Parliament. And, upon this sentence, alderman Pennington was, by the voice and clamor of the common people, against the customs and rules of election, made mayor, and accordingly installed; and the true, old, worthy mayor committed to the Tower of London, where with notable courage and constancy he continued almost to his death.

426. The other instance I think fit to mention is that of judge Mallett, who, as is before remembered, was committed to the Tower the last Lent, for having seen a petition prepared by the grand jury of Kent, for the countenance of the Book of Common Prayer, and against the imposition of the militia by ordinance without the royal assent. This judge (being this summer circuit again judge of assize for those counties) sitting at Maidstone upon the great assize, some

members of the House of Commons, under the style and title of a committee of Parliament, came to the bench; and, producing some votes and orders and declarations of one or both Houses, required him, in the name of the Parliament, to cause those papers (being on the behalf of the ordinance of the militia, and against the commission of array) to be read. He told them that 'he sat there by virtue of his majesty's commissions, and that he was authorized to do any thing comprised in those commissions; but he had no authority to do any thing else; and therefore, there being no mention in either of his commissions of those papers, or the publishing any thing of that nature, he could not, nor would, do it'; and so, finding less respect and submission than they expected both to their persons and their business from the learned judge, and that the whole county, at least the prime gentlemen and the grand jury (which [re]presented the county), condemned both much more, this committee returned to the House with great exclamations against Mr. justice Mallett, as the fomenter and protector of a malignant faction against the Parliament. And upon this charge a troop of horse was sent to attend an officer, who came with a warrant from the Houses, or some committee (whereas justice Mallett, being an assistant of the House of Peers, could not regularly be summoned by any other authority) to Kingston in Surrey, where the judge was keeping the general assizes for that county; and, to the unspeakable dishonor of the public justice of the kingdom, and the scandal of all ministers or lovers of justice, in that violent manner took the judge from the bench, and carried him prisoner to Westminster; from whence by the two Houses he was committed to the Tower of London, where he remained for the space of above two years, without ever being charged with any particular crime, till he was redeemed by his majesty by the exchange of another, whose liberty they desired.

427. By these heightened acts of power and terror they quickly demonstrated how unsecure it would be for any man at least not to concur with them. And, having a general, arms, money, and men enough at their devotion, they easily formed an army, publicly disposing such troops and regiments as had been raised for Ireland, and at one time one

hundred thousand pounds of that money which by Act of Parliament had been paid for that purpose, towards the constituting that army which was to be led against their lawful sovereign. So that it was very evident they would be in such an equipage within few weeks, both with a train of artillery, horse, and foot, all taken, armed, furnished, and supplied out of his majesty's own magazines and stores, that they had not reason to fear any opposition. In the mean time, they declared, and published to the people, that:

428. They raised that army only for the defense of the Parliament, the King's person, and the religion, liberty, and laws of the kingdom, and of those who, for their sakes and for those ends, had obeyed their orders: that the King, by the instigation of evil counsellors, had raised a great army of Papists, by which he intended to awe and destroy the Parliament, to introduce Popery and tyranny: of which intention, they said, his requiring Hull, his sending out commissions of array, his bespeaking arms and ammunition beyond the seas (there having been some brought to him by the ship called Providence); his declaring sir John Hotham traitor, and the putting out the earl of Northumberland from being Lord High Admiral of England, his removing the earls of Pembroke, Essex, Holland, the lord Fielding, and sir H. Vane, from their several places and employments, were sufficient and ample evidences: and therefore they conjured all men to assist their general, the earl of Essex.

429. And for their better and more secret transaction of all such counsels as were necessary to be entered upon or followed, they chose a committee of some choice members of either House, to intend the great business of the kingdom with reference to the army; who had authority, without so much as communicating their matter to the House, to imprison persons, seize upon estates, and many other particulars, which the two Houses, in full Parliament, had not the least regular, legal, justifiable authority to do. And for the better encouragement of men to engage in the service, the lord Kimbolton, and the five members of the House of Commons formerly accused by his majesty of high treason, upon

solemn debate, had several regiments conferred on them; and, by their example, many other members of both Houses, some upon their lowness and decayedness of their fortunes, others to get name and reputation to be in the number of reformers (amongst whom they doubted not all places of honor, or offices of profit, would be bestowed), most upon the confidence that all would be ended without a blow by the King's want of power to gather strength, desired and obtained command of horse or foot; their quality making amends for their want of experience, and their other defects, which were repaired by many good officers, both English and Scotch; the late troubles having brought many of that tribe to London, and the reputation of the earl of Essex having drawn others out of the Low Countries to engage in that service. In the choice of whom, whilst they accused the King of a purpose to bring in foreign force, and of entertaining Papists, they neither considered nation or religion, but entertained all strangers and foreigners, of what religion soever, who desired to run their fortune in war.

430. On the other side, preparations were not made with equal expedition and success by the King towards a war: for, though he well understood and discerned that he had nothing else to trust to, he was to encounter strange difficulties to do that. He was so far from having money to levy or pay soldiers that he was at this very time compelled, for very real want, to let fall all the tables kept by his officers of state in Court, by which so many of all qualities subsisted; and the prince and duke of York eat with his majesty; which only table was kept. And whoever knows the constitution of a Court, well knows what indispositions naturally flow from those declensions, and how ill those tempers bear any diminutions of their own interest, and, being once indisposed themselves, how easily they infect others. And that which made the present want of money the more intolerable, there was no visible hope from whence supply could come in any reasonable time: and that which was a greater want than money, which men rather feared than found, there were no arms; for, notwithstanding the fame of the great store of ammunition brought in by that ship, it consisted only in truth of cannon, powder, and bullet, with eight hundred

muskets, which was all the King's magazine. So that the hastening of levies, which at that time was believed would not prove difficult, would be to little purpose, when they should continue unarmed. But that which troubled the King more than all these real incapacities of making war, was the temper and constitution of his own party; which was compounded, for the most part, in Court, Council, and country, of men drawn to him by the impulsion of conscience, and abhorring the unjust and irregular proceedings of Parliament; otherwise, unexperienced in action, and unacquainted with the mysteries and necessary policy of government, severe observers of the law, and as scrupulous in all matters of relation as the other pretended to be: all his majesty's ancient counsellors and servants (except some few of lasting honor, whom we shall have occasion often to mention), being, to redeem former oversights, or for other unworthy designs, either publicly against him in London, or privately discrediting his interests and actions in his own Court. These men still urged the execution of the law; that what extravagances soever the Parliament practiced, the King's observation of the law would, in the end, suppress them all: and, indeed, believed the raising a war to be so wicked a thing that they thought it impossible the Parliament should intend it, even when they knew what they were doing; however, concluded that he that was forwardest in the preparing an army would be first odious to the people; by the affections of whom the other would be easily suppressed.

431. This was the general, received doctrine; and though it appeared plainly to others (of equal affection to the public peace), how fatal those conclusions, in that sense in which they were urged, must prove to the whole kingdom, and how soon the King must be irrecoverably lost if he proceeded not more vigorously in his defense, yet even those men durst not in any formed and public debate declare themselves, or speak that plain English the state of affairs required, but satisfied themselves with speaking what they thought necessary to the King in private; so that by this means the King wanted those firm and solid foundations of counsel and foresight as were most necessary for his condition: so that he could neither impart the true motives and grounds of any important ac-

tion, nor discover the utmost of his designs. And so he still pretended (notwithstanding the greatest and avowed preparations of the enemy) to intend nothing of hostility but in order to the reducing of Hull; the benefit of which he hoped would engage the train-bands of that great county (which was the sole strength he yet drew thither) till he could bring other forces thither which might be fit for that or any other design.

2. THE SELF-DENYING ORDINANCE [3 April 1645]

An Ordinance of the Lords and Commons assembled in Parliament, for the discharging of the Members of both Houses from all offices, both military and civil.

Be it ordained by the Lords and Commons assembled in Parliament, that all and every of the members of either House of Parliament shall be, and by authority of this Ordinance are discharged at the end of forty days after the passing of this Ordinance, of and from all and every office or command military or civil, granted or conferred by both or either of the said Houses of this present Parliament, or by any authority derived from both or either of them since the 20th day of November, 1640.

And be it further ordained, that all other governors and commanders of an island, town, castle or fort, and all other colonels and officers inferior to colonels in the several armies, not being members of either of the Houses of Parliament, shall, according to their respective commissions, continue in their several places and commands, wherein they were employed and intrusted the 20th day of March, 1644, as if this Ordinance had not been made. And that the vice-admiral, rear-admiral, and all other captains and other inferior officers in the fleet, shall, according to their several and respective commissions, continue in their several places and commands, wherein they were employed and intrusted the said 20th day of March, as if this Ordinance had not been made.

Provided always, and it is further ordained and declared, that during this war, the benefit of all offices, being neither military nor judicial, hereafter to be granted, or any way to be appointed to any person or persons by both or either House of Parliament, or by authority derived from thence, shall go and inure to such public uses as both Houses of Parliament shall appoint. And the grantees and persons executing all such offices shall be accountable to the Parliament for all the profits and perquisites thereof, and shall have no profit out of any such office, other than a competent salary for the execution of the same, in such manner as both Houses of Parliament shall order and ordain.

Provided that this Ordinance shall not extend to take away the power and authority of any Lieutenancy or Deputy-Lieutenancy in the several counties, cities or places, or of any *Custos Rotulorum* [Keeper of the Rolls], or of any commission for Justices of Peace, or sewers, or any commission of *Oyer* and *Terminer* [Hearing and Deciding], or jail-delivery.

Provided always, and it is hereby declared, that those members of either House who had offices by grant from His Majesty before this Parliament, and were by His Majesty displaced sitting this Parliament, and have since by authority of both Houses been restored, shall not by this Ordinance be discharged from their said offices or profits thereof, but shall enjoy the same; anything in this Ordinance to the contrary thereof notwithstanding.

3. LETTER FROM CROMWELL
[*Dated from Bristol, 14 September 1645*]

For the Honorable William Lenthall, Speaker of the Commons House of Parliament: These

SIR,

It hath pleased the General to give me in charge to represent unto you a particular account of the taking of Bristol, the which I gladly undertake.

After the finishing of that service at Sherborne, it was disputed at a council of war, whether we should march into the West or to Bristol. Amongst other arguments, the leaving so considerable an enemy at our backs, to march into the heart of the Kingdom; the undoing of the country about Bristol, which was exceedingly harassed by the Prince his being but a fortnight thereabouts; the correspondence he might hold in Wales; the possibility of uniting the enemy's forces where they pleased, and especially the drawing to an head the disaffected clubmen of Somerset, Wilts and Dorset, when once our backs were towards them: these considerations, together with the taking so important a place, so advantageous for the opening of trade to London, did sway the balance, and begat that conclusion.

When we came within four miles of the city, we had a new debate, whether we should endeavor to block it up, or make a regular siege. The latter being overruled, Colonel Welden with his brigade marched to Pile Hill, on the south side of the city, being within musket-shot thereof, where in a few days they made a good quarter, overlooking the city. Upon our advance, the enemy fired Bedminster, Clifton, and some other villages, and would have fired the country thereabouts if our unexpected coming had not hindered. The General caused some horse and dragooners under Commissary-General Ireton to advance over Avon, to keep-in the enemy on the north side of the town, until the foot could come up; and after a day, the General, with Colonel Montague's and Colonel Rainsborowe's brigades, marched over at Keynsham to Stapleton, where he quartered that night. The next day, Colonel Montague, having his post assigned with his brigade, was to secure all between Frome and Avon. He came up to Lawford's Gate, within musket-shot thereof. Colonel Rainsborowe's post was near to Durdham Down, where the dragooners and three regiments of horse made good a post upon the Down, between him and the River Avon, on his right hand, and from Colonel Rainsborowe's quarters to Frome River, on his left. A part of Colonel Birch and Major-General Skippon's regiments were to maintain that post.

These posts being thus settled, our horse were forced to be upon exceeding great duty, to stand by the foot, lest the foot, being so weak in all their posts, might receive an affront; and truly herein we were very happy, that we should receive so little loss by sallies, considering the paucity of our men to make good their posts, and the strength of the enemy within. By sallies (which were three or four) I know not that we lost thirty men, in all the time of our siege. Of officers of quality, only Colonel Okey was taken, by mistake going to the enemy, thinking them to be friends, and Captain Guilliams slain in a charge. We took Sir Bernard Asteley; and killed Sir Richard Crane, men very considerable with the Prince.

We had a council of war concerning the storming of the town, about eight days before we took it; and in that there appeared great unwillingness to the work, through the unseasonableness of the weather, and other apparent difficulties. Some inducement to bring us thither was the report of the good affection of the townsmen to us; but that did not answer expectation. Upon a second consideration, it was overruled for a storm, which no sooner concluded, but difficulties were removed, and all things seemed to favor the design; and indeed there hath been seldom the like cheerfulness in officers and soldiers to any work like to this, after it was once resolved on. The day and hour of our storm was appointed to be Wednesday morning, the tenth, about one of the clock. We chose to act it so early because we hoped thereby to surprise the enemy; with this resolution also (to avoid confusion and falling foul one upon another), that when we had recovered the line, and forts upon it, we would not to (sic) advance further until day. The general signal unto the storm was the firing of straw, and discharging four piece of cannon at Prior Hill Fort.

The signal was very well perceived by all, and truly the men went on with great resolution, and very presently recovered the line, making way for the horse to enter. Colonel Montague and Colonel Pickering, who stormed at Lawford's Gate, where was a double work, well filled with men and cannon, presently entered, and with great resolution beat the enemy from their works, and possessed their cannon. Their expedition was such that they forced the enemy from their advantages, without any considerable loss to themselves. They laid down the bridges for the horse to enter; Major Desborowe commanding the horse, who very gallantly seconded the foot. Then our foot advanced to the city walls, where they possessed the gate against the Castle Street whereinto were put an hundred men, who made it good. Sir Hardresse Waller, with his and the General's regiment, with no less resolution, entered on the other side of Lawford's Gate, towards Avon River; and put themselves into an immediate conjunction with the rest of the brigade.

During this, Colonel Rainsborowe and Colonel Hammond attempted Prior Hill Fort, and the line downwards towards Frome; Colonel Birch and the Major-General's regiment being to storm towards Frome River. Colonel Hammond possessed the line immediately, and beating the enemy from it, made way for our horse to enter. Colonel Rainsborowe, who had the hardest task of all at Prior Hill Fort, attempted it, and fought near three hours for it, and indeed there was great despair of carrying the place, it being exceeding high, a ladder of thirty rounds scarcely reaching the top thereof; but his resolution was such that, notwithstanding the inaccessibleness and difficulty, he would not give it over. The enemy had four piece of cannon upon it; which they played with round and case shot upon our men: his Lieutenant-Colonel Bowen and others were two hours at push of pike, standing upon the palisadoes, but could not enter. Colonel Hammond being entered the line, Captain Ireton,[1] with a forlorn of Colonel Riche's regiment (interposing with his horse between the enemy's horse and Colonel Hammond), received a shot with two pistol-bullets, which broke his arm. By means of his entrance, Colonel Hammond did storm the Fort on that part which was inward; by which means, Colonel Rainsborowe and Colonel Hammond's men entered the Fort, and immediately put to the sword almost all in it, and as this was the place of most difficulty, so of most loss to us on that side, and of very great honor to the undertakers. The horse did second them with great resolution: both those Colonels do acknowledge that their interposition between the enemy's horse and their foot was a great means of obtaining this strong Fort, without which all the rest of the line to Frome River would have done us little good:

[1] The brother of Henry Ireton.

and indeed neither horse nor foot would have stood in all that way, in any manner of security, had not the Fort been taken. Major Bethel's were the first horse entered the line; who did behave himself very gallantly, and was shot in the thigh, had one or two shot more, and his horse shot under him. Colonel Birch with his men, and the Major-General's regiment, entered with very great resolution where their post was; possessing the enemy's guns, and turning them upon them.

By this, all the line from Prior Hill Fort to Avon, which was a full mile, with all the forts, ordnance and bulwarks, were possessed by us but one, wherein there were about 120 men of the enemy which the General summoned, and all the men submitted.

The success on Colonel Welden's side did not answer with this; and although the colonels, and other the officers and soldiers both horse and foot testified very much resolution, as could be expected, Colonel Welden, Colonel Ingoldsby, Colonel Herbert, and the rest of the colonels and officers, both of horse and foot, doing what could be well looked for from men of honor; yet what by reason of the height of the works, which proved higher than report made them, and the shortness of the ladders, they were repulsed, with the loss of about 100 men. Colonel Fortescue's Lieutenant-Colonel was killed, Major Cromwell[2] dangerously shot and two of Colonel Ingoldsby's brothers hurt; with some officers.

Being possessed of thus much as hath been related, the town was fired in three places by the enemy, which we could not put out; and this begat a great trouble to the General and us all, fearing to see so famous a city burnt to ashes before our faces. Whiles we were viewing so sad a spectacle, and consulting which way to make further advantage of our success, the Prince sent a trumpet to the General to desire a treaty for the surrender of the town, to which the General agreed; and deputed Colonel Montague, Colonel Rainsborowe, and Colonel Pickering for that service; authorising them with instructions to treat and conclude the Articles,

[2] Richard, second son of Sir Philip Cromwell, Oliver's uncle.

which are these enclosed; for performance whereof hostages were mutually given.

On Thursday about two of the clock in the afternoon, the Prince marched out; having a convoy of two regiments of horse from us; and making election of Oxford for the place he would go to, which he had liberty to do by his Articles.

The cannon which we have taken are about 140 mounted; about 100 barrels of powder already come to our hands, with a good quantity of shot, ammunition, and arms. We have found already between 2000 and 3000 muskets. The Royal Fort had in it victuals for one-hundred-and-fifty men, for three-hundred-and-twenty days; the Castle victualled for near half so long. The Prince had foot of the garrison (as the mayor of the city informed me), two-thousand five-hundred, and about one thousand horse, besides the trained bands of the town, and auxiliaries 1200, some say 1500. I hear but one man hath died of the plague in all our army, although we have quartered amongst and in the midst of infected persons and places. We had not killed of ours in this storm, nor all this siege, 200 men.

Thus I have given you a true, but not a full account of this great business; wherein he that runs may read, that all this is none other than the work of God. He must be a very Atheist that doth not acknowledge it.

It may be thought that some praises are due to these gallant men, of whose valor so much mention is made: their humble suit to you and all that have an interest in this blessing, is, that in the remembrance of God's praises they may be forgotten. It's their joy that they are instruments to God's glory, and their country's good; it's their honor that God vouchsafes to use them. Sir, they that have been employed in this service know that faith and prayer obtained this city for you. I do not say ours only, but of the people of God with you and all England over, who have wrestled with God for a blessing in this very thing. Our desires are, that God may be glorified by the same spirit of faith by which we asked all our sufficiency, and having received it, it's meet that He have all the praise. Presbyterians, Independents, all had here the same spirit of faith and prayer; the same pretense and answer; they agree here, know no names

of difference: pity it is it should be otherwise anywhere. All
that believe, have the real unity, which is most glorious, because inward and spiritual, in the Body, and to the Head. As
for being united in forms, commonly called Uniformity, every Christian will for peace-sake study and do, as far as conscience will permit; and from brethren, in things of the mind
we look for no compulsion, but that of light and reason. In
other things, God hath put the sword into the Parliament's
hands, for the terror of evil-doers, and the praise of them
that do well. If any plead exemption from it, he knows not
the Gospel: if any would wring it out of your hands, or steal
it from you under what pretense soever, I hope they shall do
it without effect. That God may maintain it in your hands,
and direct you in the use thereof, is the prayer of

Your humble servant,
OLIVER CROMWELL.

4. *THE CASE OF THE ARMY TRULY STATED, together with the mischiefs and dangers that are imminent,
and some suitable remedies, Humbly proposed by the Agents
of five Regiments of Horse, to the respective Regiments
and the whole Army* [1647]

Whereas the grievances, dissatisfactions, and desires of the
Army, both as Commoners and Soldiers, hath been many
months since represented to the Parliament; and the Army
hath waited with much patience, to see their common grievances redressed and the rights and freedoms of the Nation
cleared and secured; yet, upon a most serious and conscientious view of our Narratives, Representations, Engagement,
Declarations, Remonstrances, and comparing with those the
present state of the Army and Kingdom, and the present
manner of actings of many at the Head Quarters, we not
only apprehend nothing to have been done effectually, either
for the Army or the poor oppressed people of the nation, but
we also conceive, that there is little probability of any good,
without some more speedy and vigorous actings.

In respect of the Army, there hath been hitherto no public
vindication thereof, about their first Petition, answerable to

the Ignominy, by declaring them enemies to the State, & disturbers of the peace: No public clearing nor repairing of the credit of the Officers, sent for about that petition as Delinquents: No provision for Apprentices, Widows, Orphans, or maimed Soldiers, answerable to our reasonable addresses propounded in their behalf: No such Indemnity, as provideth security, for the quiet, ease, or safety of the Soldiers, disbanded or to be disbanded. No security for our Arrears, or provision for present pay, to enable the Army to subsist, without burdening the distressed Country. And in respect to the rights and freedoms of ourselves and the people, that we declared we would insist upon, we conceive there is no kind or degree of satisfaction given: there is no determinate period of time set when the Parliament shall certainly end: The house is in no measure purged, either from persons unduly elected, or from Delinquents, that appeared to be such at the Army's last insisting upon their rights, or since: the honor of the Parliamentary authority not cleared, and vindicated from the most horrid injustice of that Declaration against the Army for petitioning, nor of suppressing and burning Petitions, abusing and imprisoning Petitioners: But those strange precedents remain upon Record, to the infamy of Parliamentary authority; and the danger of our own and the people's freedoms: The people are not righted, nor satisfied in point of accounts, for the vast sums of money disbursed by them. None of the public burdens, or oppressions, by arbitrary Committees, injustice in the Law, Tithes, Monopolies, and restraint of free trade, burdensome Oaths, inequality of Assessments, Excise, and otherwise are removed or lightened, the rights of the people in their Parliaments concerning the nature and extent of that power, are not cleared and declared. So that we apprehend our own & the people's case, little (if in any measure) better, since the Army last hazarded themselves for their own and the people's rights and freedoms. Nay, to the grief of our hearts, we must declare, that we conceive, the people and the Army's case much impaired, since the first Rendezvouz at *New Market*, when that solemn engagement was entered into: And that from the consideration.

That the Army's Engagement, Representations, Declarations, and Remonstrances, and promises in them contained, are declined, and more and more daily broken, and not only in some smaller matters, wherein the Army and the Kingdom are not so nearly concerned, but in divers particulars of dangerous consequence to the Army and the whole Nation. As,

First, In the Engagement, page the 5th, the Army promised every Member thereof each to other, and to the Parliament and Kingdom, that they would neither disband nor divide, nor suffer themselves to be disbanded or divided until satisfaction should be given to the Army in relation to their grievances, and desires; and security that neither the Army nor the free-born people of *England,* should remain subject to such injuries, oppression, and abuse, as the corrupt party in the Parliament then had attempted against them.

Secondly, The Train of Artillery is now to be disbanded, before satisfaction or security is given to the whole Army in relation to themselves, or other the free-born people, either in respect to their grievances or desires. And when the strength or sinews of the Army be broken, what effectual good can be secured for themselves or the people in case of opposition?

Thirdly, The Army is divided into quarters so far distant, that one part is in no capability to give timely assistance to another, if any design should be to disband any part by violence suddenly, although neither our grievances nor desires as Soldiers or Commoners are redressed or answered. And as we conceive this dividing of the Army before satisfaction or security as aforesaid, to be contrary to the Army's intention in their Engagement, at the said Rendezvouz, so we conceive it hath from that time given all the advantage to the enemies, to band and design against the Army, whereby not only pay hath been kept from the Soldiers, and security for arrears prevented, but the kingdom was endangered to have been imbroiled in blood, and the settlement of the peace and freedom of the Nation, hath been thus long delayed.

The whole intent of the Engagement, and the equitable sense of it, hath been perverted openly, by affirming, and by sinister means making seeming determinations in the

Council, that the Army was not to insist upon, or demand any security, for any of their own or other the free-born people's freedoms or rights, though they might propound any thing to the Parliament's consideration; and according to that high breach of their Engagement, their actions have been regulated, and nothing that was declared formerly, to be insisted upon, hath been resolvedly adhered to, or claimed as the Army's or the people's due, and we conceive it hath been by this means, that the Soldier hath had no pay constantly provided, nor any security for Arrears given them, & that hitherto they could not obtain so much, as to be paid up equally with those that did desert the Army, it not being positively insisted upon, although in the Remonstrance of *June* 23, page 11. It was declared, that it should be insisted upon resolvedly, to be done before the *Thursday* night after the sending that Remonstrance, and it's now many months since.

Fourthly, In the prosecution of this breach, there hath been many discouragements of the Agitators of the Regiments, in consulting about the most effectual means, for procuring the speedy redress of the people's grievances, and clearing and securing the native rights of the Army, and all others the free Commons.

It hath been instilled into them, that they ought not to intermeddle with those matters, thereby to induce them, to betray the trust the Regiments reposed in them; and for that purpose, the endeavors of some hath been to persuade the Soldiery, that their Agitators have meddled with more than concerned them. In the Declaration of *June* 14 it was declared that the Army would adhere to their desires of full and equal satisfaction to the whole Soldiery of the Kingdom in Arrears, Indemnity, and all other things mentioned in the papers, that contained the grievances, dissatisfactions and desires who did then, or should afterward concur with this Army in these desires.

But many thousands who have concurred with this Army, are now to be sent for *Ireland*, or to be disbanded with two months pay, before any security for Arrears, or sufficient Indemnity, or any satisfaction to any desires as Soldiers or Commoners, then propounded; so now our Declaration is forgotten, and the faith of the Army, and his Excellency broken, for it may be remembered, that his excellency often promised, that the same care should be taken for those, that concurred, that should be for this Army, therefore if this course be driven on, what better can we expect for ourselves in the end?

Sixthly, In the same Declaration, *June* 14, page 6, it is declared that the Army took up Arms, in judgment and conscience, for the people's just rights and liberties, and not as mercenary Soldiers, hired to serve an arbitrary power of the State, and that in the same manner it continued in arms at that time, and page 7 of the same Declaration, it was declared that they proceeded upon the principles of right and freedom, and upon the law of nature and Nations: But the strength of the endeavors of many hath been, and are now, spent to persuade the Soldiers and Agitators, that they stand as Soldiers only to serve the State, and may not as free Commons claim their right and freedom as due to them, as those ends for which they have hazarded their lives, and that the ground of their refusing to disband, was only the want of Arrears and Indemnity.

Seventhly, In the Remonstrance *June* 23, page 14 compared with page 15, it was declared, that such extraordinary courses should be taken as God should direct & enable them thereunto, to put things to a speedy issue, unless by the *Thursday* then immediately following, assurance and security were given to the Army and Kingdom, that the things desired in the Declaration, *June* the 14 should be speedily granted and settled.

But there hath been ever since, a total neglect of insisting positively upon the redress of those grievances, or granting those desires of the Army as Soldiers. That the Declaration of *June* the 14, page the 3, refers unto, as formerly expressed, and not so much as one of those desires, as Commoners of *England* in the behalf of themselves and others (propounded in the same Declaration, pages 6, 9, 10, 11) hath been insisted upon positively; neither settling a determinate period, wherein the Parliament shall certainly end, nor purging the House, nor clearing the rights of the people, in petitioning, nor the righting of them in accounts, etc. so that by these declinings of the Army, from insisting resolvedly upon the people's, and the Army's own rights, both are after long expectations, as far from right and freedom, as though there had been no man to plead their cause. And herein it is to be observed, that the neglect of insisting upon our most just desires, hath given enemies such secret encouragement, that they shuffle off any desires, though propounded, as to be insisted upon, as may be mentioned in that our just desire, of recalling publicly the Declaration, inviting all to desert the Army, & professed to be insisted upon, in the same Declaration, *June* 23, page 11, which notwithstanding to this day was never publicly recalled; so likewise the desire of vindicating the Parliament's honor, in relation to a public disowning the order to suppress our first Petition, and many others.

Eighthly, In the Declaration of *June* 14, page 10, as in all other Remonstrances and Declarations, it was desired, that the rights and liberties of the people might be secured, before the King's business should be considered. But now the grievances of the people are propounded to be considered after the restoring him to the regal power, and that in such a way according to the proposals *viz*, with a negative voice, that the people that have purchased by blood what was their right, of which the King endeavored to deprive them, should yet solely depend on his will, for their relief in their grievances and oppressions; and in like manner the security for the Army's Arrears is proposed, to be considered after the business of the King be determined, so that there is a total declension since the method formerly desired, in the settling of the peace of the Nation.

Ninthly, It hath been always professed and declared, that the Army was called forth and conjured by the Parliament's Declarations, for defense of the people's rights, against the forces raised by the King, and for delivering the King from his evil Council, who seduced him to raise the war, and bringing Delinquents to condign punishment, But now through the Army's countenance and indulgence, those conquered enemies, that were the King's forces, abuse, reproach, and again insult over the people, whose freedom was the grounds of the Army's engagement, yea, the King's evil Counselors, that concurred in designing all the mischiefs in the

King's late war against the people, are again restored to him, and are admitted free access without check into all the Army's quarrels, whereby they are restored to a capacity of plotting and designing mischief against the Army and kingdom.

Tenthly, When imminent ruin, to the whole nation was apprehended, by means of the multitudes of corrupted Members in Parliament, diverting and obstructing all good proceedings; then the purging of the House in part, from one kind of Delinquents, was again insisted upon, and a solemn Protestation was passed in the remonstrance from *Kingston*, page 21, That the Army would not permit those to sit in the House, that usurped the name and power of Parliamentary authority, when the Parliament was by violence suspended, and endeavored to raise a war to destroy the Parliament and Army, but that they would take some effectual course to restrain them from sitting there, that the people might be concluded only by those Members that are free from such apparent treacherous breaches of their trust.

But hitherto this Engagement for purging the House from those Delinquents (whose interest engages them to be designing mischief against the people and Army) is declined and broken, to the black reproach and foulest infamy of the Army; and now these strong cords are cut in sunder and so forgotten, that there are no visible endeavors or intentions, to preserve the honor of the Army, in its faithfulness to its Engagement and Protestation.

Thus all promises of the Army to the people that Petitioned his Excellency and the Army to stand for the National interest, freedoms and rights, are hitherto wholly declined, and the law of nature and nations now refused by many to be the rule by which their proceedings should be regulated; they now strip themselves of the interest of English men, which was so ill resented when it was attempted by the malice of the enemies. And thus the people's expectations that were much greatened, and their hopes of relief in their miseries and oppressions which were so much heightened are like to be frustrate, and while you look for peace and freedom, the flood-gates of slavery, oppression and misery are opened upon the Nation, as may appear by the present manifold dangers that incompass about the Army and the whole Nation.

> *The mischiefs, evils, and dangers, which are and will be the necessary consequence of the Army's declining or delaying the effectual fulfilling of its first Engagement, Promises and Declarations or of its neglect to insist positively upon its first principles of common right and freedom.*

Whereas it's now many months since the Army declared (In answer to the Petitions of divers Counties, and from the sense of an absolute necessity thereof) that they would insist upon the people's interest; as in the Declaration of June 14, page 13, And yet no relief for the people in any of their oppressions, by arbitrary powers, Monopolies, injustice in the proceeding at Law, Tithes, Excise, etc. is effectually procured; nor any greater probability of future help is visible than was before, no foundations of freedom being yet laid; and yet the Soldiery burdening the country with free quarters and occasioning greater taxes. These five mischiefs and dangers ensue inevitably.

First, The love and affection of the people to the Army, which is (an army's greatest strength) is decayed, cooled, and near lost; it's already the common voice of the people, what good hath our new Saviors done for us? What grievances have they procured to be redressed? Wherein is our condition bettered? or how are we more free than before?

Secondly, Not only so, but the Army is rendered as an heavy burden to the people, in regard more pay is exacted daily for them, and the people find no good procured by them, that's answerable or equivalent to the charge, so that now the people begin to cry louder for disbanding the Army than they did formerly for keeping us in Arms, because they see no benefit accruing, they say they are as likely to be oppressed and enslaved both by King and Parliament, as they were before the Army engaged professedly to see their freedoms cleared and secured.

Thirdly, Whilst the people's old oppressions are continued,

and more taxes also are imposed for pay for the Army, they are disabled daily more & more for the maintaining of an Army for their preservation, for they begin to say, they can but be destroyed by oppression, and it's all one to them, whether it be by pretended friends or professed enemies, it were as good, say they, that the King should rule again by prerogative; we were slaves then to his will and we are now no better; we had rather have one tyrant than hundreds.

Fourthly, By this means, distractions, divisions, heart-burnings and jealousies are increased, to the imminent danger of ruin to the Army and Kingdom; the people are inclined to tumults crying out, will none procure relief for us: shall we always be deluded with fair words, and be devoured by oppressors? we must ere long rise up in arms, and every one catch what he can: thus confusion is threatened.

Fifthly, The Army is exposed to contempt and scandal, and the most black reproaches, and infamies are cast upon them, the people say, that their resolutions not to disband, were because they would live idly on the people's labors, and when the Soldiers are constrained to take free quarters, this (saith the people) is for freedom, and right, to eat the bread out of our children's mouths: so that many Soldiers are ashamed of themselves, and fear that the people should rise to destroy them: you will do nothing for us (say they), we are vexed by malignant Judges for conscience sake, by arbitrary Committees in the Country, and at Parliament, ordering one thing this day, and recalling it the next, to our intolerable vexation, injustice in the law is the same, and we buy our right at as a dear rate as ever, Tithes are enforced from us double and treble, Excise continues, we can have no accounts of all our moneys disbursed for the public, more is daily required, and we know not what is become of all we have paid already, the Soldiers have little pay, and the maimed Soldiers, Widows and Orphans are thrust upon us to be parish charges.

Secondly, Whereas the Engagement is broken, and the first principles deserted or neglected, these mischiefs and dangers have ensued.

1. The enemies are encouraged and emboldened to proceed in prejudice to the people & the Army as formerly: they

may receive hopes upon the Army's own words in their General Councils, that the Army will not oppose or disturb them in their proceedings, to deprive the Army and people of their native rights, if they can abuse the Parliament, or surprise them as formerly, they may say for themselves, the Army hath declared that they stand only as Soldiers, and will not insist upon any positive demand of their own and the Nation's freedoms: and was it not this that emboldened the enemies formerly to suppress our first petition, and declare us enemies, for petitioning? they thought we would have stood only as mercenary Soldiers, hired to serve their arbitrary power, and not remembered that we by their invitation took up arms in judgment and conscience, to preserve the nation from tyranny and oppression, and therefore were obliged to insist upon our rights and freedoms as Commoners, and surely it hath been upon this ground, that they kept us without money so long, thinking we would not or durst not insist upon our demands of that which is due to us, and upon this ground we judge the Parliament hath proceeded of late to increase the people's oppressions, by an Ordinance for triple damages, to be paid by all that refuse (though for conscience sake) to Pay Tithes, and an Ordinance to lock up the printing presses against whom they please, which was in the Bishops' time complained of, as one of the great oppressions, and have slighted just petitions, and neglected to consider, and redress the prisoners' grievances and oppressions and the sufferings of conscientious persons, by the unjust statutes against Conventicles so styied, & statutes for Common Prayer Book, and enforcing all to come to Church, and all other the people's grievances.

2. From the Army's declining their first principles, the same corrupt Members remain in Parliament that caused the *Army* to be proclaimed enemies for petitioning, and it's to be observed that through the influence of those in the house, there was never any public vindication of the Army's honor, and of the justice of their petitioning at that time, and can the Army be safe, so long as its old declared enemies are in power and do but watch the fittest opportunity to work any mischief, but not only those enemies remain in power, and watch to destroy you, but 65 at least that lately

voted and endeavored to raise a new work to destroy the Army, are suffered to vote in the Parliament though the Army hath protested solemnly, they would not suffer those usurpers to sit there, or that they would be concluded by those that were co-actors in such treasonable breaches of their trust.

3. Through the Army's dividing contrary to the Engagement, and neglecting to insist upon the first Declaration, the enemies have had power and opportunity, to prevent them of their constant pay, and obstruct all proceedings to security for Arrears, whereas otherwise the enemies would not have dared to presume to obstruct good proceedings, and to prosecute their designs against the Army.

4. *Through the Army's back-sliding from the Remonstrance, and Protestation from Kingston, August 18, those that lately endeavored to raise a war against the Parliament and Army, continue in the House, and have passed an Ordinance, wherein those betrayers of their trust are acknowledged to have been a House of Parliament, when the Parliament was forced away and suspended, and the Army having declared them to be no Parliament, and his Excellency slighted their Command, at* Colebrook, *professing he knew no Parliament, to which he should send, are by this made guilty of the highest treason, and so a snare is laid for his Excellency and the Army, that when the enemies shall have the advantage, they may be declared traitors, for declaring against the Parliament, and disowning their authority, so that if some speedy remedy be not applied, no man knows how soon the enemy may prevail to destroy his Excellency, the Army and Kingdom by this means: and the policy of the enemy is to be observed, that they would never suffer that Declaration to be debated in the House, that was published at the Army's marching towards* London; *wherein those that usurped the power of a Parliament, when the Parliament was suspended, were declared to be no legal Parliament: but the Declaration and Remonstrance of August 18, wherein the Army protested against the sitting of those usurpers in the House, may together be made the ground of their declaring us Traitors upon any advantage, for disowning, and declaring against the supreme authority of the Nation, in case those*

usurpers shall continue to be acknowledged an House of Parliament, as it remains at present by the late Ordinance of August 20 procured to be passed by those usurpers themselves sitting judges of their own case.

5. *By this neglect and declining of the Army, the Parliament is returned to their old dilatory way of proceeding, neither insisting upon the relieving the people speedily and effectually in any of their grievances, nor providing constant pay for the Army, nor security for Arrears; so that the delays that are occasioned through the Army's declining their first principles are as distinctive to the Army and Kingdom, as if there were direct actings by the Army against the Kingdom's peace.*

6. *Through the same declension of the Army's first principles, and the good and necessary method propounded for settling the nation in peace and freedom before the King's business be considered, the King is likely to recover his old capacity, before the people's freedoms (which they have redeemed out of the hands of him and his forces by blood) be cleared and established securely, and likewise before any security be given for Arrears; and then what probability there is, that then there should be any good security of pay obtained for the Army that conquered him, and for the freedoms of those that assisted them, let any rational man judge? It may more certainly be expected, that he will provide for the pay and Arrears of his own Soldiery rather than of ours. And likewise by the same means, the Armies and their assistants indemnity, is propounded to receive its strength from the King's consent; whereas not only his sign of, or consent to any act is wholly null and void in Law, because he is under restraint, and so our indemnity, will be insufficient, if it shall depend in the least, on his confirmation. But also it's the highest disparagement to the supreme authority of this Nation, the Parliament, that when they have commanded an Army upon service against the King, they should not have sufficient power to save them harmless for obedience to their commands, and also it's the highest dishonor to the Army, that they should seek to the conquered enemy to save them harmless for fighting against them, which is to ask him par-*

don, and so will remain as a perpetual reproach upon them, & render them traitors to posterity.

7. Through the Army's declining its first principles, to insist upon satisfaction and security as Soldiers and Commoners before disbanding or dividing the Army, is it now likely to be so far scattered into several quarters, that it shall be in no capacity, to insist upon security for arrears, sufficient indemnity, or upon any its own or the nation's rights, in case they shall be still denied them.

8. It is to be considered that the enemies on the one hand, and the other increase daily in their boldness, confidence, and strength, while security for the Army's arrears, and constant future pay (so long as it shall be continued) are not provided, and the rights and freedoms of the people are not cleared and secured, & the Army may divide, in case one part should insist upon the first just principles, and be faithful thereunto, and another part should by flatteries, preferments, fear or negligence decline or desert them, and let it be considered what strength that would add to the enemies, and how far it will endanger the ruin of the Army and Kingdom.

Now we cannot but declare, that these sad apprehensions of mischiefs, dangers and confusion gaping to devour the Army hath filled our hearts with troubles, that we never did, nor do regard the worst of evils or mischiefs that can befall ourselves in comparison to the consequence of them to the poor Nation, or to the security of common right and freedom, we could not but in (real not formal fained) trouble of heart for the poor Nation and oppressed people, break forth and cry, O our bowels! our bowels! we are troubled at the very heart to hear the people's doleful groans, and yet their expected deliverers will not hear or consider, they have run to and fro, and sighed & even wept forth their sorrows and miseries, in petitions, first to the King then to the Parliament, and then to the Army, yet they have all been like broken reeds, even the Army itself upon whom they leaned have pierced their hands, their eyes even fail with looking for peace and freedom, but behold nothing but distraction, oppression and trouble, and could we hope that help is intended, yet the people perish by delays, we wish therefore that the bowels of compassion in the whole Army might yearn towards their distressed brethren, and that they might with one consent say each to other, come let us join together speedily to demand present redress for the people's grievances, and security for all their and our own rights and freedoms as Soldiers and Commoners. Let us never divide each from other till those just demands be answered really and effectually, that so for the people's case as many forces as are not absolutely necessary may be speedily disbanded and our honor may be preserved unspotted, when they shall see, that we minded not our own interest, but the good, freedom, and welfare of the whole Nation. Now to all that shall thus appear we propound.

That whatsoever was proposed to be insisted on either, in the Declaration of *June* the 14 or the Remonstrance *June* 23 and in the Remon. from *Kingston, August* 18, be adhered to resolvedly, so as not to recede from those desires, until they be thoroughly and effectually answered: more particularly, that whereas it appears by positive laws and ancient just customs, that the people have right to new successive elections for Parliaments, at certain periods of time, and that it ought not to be denied them, being so essential to their freedom, that without it they are no better than slaves, the nature of that legislative power, being arbitrary: and that therefore it be insisted on so positively, and resolvedly, as not to recede from it.

1. That a determined period of time, be forthwith set, wherein this Parliament shall certainly be dissolved, provided also that the said period be within 9 or 10 months, next ensuing, that so there may be sufficient time for settling of peace and freedom.

2. Whereas all good is obstructed and diverted by the power & influence of Delinquents, the late usurpers, & undue elected ones in the Parliament, that therefore it be positively & resolvedly insisted on; that the house be forthwith purged, from all that have forfeited their trust, or were unduly elected, but especially that an order be passed forthwith, for the expelling all those from the house, who sat in the late pretended Parliament, & that likewise a severe penalty be ordered to be imposed on every of those usurpers that shall presume to sit in the House, for the passing of

such an order, before they shall have given sufficient evidence, that they neither voted for a new war, or for the King's coming to London upon his own terms.

3. Whereas his Excellency & the whole Army, were guilty of the highest treason if the pretended Parliament had been a legal Parliament, and it's apparent that they were no legal Parliament, that therefore it be positively and resolvedly insisted upon, that the Declaration of the Army upon their last march up to London be forthwith publicly owned, and approved of by the Parliament, and that the same public approbation be Passed upon the Remonstrance, & protest sent from *Kingston August* 18.

4. Whereas Parliaments rightly constituted are the foundation of the hopes of right and freedom to this people, and whereas the people have been prevented of Parliaments, though many positive laws have been made for a constant succession of Parliaments, that therefore it be positively and resolvedly insisted upon, that a law paramount be made, enacting it, to be unalterable by Parliaments that the people shall of course meet without any warrants or writs once in every two years upon an appointed day in their respective Counties, for the election of their representors in Parliament, & that all the freeborn at the age of 21 years and upwards, be the electors, excepting those that have or shall deprive themselves of that their freedom, either for some years, or wholly by delinquency, and that the Parliament so elected and called, may have a certain period of time set, wherein they shall of course determine, and that before the same period they may not be adjournable and dissolvable by the King, or any other except themselves.

Whereas all power is originally and essentially in the whole body of the people of this Nation, and whereas their free choice or consent by their Representors is the only original or foundation of all just government; and the reason and end of the choice of all just Governors whatsoever is their apprehension of safety and good by them, that it be insisted upon positively. That the supreme power of the people's representors or Commons assembled in Parliament, be forthwith clearly declared as their power to make laws, or repeal laws (which are not, or ought not to be unalterable), as also their power to call to an account all officers in this Nation whatsoever, for their neglect or treacheries in their trust for the people's good, and to continue or displace and remove them from their offices, dignities or trust, according to their demerits by their faithfulness or treachery in the business or matters where with they are entrusted. And further, that this power to constitute any kind of Governors or officers, that they shall judge to be for the people's good, be declared, and that upon the aforesaid considerations it be insisted upon, that all obstructions to the freedom and equality of the people's choice of their Representors, either by Patents, Charters or usurpations, by pretended customs, be removed by these present Commons in Parliament, and that such a freedom of choice be provided for, as the people may be equally represented. This power of Commons in Parliament, is the thing against which the King hath contended, and the people have defended with their lives, and therefore ought now to be demanded as the price of their blood.

That all the oppressions of the poor by Excise upon Bear, Cloth, Stuffs, and all manufactures, and English commodities; be forthwith taken off, and that all Excise be better regulated, and imposed upon foreign commodities, and a time set wherein it shall certainly end, if there be a necessity of its present continuance on such commodities.

5. Whereas the people have disbursed such vast sums of money, by Pole-money, Subsidies, proposition money, Contribution, the five and twentieth part, views and reviews of the same monthly assessments, Excise, and other ways, and such vast sums have been collected and enforced by Sequestrations, Compositions, sale of Bishops' lands, and other ways, that the whole charge of the forces by sea and land might have been defrayed to the utmost farthing, and yet many millions of money remained if all that have been disbursed freely or enforced, had been faithfully brought into the public treasury, and improved for the public use only: therefore, in respect to the people's right, and for their ease, and for better and more easy provision of money for the Soldiery, that it be insisted upon positively, that faithful

persons be chosen to receive accounts in every part of the Kingdom, especially considering that former Committees for accounts were constituted in a time when corrupt men over powered the Parliament, and that they have done no service in discovering monies since their constitution; and herein it's to be insisted on that all without distinction, as well Parliament men as others, may be equally accountable to persons chosen for that purpose.

Now herein it's further to be insisted on, that whereas the time was wholly corrupt when persons were appointed to make sale of Bishops' lands, and whereas Parliamentmen, Committeemen, and their kinfolk were the only buyers, and much is sold, and yet it's pretended, that little or no money is received, and whereas Lords, Parliamentmen, and some other rich men, have vast sums of arrears allowed them in their purchase, and all their monies lent to the state paid them, while others are left in necessity, to whom the state is much indebted, and so present money that might be for the equal advantage of all, is not brought into the public Treasury by those sales. It's therefore to be insisted on that the sale of Bishops' lands be reviewed, and that they may be sold to their worth, and for present monies, for the public use, & that the sale of all such be recalled, as have not been sold to their worth, or for present monies.

And it is further offered, in consideration that the Court have occasioned the late war, and reduced the state to such necessity, by causing such vast expense of treasure, that therefore whereas the many oppressions of the people, and the danger of absolute tyranny, were the occasion of the expense of so much blood, and whereas the people have bought their rights and freedoms, by the price of blood, and have in vain waited long since, the common enemy, hath been subdued for the redress of their grievances and oppressions, that therefore it be demanded as the people's due, which ought not to be denied to the Army or to them, that before the King hath his Court and lives in honor, yet before his business be further considered, because the people are under much oppression and misery, it be forthwith the whole work of the Parliament, to hear or consider of, & study effectually redress for all common grievances and oppressions, and for the securing all other the people's rights and freedoms, besides all these aforementioned, and in particular.

First, that all the orders, votes, ordinances or declarations, that have passed either to discountenance petitions, suppress, prevent or burn petitions, imprison or declare against petitioners, being dangerous precedents against the freedom of the people, may be forthwith expunged the Journal books, and the injustice of them clearly declared to all the people, and that in such a declaration the soldiery be vindicated, as to the right and equity of their first petition.

That all those large sums of money that were allowed to needless pretended Officers of the Court which did but increase wickedness and profaneness, may be reserved for a public treasure to be expended in paying those forces that must be maintained for the people's safety, that so through a good and faithful improvement of all the Lands pertaining to the Court, there might be much reserved for leaving public charges, and easing the people.

And it's further offered, that whereas millions of money have been kept in dead stocks in the City of *London* the Halls and Companies, and the free men of the City could never obtain any account thereof, according to their right; That therefore a just and strict account may be forthwith given to all the freemen of all those dead stocks, & whereas there hath been nothing paid out of those, nor for the lands pertaining to the City, while the estates of others have been much wasted, by continual payments, that therefore proportionable sums to what other estates have paid, may be taken out of those dead stocks, and lands which would amount to such vast sums, as would pay much of the soldiers' arrears, without burdening the oppressed people.

And it's further offered, that forest lands, and Deans' and Chapters' lands be immediately set apart for the arrears of the Army, and that the revenue of these and the residue of Bishops' lands unsold till the time of sale may be forthwith appointed to be paid unto our Treasury, to be reserved for the soldiers' constant pay. And it's to be wished that only such part of the aforesaid lands be sold as necessity requires, to satisfy the Soldiery for arrears, and that the residue be reserved and improved for a constant revenue for the State that the people may not be burdened, and that out of the revenues public debts may be paid, and not first taken out of their own purses to be repayed to them.

And it's further offered for the people's ease, that the arrears of all former assessments be duly collected from those who have sufficient estates, and have not been impoverished by the war.

And whereas it's conceived that the fees of receivers of customs and Excise if they were justly computed, would amount to near as much as the Army's pay, it's therefore offered that speedy consideration be had of the multitude of those officers and their excessive fees, & profits, as £500, 600, 1000, 1200 *per annum*. And whereas that many Excisemen appoint whom they please as their substitute, and allow what they please for their pay, that the officers may be few, and constant stipends allowed them, none exceeding £200 *per annum*, that so more monies may be brought into the public treasury.

And for the ease and satisfaction of the people, it's further to be insisted on, that the charge of all the forces to be kept up in the Kingdom by sea or land, be particularly computed and published, and that all taxes that shall be necessary, may be wholly proportioned, according to that charge; and that there be an equal rate propounded throughout the Kingdom in all assessments, that so one town may not bear double the proportion of another of the same value.

4. That all Monopolies be forthwith removed, and no persons whatsoever may be permitted to restrain others from free trade.

5. That the most sad oppressions of prisoners be forthwith eased and removed, and that no person that hath no estate real or personal, nor any person that shall willingly yield up his estate to satisfy his creditors may be detained in prison to the ruin of their persons and families, and likewise, that no person imprisoned in a criminal cause, may be detained from his legal trial any longer than the next term.

6. That all Statutes, for the Common Prayer Book, and

for enforcing all to come to Church, whereby many religious and conscientious people are daily vexed and oppressed, be forthwith repealed and nulled. As also that all Statutes against Conventicles, under the pretense of which, religious people are vexed for private meetings about the worship of God, may be likewise repealed and nulled.

7. That all the oppressive Statutes, enforcing all persons though against their consciences to pay Tithes, whereby the husbandman cannot eat the fruit of his labors, may be forthwith repealed and nulled.

8. That all Statutes enforcing the taking of oaths, as in towns corporate, the oath of Supremacy, &c. Wherein either the whole oaths, or some clauses in them, are burdens, and snares to conscientious people may be repealed and nulled.

9. That it be declared that no person or Court shall have power or be permitted to enforce any person to make oath, or answer to any Interrogatories concerning himself, in any criminal case.

10. That a Committee of conscientious persons be forthwith selected to consider of the most intolerable oppressions by unjust proceedings in the law, that with all the laws might be reduced to a smaller number, to be comprised in one volume in the English tongue, that every free Commoner might understand his own proceedings, that Courts might be in the respective Counties or Hundreds, that proceedings might become short and speedy, and that the numberless grievances in the law and Lawyers, might be redressed as soon as possible.

11. That all privileges and protections above the law, whereby some persons are exempted from the force and power thereof, to the insufferable vexation and ruin of multitudes of distressed people, may be forthwith abrogated.

12. That all the ancient rights and donations belonging to the poor, now embezzled and converted to other uses, as inclosed Commons, Alms-houses, &c. throughout all parts of the land, may be forthwith restored to the ancient public use and service of the poor, in whose hands soever they be detained.

Many other grievances are and ought to be redressed, but

these as they are propounded, we conceive might be in a very short time redressed to the relief of many distressed ones, and to a general ease; or at least, put into a way, wherein there might be visible hopes of remedy, and therefore these might be demanded as due to the people, though we desire the Counties might be encouraged to represent all their other grievances also for speedy redress.

7. General head. That it be insisted on, that such Indemnity be forthwith given both for the Soldiery and all that gave them assistance, and shall provide securely for their quiet, ease and safety, and prevent all chargeable journeys to London, to seek after and wait upon Committees.

8. That in some of the forementioned ways, security be given for arrears forthwith, that as soon as the rights and freedoms of the people be secured according as it's hereupon propounded, and the other desires of the Army in relation to their particular freedom from pressing, and provision to be made in a certain and no dishonorable way for maimed Soldiers, Widows, and Orphans, that shall continue during their lives, that then the Armies may be disposed into the hands of the faithful well-affected of the Nation, which may be so formed into a military posture, as to be ready on all occasions of service, and as many of the forces that are kept in constant pay, as shall not be absolutely necessary for the preservation and safety of the people, may be as speedily as possible disbanded, that they may not be a burden to the Nation.

9. Whereas mercy and justice are the foundations of a lasting peace, it's necessary to be insisted on (for the healing differences as far as possible), That all those whose estates have been sequestered, and yet were not in arms for the King, or gave any actual assistance to him in men, money, or arms, plate, horse, &c. in the late war, that all such be discharged forthwith from their sequestrations; and that all such as have compounded, may not be enforced, to pay the five or twentieth part, seeing their whole estates were so long under sequestration: and that all those that have not compounded, who were in Arms for the King, may be compelled forthwith to compound, provided, that their Compositions be so mod-

erate, as none may exceed two years' revenue, that their families be not ruined, and they put upon desperate attempts against the peace of the Nation to preserve themselves.

These things propounded are no more than what we conceived, should have been thoroughly done long since, being as to the principal of them but the substance and equitable sense of our former declarations, Remonstrances, and representations, And therefore though our restless desires of the people's good, and of the welfare of the Army, have constrained us, thus publicly to state our case, and the remedy according to the best improvement of the small Talent of understanding that God hath given freely to us? yet let not the matter be prejudged because of the unworthy Authors, neither let it be thought presumption. It may be remembered that the Father's danger made a dumb child to speak, and the Army's, yea all the people's dangers and miseries have wrested open our mouths, who had otherwise been silent in this kind to the grave, and let it not be thought that we intend the division of the Army, we profess we are deeply sensible and desire all our fellow soldiers to consider it.

In case the union of the Army should be broken (which the enemy wait for), ruin and destruction will break in upon us like a roaring sea, but we are much confident that the adhering to those desires and to that speedy way of attaining our just ends for which we first engaged, cannot be interpreted to be a desire of division, but the strongest vigorous endeavors after union, and though many whom we did betrust have been guilty of most supine negligence, yet we expect that the same impulsion of judgment and conscience that we have all professed, did command us forth at first for the people's Freedom, will be again so effectual, that all will unanimously concur with us, so that a demand of the people's and Army's rights shall be made by the whole Army as by one man, that then all the enemies to, or obstructors of the happy settlement of common right, peace and freedom, may hear of our union and resolution, and their hands may be weak, and their hearts may fail them, and so this Army that God hath clothed with honor in subduing the common enemy, may yet be more honorable in the people's eyes, when they shall be called the Repairers of their breaches, and the restorers of their peace, right, and freedom.

And this is the prayer, and shall always be the earnest endeavors of.

The Army's and all the people's most faithful servants,

Lieut. Gen. {*Robert Everard.* *George Sadler.* Com. Gen. {*George Garret.* *Thomas Beverly.*

Col. Fleetwood. {*William Priar.* *William Bryan.*

Col. Whalyes. {*Matthew Wealy.* *William Russell.* *Richard Seale.* C. Riches. {*John Dober.* *William Hudson.* Agitators.

Gilford, October 9. 1647.

IV

THE LEVELLERS AND THE DIGGERS

As was seen in Chapter III, the common soldier and his elected leaders, the Agitators, provided the principal radical element found in the Puritan Revolution. From 1647 until 1653 these men questioned and challenged almost all the ancient institutions that had been part and parcel of English life. The years from 1642 to 1649 had really witnessed a civil war, but now a true revolution was at hand. The total victory of the New Model Army and its nominal superior, the Long Parliament, unleashed a flood of books, pamphlets, and petitions demanding a new beginning in England. Yet the Long Parliament, a mere rump after the expulsion of the Presbyterians in 1648, showed little interest in anything other than the enjoyment of the fruits of power and the perpetuation of it for as long as possible. In the writings of "Free-born John" Lilburne [1, 2] we see the disillusionment with the new Commonwealth already far advanced, within a month of the king's execution. For Lilburne there was truth in the saying that "new Presbyter was but old bishop writ large" and perhaps the Rump was but the old king writ large.

In the Introduction it was pointed out that the Puritan Revolution did resemble the great revolutions of the modern world. The writings of Lilburne and his Levellers[1] provide this revolutionary element. They have attracted a great deal

[1] According to Marchamont Needham in his newspaper *Mercurius Politicus* for November 16, 1647, it was the king who first dubbed the Agitators Levellers. Riotous peasants who opposed the enclosure movement had been called "levellers" throughout the early seventeenth century. From that point on, the name was in use, although the Leveller leaders frequently felt called upon to deny any desire to "level men's estates."

of attention from historians and are often the focal point of attention for both those who sympathize with and those who abhor the English Revolution. In their own eyes they were the conscience of the people of England, organizing them and, in their name, bombarding those in the seats of power with their demands for equality and democracy. To Cromwell and all those with tangible interests to be defended, they constituted the grave threat of anarchy. This "threat" of anarchy contributed mightily to Cromwell's turning away from alliance with the common soldiers and toward a more conservative alignment.

The yeomen, artisans, and "mechanic-sort of men" who were the Levellers constituted a powerful element in the army and, therefore, could bring great influence to bear in national politics. The Diggers on the other hand were few in numbers and were led by men more visionary and less practical than the Levellers. The Diggers[2] called themselves "True Levellers" [3] and sought not just religious, political, and social equality, but economic equality as well. To them the whole system of private property had entered English life with the Norman Conquest. The land of England rightfully belonged to the common Englishman, who should reclaim it. Naturally the opposition often tried to paint the Levellers with the Diggers' brush.

1. ENGLAND'S NEW CHAINS DISCOVERED

England's/ New Chains/ Discovered:/ Or/ The serious apprehensions of a part of the People, in behalf of the Commonwealth; (being Presenters, Promoters, and Approvers of the Large Petition of September 11. 1648.)/ Presented to the Supreme Authority of England, the Representers of the people in Parliament assembled./ By Lieut. Col. John Lilburne, *and divers other Citizens*

[2] The name "Digger" was taken from the song the members of the group sang while digging: "You noble Diggers all, stand up now, stand up now. . . ." [See Brailsford, *The Levellers and the English Revolution,* p. 656.]

of London, and Borough of Southwark; February 26.
1648. *whereunto his speech delivered at the Bar is annexed./*

Since you have done the Nation so much right, and yourselves so much honor as to declare that the People (under
God) are the original of all just Powers; and given us thereby
fair grounds to hope, that you really intend their Freedom
and Prosperity; yet the way thereunto being frequently mistaken, and through haste or error of judgment, those who
mean the best, are many times mis-led so far to the prejudice
of those that trust them, as to leave them in a condition
nearest to bondage, when they have thought they had brought
them into a way of Freedom. And since woeful experience
hath manifested this to be a Truth, there seemeth no small
reason that you should seriously lay to heart what at present
we have to offer, for discovery and prevention of so great a
danger.

And because we have been the first movers in and concerning an Agreement of the People, as the most proper and
just means for the settling the long and tedious distractions
of this Nation, occasioned by nothing more than the uncertainty of our government; and since there hath been an Agreement prepared and presented by some Officers of the Army
to this honorable House, as what they thought requisite to
be agreed unto by the People (you approving thereof) we
shall in the first place deliver our apprehensions thereupon.

That an Agreement between those that trust, and those
who are trusted, hath appeared a thing acceptable to this
honorable House, his Excellency, and the Officers of the
Army, is as much to our rejoicing, as we conceive it just in
itself, and profitable for the Commonwealth, and cannot
doubt but that you will protect those of the people, who
have no ways forfeited their Birthright, in their proper liberty
of taking this, or any other, as God and their own Considerations shall direct them.

Which we the rather mention, for that many particulars
in the Agreement before you, are upon serious examination
thereof, dis-satisfactory to most of those who are very earnestly desirous of an Agreement, and many very material

things seem to be wanting therein, which may be supplied in another: As

1. They are now much troubled there should be any Intervals between the ending of this Representative, and the beginning of the next as being desirous that this present Parliament that hath lately done so great things in so short a time, tending to their Liberties, should sit; until with certainty and safety they can see them delivered into the hands of another Representative, rather than to leave them (though never so small a time) under the dominion of a Council of State; a Constitution of a new and inexperienced Nature, and which they fear, as the case now stands, may design to perpetuate their power, and to keep off Parliaments for ever.

2. They now conceive no less danger, in that it is provided that Parliaments for the future are to continue but 6 months, and a Council of State 18. In which time, if they should prove corrupt, having command of all Forces by Sea and Land, they will have great opportunities to make themselves absolute and unaccountable: And because this is a danger, than which there cannot well be a greater; they generally encline to Annual Parliaments, bounded and limited as reason shall devise, not dissolvable, but to be continued or adjourned as shall seem good in their discretion, during that year, but no longer; and then to dissolve of course, and give way to those who shall be chosen immediately to succeed them, and in the Intervals of their adjournments, to entrust an ordinary Committee of their own members, as in other cases limited and bounded with express instructions, and accountable to the next Session, which will avoid all those dangers feared from a Council of State, as at present this is constituted.

3. They are not satisfied with the clause, wherein it is said, that the power of the Representatives shall extend to the erecting and abolishing of Courts of Justice; since the alteration of the usual way of Trials by twelve sworn men of the Neighborhood, may be included therein: a constitution so equal and just in itself, as that they conceive it ought to remain unalterable. Neither is it clear what is meant by these words (viz.), That the Representatives have the highest final judgment. They conceiving that their Authority in these

cases, is only to make Laws, Rules, and Directions for other Courts and Persons assigned by Law for the execution thereof; unto which every member of the Commonwealth, as well those of the Representative, as others, should be alike subject; it being likewise unreasonable in itself, and an occasion of much partiality, injustice, and vexation to the people, that the Lawmakers, should be Law-executors.

4. Although it doth provide that in the Laws hereafter to be made, no person by virtue of any Tenure, Grant, Charter, Patent, Degree, or Birth, shall be privileged from subjection thereunto, or from being bound thereby, as well as others; Yet doth it not null and make void those present Protections by Law, or otherwise; nor leave all persons, as well Lords as others, alike liable in person and estate, as in reason and conscience they ought to be.

5. They are very much unsatisfied with what is expressed as a reserve from the Representative, in matters of Religion, as being very obscure, and full of perplexity, that ought to be most plain and clear; there having occurred no greater trouble to the Nation about anything than by the intermeddling of Parliaments in matters of Religion.

6. They seem to conceive it absolutely necessary, that there be in their Agreement, a reserve from ever having any Kingly Government, and a bar against restoring the House of Lords, both which are wanting in the Agreement which is before you.

7. They seem to be resolved to take away all known and burdensome grievances, as Tithes, that great oppression of the Country's industry and hindrance of Tillage: Excise, and Customs, Those secret thieves, and Robbers, Drainers of the poor and middle sort of People, and the greatest Obstructers of Trade, surmounting all the prejudices of Ship-money, Patents, and Projects, before this Parliament: also to take away all Monopolizing Companies of Merchants, the hinderers and decayers of Clothing and Cloth-working, Dying, and the like useful professions; by which thousands of poor people might be set at work, that are now ready to starve, were Merchandizing restored to its due and proper freedom: they conceive likewise that the three grievances before mentioned, (viz.) Monopolizing Companies, Excise, and Customs, do

exceedingly prejudice Shipping, and Navigation, and Consequently discourage Seamen, and Mariners, and which have had no small influence upon the late unhappy revolts which have so much endangered the Nation, and so much advantaged your enemies. They also incline to direct a more equal and less burdensome way for levying monies for the future, those other fore-mentioned being so chargeable in the receipt, as that the very stipends and allowance to the Officers attending thereupon would defray a very great part of the charge of the Army; whereas now they engender and support a corrupt interest. They also have in mind to take away all imprisonment of disabled men, for debt; and to provide some effectual course to enforce all that are able to a speedy payment, and not suffer them to be sheltered in Prisons, where they live in plenty, whilst their Creditors are undone. They have also in mind to provide work, and comfortable maintainance for all sorts of poor, aged, and impotent people, and to establish some more speedy, less troublesome and chargeable way for deciding of Controversies in Law, whole families having been ruined by seeking right in the ways yet in being: All which, though of greatest and most immediate concernment to the People, are yet omitted in their Agreement before you.

These and the like are their intentions in what they purpose for an Agreement of the People, as being resolved (so far as they are able) to lay an impossibility upon all whom they shall hereafter trust, of ever wronging the Commonwealth in any considerable measure, without certainty of ruining themselves, and as conceiving it to be an improper tedious, and unprofitable thing for the People, to be ever running after their Representatives with Petitions for redress of such Grievances as may at once be removed by themselves, or to depend for these things so essential to their happiness and freedom, upon the uncertain judgments of several Representatives, the one being apt to renew what the other hath taken away.

And as to the use of their Rights and Liberties herein as becometh, and is due to the people, from whom all just powers are derived; they hoped for and expect what protection is in you and the Army to afford: and we likewise in their and our own behalfs do earnestly desire, that you will publicly declare your resolution to protect those who have not forfeited their liberties in the use thereof, lest they should conceive that the Agreement before you being published abroad, and the Commissioners therein nominated being at work in persuance thereof, is intended to be imposed upon them, which as it is absolutely contrary to the nature of a free Agreement, so we are persuaded it cannot enter into your thoughts to use any impulsion therein.

But although we have presented our apprehensions and desires concerning this great work of an Agreement, and are apt to persuade ourselves that nothing shall be able to frustrate our hopes which we have built thereupon; yet have we seen and heard many things of late, which occasions not only apprehensions of other matters intended to be brought upon us of danger to such an Agreement, but of bondage and ruin to all such as shall pursue it.

Insomuch that we are even aghast and astonished to see that notwithstanding the productions of the highest notions of freedom that ever this Nation, or any people in the world, have brought to light, notwithstanding the vast expense of blood and treasure that hath been made to purchase those freedoms, notwithstanding the many eminent and even miraculous Victories God hath been pleased to honor our just Cause withall, notwithstanding the extraordinary gripes and pangs, this House hath suffered more than once at the hands of your own servants, and that at least seemingly for the obtaining these our Native Liberties.

When we consider what rackings and tortures the People in general have suffered through decay of Trade, and dearness of food, and very many families in particular, through Freequarter, Violence, and other miseries, incident to war, having nothing to support them therein, but hopes of Freedom, and a well-settled Commonwealth in the end.

That yet after all these things have been done and suffered, and whilst the way of an Agreement of the People is owned, and approved, even by yourselves, and that all men are in expectation of being put into possession of so dear a purchase; Behold! in the close of all, we hear and see what gives us fresh and pregnant cause to believe that the contrary is really intended, and that all those specious pretenses, and high Notions of Liberty, with those extraordinary courses that have of late been taken (as if of necessity for liberty, and which indeed can never be justified, but deserve the greatest punishments, unless they end in just liberty, and an equal Government) appear to us to have been done and directed by some secret powerful influences, the more securely and unsuspectedly to attain to an absolute domination over the Commonwealth: It being impossible for them, but by assuming our generally approved Principles, and hiding under the fair show thereof their other designs, to have drawn in so many good and godly men (really aiming at what the other had but in show and pretense) and making them unwittingly instrumental to their own and their Country's Bondage.

For where is that good, or where is that liberty so much pretended, so dearly purchased? If we look upon what this House hath done since it hath voted itself the Supreme Authority, and disburdened themselves of the power of the Lords. First, we find a high Court of Justice erected, for Trial of Criminal causes; whereby that great and strong hold of our preservation, the way of trial by 12 sworn men of the Neighborhood is infringed, all liberty of exception against the triers, is over-ruled by a Court consisting of persons picked and chosen in an unusual way; the practice whereof we cannot allow of, though against open and notorious enemies; as well because we know it to be an usual policy to introduce by such means all usurpations, first against Adversaries, in hope of easier admission; as also, for that the same being so admitted, may at pleasure be exercised against any person or persons whatsoever. This is the first part of our new liberty. The next is the censuring of a Member of this House, for declaring his judgment in a point of Religion, which is directly opposite to the Reserve in the Agreement concerning Religion. Besides the Act for pressing of Seamen, directly contrary to the Agreement of the Officers. Then the stopping of our mouths from Printing, is carefully provided for, and the most severe and unreasonable Ordinances of Parliament that were made in the time of Hollis and Stapleton's reign, to gag us from speaking truth, and discovering the tyrannies of bad men, are referred to the care of the General, and by him to his Marshal, to be put in execution; in searching, fining, imprisoning, and other ways corporally punishing all that any ways be guilty of unlicensed Printing; They dealing with us as the Bishops of old did with the honest Puritan, who were exact in getting Laws made against the Papist, but really intended them against the Puritan, and made them feel the smart of them: Which also hath been, and is daily exercised most violently, whereby our Liberties have been more deeply wounded, than since the beginning of this Parliament; and that to the dislike of the Soldiery, as by their late Petition in that behalf plainly appeareth. Then whereas it was expected that the Chancery, and Courts of Justice in Westminster, and the Judges and Officers thereof should have been surveyed, and for the present regulated, till a better and more equal way of deciding controversies could have been constituted, that the trouble and charge of the people in their suits should have been abated: Instead hereof, the old and advanced fees are continued, and new thousand pounds Annual stipends allotted; when in the corruptest times the ordinary fees were thought a great and a sore burden; in the meantime, and in lieu thereof, there is not one perplexity or absurdity in proceedings taken away. Those Petitioners that have moved in behalf of the people, how have they been entertained? Sometimes with the compliment of empty thanks, their desires in the meantime not at all considered; at other times meeting with Reproaches and Threats for their constancy and public affections, and with violent motions, that their Petitions be burnt by the common Hangman, whilst others are not taken in at all; to so small an account are the people brought, even while they are flattered with notions of being the Original of all just power. And lastly, for completing this new kind of liberty, a Council of State is hastily erected for Guardians thereof, who to that end are possessed with power to order and dispose all the forces appertaining to England by Sea or Land, to dispose of the public Treasure, to command any person whatsoever before them, to give oath for the discovering of Truth, to imprison any that shall disobey their commands, and such as they shall judge contumacious. What now is become of that liberty that no man's person shall be attached or imprisoned, or otherwise diseased of his Freehold, or free Customs, but by lawful judgment of his equals? We entreat you give us leave to lay these things open to your view, and judge impartially of our present condition, and of your own also, that by strong and powerful influences of some persons, are put upon these and the like proceedings, which both you and we ere long (if we look not to it) shall be enforced to subject ourselves unto; then we have further cause to complain, when we consider the persons: as first, the chief of the Army directly contrary to what themselves thought meet in their Agreement for the People. 2 Judges of the Law and Treasurers for monies. Then 5 that were Members of the Lords' House, and most of them such as have refused to approve of your Votes and proceedings, concerning the King and Lords. 2 of them Judges in the Star Chamber, and approvers of the bloody and tyrannical sentences issuing from thence.

Some of your own House, forward men in the Treaty, and decliners of your last proceedings; all which do clearly manifest to our understandings that the secret contrivers of those things do think themselves now so surely guarded by the strength of an Army, by their daily Acts and Stratagems, to their ends inclined, and the captivation of this House, that they may now take off the Veil and Cloak of their designs as dreadless of whatever can be done against them. By this Council of State, all power is got into their own hands, a project which hath been long and industriously labored for; and which being once firmly and to their liking established their next motions may be upon pretense of ease to the People, for the dissolution of this Parliament, half of whose time is already swallowed up by the said Council now, because no obstacle lies in their way, to the full establishment of these their ends, but the uncorrupted part of the Soldiery, that have their eyes fixed upon their engagements and promises of good to the People, and resolve by no threats or allurements to decline the same; together with that part of the people in City and Countries, that remain constant in their motions for Common good, and still persist to run their utmost hazards for procurement of the same, by whom all

evil men's designs both have, and are still likely to find a
check and discovery. Hereupon the grand contrivers fore-
mentioned, whom we can particular by name, do begin to
raise their spleen, and manifest a more violent enmity
against Soldiers and People, disposed as aforesaid, than ever
heretofore, as appeareth by what lately past, at a meeting of
Officers, on Feb. 22 last, at Whitehall, where after expressions of much bitterness against the most Conscientious part
of the Soldiery, and others, it was insisted upon (as we are
from very credible hands certainly informed) that a motion
should be made to this House for the procurement of a Law
enabling them to put to death all such as they should judge
by Petitions or otherwise to disturb the present proceedings;
and upon urging that the Civil Magistrate should do it, It
was answered, that they could hang twenty ere the Magistrate
one. It was likewise urged that Orders might be given to
seize upon the Petitioners, Soldiers, or others, at their meetings, with much exclamation against some of greatest integrity
to your just Authority, whereof they have given continual and
undeniable assurances. A Proclamation was likewise appointed, forbidding the Soldiers to Petition you, or any but
their Officers, prohibiting their correspondencies: And
private Orders to be given out for seizing upon Citizens and
Soldiers at their meetings. And thus after these fair blossoms
of hopeful liberty, breaks forth this bitter fruit, of the vilest
and basest bondage that ever Englishmen groaned under:
whereby this notwithstanding is gained (viz.) an evident and
(we hope) a timely discovery of the instruments, from
whence all the evils, contrivances, and designs (which for
above these eighteen months have been strongly suspected)
took their rise and original, even ever since the first breach of
their Promises and engagements made at New Market,
Triploe Heath, with the Agitators and People. It being for
these ends that they have so violently opposed all such as
manifested any zeal for Common Right, or any regard to the
Faith of the Army, sentencing some to death, others to reproachful punishments, placing and displacing Officers according as they showed themselves serviceable or opposite to
their designs, listing as many as they thought good, even of
such as have served in Arms against you: And then again

upon pretense of easing the charge of the People, disbanding Supernumeraries, by advantage thereof picking out, such as were most cordial and active for Common good; thereby molding the Army (as far as they could) to their own bent and ends premised; exercising Martial Law with much cruelty, thereby to debase their spirits, and make them subservient to their wills and pleasures; extending likewise their power (in many cases) over persons not Members of the Army.

And when in case of opposition and difficult services, they have by their creatures desired a Reconciliation with such as at other times they reproached, vilified, and otherwise abased; and through fair promises of good, and dissembled repentance gained their association and assistance, to the great advantage of their proceedings: yet their necessities being over, and the Common enemy subdued, they have slighted their former promises, and renewed their hate and bitterness against such their assistances, reproaching them with such appellations as they knew did most distaste the People, such as Levellers, Jesuits, Anarchists, Royalists, names both contradictory in themselves, and altogether groundless in relation to the men so reputed; merely relying for release thereof upon the easiness and credulity of the People.

And though the better to insinuate themselves, and get repute with the People, as also to conquer their necessities, they have been feign to make use of those very principles and productions, the men they have so much traduced, have brought to light: yet the producers themselves they have and do still more eagerly malign than ever, as such whom they know to be acquainted to their deceits, and deviations and best able to discover the same.

So that now at length, guessing all to be sure, and their own (the King being removed, the House of Lords nulled, their long plotted Council of State erected, and this House awed to their ends), the edge of their malice is turning against such as have yet so much courage left them as to appear for the well establishment of England's Liberties: and because God hath preserved a great part of the Army untainted with the guilt of the designs aforementioned, who cannot without much danger to the designers themselves be suppressed, they have resolved to put this House upon raising more new forces (notwithstanding the present necessities of the People, in maintaining those that are already), in doing whereof, though the pretense be danger, and opposition, yet the concealed end is like to be the over-balancing those in the Army, who are resolved to stand for true Freedom, as the end of all their labors, the which (if they should be permitted to do) they would not then doubt of making themselves absolute seizures, Lords and Masters, both of Parliament and People; which when they have done we expect the utmost of misery, nor shall it grieve us to expire with the liberties of our native Country: for what good man can with any comfort to himself survive then? But God hath hitherto preserved us, and the Justice of our desires, as integrity of our intentions are daily more and more manifest to the impartial and unprejudiced part of men; insomuch that it is no small comfort to us, that notwithstanding we are upon all these disadvantages that may be, having neither power nor pre-eminence, the Common Idols of the world; our Cause and principles, do through their own natural truth and luster get ground in men's understandings, so that where there was one, twelve months since, that owned our principles, we believe there are now hundreds, so that though we fail, our Truths prosper.

And posterity we doubt not shall reap the benefit of our endeavors, whatever shall become of us. However though we have neither strength nor safety before us, we have discharged our Consciences, and emptied our breasts unto you, knowing well that if you will make use of your power, and take unto you that courage which becomes men of your Trust and condition, you may yet through the goodness of God prevent the danger and mischief intended, and be instrumental in restoring this long enthralled and betrayed Nation into a good and happy condition.

For which end we most earnestly desire and propose, as the main prop and support of the work [1], that you will not dissolve this House, nor suffer yourselves to be dissolved, until as aforesaid, you see a new Representative the next day ready to take your room; which you may confidently and safely insist upon, there being no considerable number in the Army or elsewhere, that will be so unworthy as to dare to disturb you therein.

2. That you will put in practice the Self-denying Ordinance, the most just and useful that ever was made, and continually cried out for by the People; whereby a great infamy that lies upon your cause will be removed, and men of powerful influences, and dangerous designs, deprived of those means and opportunities which now they have, to prejudice the public.

3. That you will consider how dangerous it is for one and the same persons to be continued long in the highest commands of a Military power, especially acting so long distinct, and of themselves, as those now in being have done, and in such extraordinary ways whereunto they have accustomed themselves, which was the original of most Regalities and Tyrannies in the world.

4. That you appoint a Committee of such of your own members, as have been longest established upon those rules of Freedom upon which you now proceed; to hear, examine, and conclude all controversies between Officers and Officers, and between Officers and Soldiers; to consider and mitigate the Law-Martial; and to provide that it be not exercised at all upon persons not of the Army: Also to release and repair such as have thereby unduly suffered, as they shall see cause: To consider the condition of the private Soldiers, both Horse and Foot in these dear times, and to allow them such increase of pay, as wherewithal they may live comfortably, and honestly discharge their Quarters: That all disbanding be referred to the said Committee, and that such of the Army as have served the King, may be first disbanded.

5. That you will open the Press, whereby all treacherous and tyrannical designs may be the easier discovered, and so prevented, which is a liberty of greatest concernment to the Commonwealth, and which such only as intend a tyranny are engaged to prohibit: The mouths of Adversaries being best stopped, by the sensible good which the people receive from the actions of such as are in Authority.

6. That you will (whilst you have opportunity) abate the charge of the Law, and reduce the stipends of Judges, and

all other Magistrates and Officers in the Commonwealth, to a less, but competent allowance, converting the over-plus to the public Treasury, whereby the taxes of the People may be much eased.

7. But above all, that you will dissolve this present Council of State, which upon the grounds fore-mentioned so much threateneth Tyranny; and manage your affairs by Committees of short continuance, and such as may be frequently and exactly accountable for the discharge of their Trusts.

8. That you will publish a strict prohibition, and severe penalty against all such, whether Committees, Magistrates, or Officers of what kind soever, as shall exceed the limits of their Commission, Rules, or Directions, and encourage all men in their informations and complaints against them.

9. That you will speedily satisfy the expectations of the Soldiers in point of Arrears, and of the people in point of Accounts, in such a manner, as that it may not as formerly, prove a snare to such as have been most faithful, and a protection to the most corrupt, in the discharge of their trust and duties.

10. That the so many times complained of Ordinance for Tithes upon triple damages, may be forthwith taken away; all which, together with due regard shown to Petitioners, without respect to their number and strength, would so fasten you in the affections of the people, and of the honest Officers and Soldiers, as that you should not need to fear any opposite power whatsoever: and for the time to come, of yourselves enjoy the exercise of your Supreme Authority, whereof you have yet but the name only; and be enabled to vindicate your just undertakings; wherein we should not only rejoice to have occasion to manifest how ready we should be to hazard our lives in your behalf, but should also bend all our studies and endeavors to render you Honorable to all future generations.

Feb. 26. 1648. Being ushered in by the Sergeant at Arms, and called to the Bar, with all due respects given unto the House, Lieutenant Colonel John Lilburne, with divers others, coming to the Bar next the Mace, with the Address in his hand, spake these words, or to this effect, as followeth.

Mr. Speaker,

I am very glad that without any inconvenience unto myself, and those that are with me, I may freely and cheerfully address myself to this honorable House, as the Supreme Authority of England (time was when I could not) and it much refresheth my spirit, to live to see this day, that you have made such a step·to the People's Liberties, as to own and declare yourselves to be (as indeed you are) the Supreme Authority of this Nation.

Mr. Speaker, I am desired by a company of honest men, living in and about London, who in truth do rightly appropriate to themselves, the title of the Contrivers, Promoters, Presenters, and Approvers of the late Large London Petition of the 11 of Sept. last (which was the first Petition I know of in England, that was presented to this honorable House against the late destructive Personal Treaty with the late King), to present you with their serious apprehensions; And give me leave (I beseech you) for myself and them, to say thus much; That for the most part of us, we are those that in the worst of times durst own our Liberties and Freedoms, in the face of the greatest of our adversaries; and from the beginning of these Wars, never shrunk from the owning of our Freedoms, in the most tempestuous times, nor changed our Principles: Nay Sir, let me with truth tell you, that to the most of us, our Wives, our Children, our Estates, our Relations, nay our Lives, and all that upon earth we can call Ours, have not been so highly valued by us, as our Liberties and Freedoms; which our constant Actions (to the apparent hazard of our Blood and Lives) have been a clear and full demonstration of, for these many years together.

And Mr. Speaker, give me leave to tell you, that I am confident our Liberties and Freedoms (the true and just end of all the late Wars) are so dear and precious to us, that we had rather our Lives should breathe out with them, than to live one moment after the expiration of them.

Mr. Speaker, I must confess I am to present you with a paper, something of a new kind, for we have had no longer

time to consider of it, than from Thursday last, and Warrants (as we are informed) issuing out against us to take us,
from those that have no power over us; we durst not well
go our ordinary way to work, to get Subscriptions to it, lest
we should be surprised before we could present it to this
honorable House, and so be frustrated in that benefit or relief that we justly expect from you; and to present it with
a few hands, we judged inconsiderable in your estimation,
and therefore chose in the third place (being in so much
haste as we were to prevent our imminent and too apparent
ruin) in person to bring it to your Bar, and avowedly to
present it here: And therefore without any further question,
give me leave to tell you, I own it, and I know so doth all
the rest of my Friends present; and if any hazard should
ensue thereby, Give me leave resolvedly to tell you, I am
sorry I have but one life to lose, in maintaining the Truth,
Justice, and Righteousness, of so gallant a piece.

Mr. Speaker, We own this honorable House (as of right)
the true Guardian of our Liberties and Freedoms; and we
wish and most heartily desire, you would rouse up your spirits
(like men of gallantry) and now at last take unto yourselves
a magnanimous resolution, to acquit yourselves (without fear
or dread) like the chosen and betrusted Trustees of the People, from whom (as yourselves acknowledge and declare) all
just power is derived, to free us from all bondage and slavery,
and really and truly invest us into the price of all our blood,
hazards, and toils; Our Liberties and Freedoms, the true difference and distinction of men from beasts.

Mr. Speaker, Though my spirit is full in the sad apprehension of the dying condition of our Liberties and Freedoms:
Yet at present I shall say no more, but in the behalf of
myself and my friends, I shall earnestly entreat you to read
these our serious Apprehensions seriously, and debate them
deliberately.

Friends,

This we have adventured to publish for the timely information and benefit of all that adhere unto the common interest
of the people, hoping that with such, upon due consideration, it will find as large an acceptance, as our late Peti-

tion of Sept. 11, 1648. And we thought good (in regard we were not called in to receive an answer to the same) to acquaint you, that we intend to second it with a Petition sufficiently subscribed, we doubt not with many thousands, earnestly to solicit for an effectual Answer.

2. *A MANIFESTATION from* Lieutenant Colonel *John Lilburne*, Master *William Walwyn*, Master *Thomas Prince,* and Master *Richard Overton* (now prisoners in the Tower of *London*) and others, commonly (though unjustly) styled *Levellers*.

Since no man is born for himself only, but obliged by the Laws of Nature (which reaches all) of Christianity (which engages us as Christians) and of Public Society and Government, to employ our endeavors for the advancement of a communitive Happiness, of equal concernment to others as ourselves: here have we (according to that measure of understanding God hath dispensed unto us) labored with much weakness indeed, but with integrity of heart, to produce out of the Common Calamities, such a proportion of Freedom and good to the Nation, as might somewhat compensate its many grievances and lasting sufferings: And although in doing thereof we have hitherto reaped only Reproach, and hatred for our good Will, and been fain to wrestle with the violent passions of Powers and Principalities; yet since it is nothing so much as our Blessed Master and his Followers suffered before us, and but what at first we reckoned upon, we cannot be thereby any whit dismayed in the performance of our duties, supported inwardly by the Innocency and evenness of our Consciences.

'Tis a very great unhappiness we well know, to be always struggling and striving in the world, and does wholly keep us from the enjoyment of those contentments our several Conditions reach unto: So that if we should consult only with ourselves, and regard only our own ease, We should never enterpose as we have done, in behalf of the Commonwealth: But when so much has been done for recovery of our Liberties, and seeing God hath so blessed that which has been done, as thereby to clear the way, and to afford an opportunity which these 600 years has been desired, but could never be attained, of making this a *truly happy* and *wholly Free* Nation; We think ourselves bound by the greatest obligations that may be, to prevent the neglect of this opportunity, and to hinder as much as lies in us, that the blood which has been shed be not spilt like water upon the ground, nor that after the abundant Calamities, which have overspread all quarters of the Land, the change be only Notional, Nominal, Circumstantial, whilst the real Burdens, Grievances, and Bondages, be continued, even when the Monarchy is changed into a Republic.

We are no more concerned indeed than other men, and could bear the Yoke we believe as easily as others; but since a Common Duty lies upon every man to be cautious and circumspect in behalf of his Country, especially while the Government thereof is settling, other men's neglect is so far we think from being a just motive to us of the like sloth and inanimadvertency, as that it rather requires of us an increase of care and circumspection which if it produces not so good a settlement as ought to be, yet certainly it will prevent its being so bad as otherwise it would be, if we should all only mind our particular callings and employments.

So that although personally we may suffer, yet our solace is that the Commonwealth is thereby some gainer, and we doubt not but that God in his due time will so clearly dispel the Clouds of Ignominy and Obloquy which now surround us by keeping our hearts upright and our spirits sincerely public, that every good man will give us the right hand of fellowship, and be even sorry that they have been estranged, and so hardly opinionated against us: We question not but that in time the reason of such misprisions will appear to be in their eyes and not in our Actions, in the false Representation of things to them and improper glosses that are put upon everything we do or say: In our own behalfs we have as yet said nothing, trusting that either shame and Christian duty would restrain men from making so bold with others' good Name and Reputation, or that the sincerity of our actions would evince the falsehood of these scandals, and prevent the People's Belief of them; But we have found that with too much greediness they suck in Reports that tend to the discredit of others, and that our silence gives encouragement to bad Rumors of us; so that in all places they are spread, and industriously propagated as well amongst them that know us, as them that know us not, the first being fed with Jealousies that there is more in our designs than appears, that there is something of danger in the bottom of our hearts, not yet discovered: that we are driven on by others, that we are even discontented and irresolved, that nobody yet knows what we would have, or where our desires will end; whilst they that know us not are made believe any strange conceit of us, that we would Level all men's estates, that we would have no distinction of Orders and Dignities amongst men, that we are indeed for no Government, but a Popular confusion; and then again that we have been Agents for the King, and now for the Queen; That we are Atheists, Antiscripturists, Jesuits and indeed anything, that is hateful and of evil repute amongst men.

All which we could without observance pass over, remembering what is promised to be the Portion of good men, were the damage only personal, but since the ends of such Rumors are purposely to make us useless and unserviceable to the Commonwealth, we are necessitated to open our breasts and show the world our insides, for removing of those scandals that lie upon us, and likewise for manifesting plainly and particularly what our desires are, and in what we will center and acquiesce: all which we shall present to public view and consideration, not pertinaciously or Magisterially, as concluding other men's judgments, but manifesting our own, for our further vindication, and for the procuring of a Bond and lasting establishment for the Commonwealth.

First, Then it will be requisite that we express ourselves concerning Levelling, for which we suppose is commonly meant an equaling of men's estates, and taking away the proper right and Title that every man has to what is his own. This as we have formerly declared against, particularly in our petition of the 11 of Sept. so do we again profess that to attempt an inducing the same is most injurious, unless there did precede an universal assent thereunto from all and every one of the People. Nor do we, under favor, judge it within the Power of a Representative itself, because although their power is supreme, yet it is but deputative and of trust; and consequently must be restrained expressly or tacitly, to some particular essential as well to the People's safety and freedom as to the present Government.

The Community amongst the primitive Christians, was *Voluntary, not Co-active;* they *brought* their goods and laid them at the Apostles' feet, they were not enjoined to bring them, it was the effect of their Charity and heavenly mindedness, which the blessed Apostles begot in them, and not the Injunction of any Constitution, which as it was but for a short time done, and in but two or three places, that the Scripture makes mention of, so does the very doing of it there and the Apostles' answer to him that detained a part, imply that it was not esteemed a duty, but reckoned a voluntary act occasioned by the abundant measure of faith that was in those Christians and Apostles.

We profess therefore that we never had it in our thoughts to Level men's estates, it being the utmost of our aim that the Commonwealth be reduced to such a pass that every man may with as much security as may be enjoy his property.

We know very well that in all Ages those men that engage themselves against Tyranny, unjust and Arbitrary proceedings in Magistrates, have suffered under such appellations, the People being purposely frighted from that which is good by insinuations of imaginary evil.

But be it so, we must notwithstanding discharge our Duties, which being performed, the success is in God's hand to whose good pleasure we must leave the clearing of men's spirits, our only certainty being Tranquillity of mind, and peace of Conscience.

For distinction of Orders and Dignities, We think them so far needful, as they are animosities of virtue, or requisite for the maintenance of the Magistracy and Government, we think they were never intended for the nourishment of Ambition, or subjugation of the People but only to preserve the due respect and obedience in the People which is necessary for the better execution of the Laws.

That we are for Government and against Popular Confusion, we conceive all our actions declare, when rightly con-

sidered, our aim having been all along to reduce it as near
as might be to perfection, and certainly we know very well
the pravity and corruption of man's heart is such that there
could be no living without it; and that though Tyranny is
so excessively bad, yet of the two extremes, Confusion is the
worst: 'Tis somewhat a strange consequence to infer that because we have labored so earnestly for a good Government,
therefore we would have none at all; Because we would have
the dead and exorbitant Branches pruned, and better science
grafted, therefore we would pluck the Tree up by the roots.

Yet thus have we been misconceived, and misrepresented
to the world, under which we must suffer, till God sees it
fitting in his good time to clear such harsh mistakes, by which
many, even good men keep a distance from us.

For those weak suppositions of some of us being Agents
for the King or Queen, we think it needful to say no more
but this, That though we have not been any way violent
against the persons of them, or their Party, as having aimed
at the conversion of all, and the destruction of none, yet
do we verily believe that those Principles and Maxims of
Government which are most fundamentally opposite to the
Prerogative, and the King's interest, take their first rise and
original from us, many whereof though at first startled at,
and disowned by those that professed the greatest opposition
to him, have yet since been taken up by them and put in
practice: and this we think is sufficient, though much more
might be said to clear us from any Agency for that Party.

It is likewise suggested that we are acted by others, who
have other ends than appear to us; we answer. That that cannot be, since everything has its rise amongst ourselves, and
since those things we bring to light cannot conduce to the
ends of any but the public weal of the Nation.

All our Desires, Petitions and Papers are directly opposite
to all corrupt Interests; nor have any, credit with us, but
persons well known, and of certain abodes, and such as have
given sound and undeniable testimonies of the truth of their
affection to their Country: Besides, the things we promote, are not good only in appearance, but sensibly so: not
molded nor contrived by the subtle or politic Principles of
the World, but plainly produced and nakedly sent, with-

out any insinuating arts, relying wholly upon the apparent and universal belief they carry in themselves; and that is it which convinces and engages us in the promotion thereof. So that that suggestion has not indeed any foundation in itself, but is purposely framed, as we conceive, to make us afraid one of another, and to disable us in the promotion of those good things that tend to the freedom and happiness of the Commonwealth.

For our being Jesuits, either in Order or Principles, as 'tis severally reported of us; Though the easiest Negative is hardly proved; yet we can say, That those on whom the first is principally fixed, are married, and were never over Sea: and we think Marriage is never dispensed withall in that Order, and that none can be admitted into the Order but such as are personally present. 'Tis hard that we are put to express thus much; and happily we might better pass such reports over in silence; but that we believe the very mentioning of them publicly, will be an answer to them, and make such as foment them ashamed of such generally condemned ways of discrediting and blasting the Reputation of other men. For the principles of Jesuits, we profess we know not what they are; but they are generally said to be full of craft and worldly policy; and therefore exceedingly different from that plainness and simplicity that is apparently visible in all our proceedings.

Whereas it's said, we are Atheists and Antiscripturists, we profess that we believe there is one eternal and omnipotent God, the Author and Preserver of all things in the world. To whose will and directions, written first in our hearts, and afterwards in his blessed Word, we ought to square our actions and conversations. And though we are not so strict upon the formal and Ceremonial part of his Service, the method, manner, and personal injunction being not so clearly made out unto us, nor the necessary requisites which his Officers and Ministers ought to be furnished withall as yet appearing to some of us in any that pretend thereunto: yet for the manifestation of God's love in Christ, it is clearly assented unto by us; and the practical and most real part of Religion is as readily submitted unto by us, as being, in our apprehensions, the most eminent and the most excellent in the world, and as proceeding from no other but that God who is Goodness itself: and we humbly desire his Goodness daily more and more to conform our hearts to a willing and sincere obedience thereunto.

For our not being preferred to Offices and Places of profit and credit, which is urged to be the ground of our dissatisfaction, we say, That although we know no reason why we should not be equally capable of them with other men, nor why our public Affection should be any bar or hindrance thereunto: Yet on the other side, we suppose we can truly say of ourselves, that we have not been so earnest and solicitous after them as others: and that in the Catalog of Suitors, very few that are reckoned of us, are to be found. We are very sorry that so general a change of Officers is proposed, which we judge of no small disparagement to our Cause; and do think it best, that in removals of that kind, the ground should not be difference in opinion, either in Religious or Civil Matters, but corruption or breach of Trust; considering the misery which befalls whole Families upon such Changes; and that discontents are thereby increased: Whereas we hold it necessary that all ways of composure and acquieting those storms which the preceding differences and distractions have begotten, be with utmost care and prudence endeavored.

And whereas 'tis urged, That if we were in power, we would bear ourselves as Tyrannically as others have done: We confess indeed, that the experimental defections of so many men as have succeeded in Authority, and the exceeding difference we have hitherto found in the same men in a low, and in an exalted condition, makes us even mistrust our own hearts, and hardly believe our own Resolutions of the contrary. And therefore we have proposed such an Establishment, as supposing men to be too flexible and yielding to worldly Temptations, they should not yet have a means or opportunity either to injure particulars, or prejudice the Public, without extreme hazard, and apparent danger to themselves. Besides, to the objection we have further to say, That we aim not at power in ourselves, our Principles and Desires being in no measure of self-concernment: nor do we rely for obtaining the same upon strength, or a forcible obstruction; but solely upon that inbred and persuasive power that is all good and just things, to make their own way in the hearts of men, and so to procure their own Establishments.

And that makes us at this time naked and defenseless as we are, and amidst so many discouragements on all hands to persevere in our motions and desires of good to the Nation; although disowned therein at such a time when the doing thereof can be interpreted no other but a politic delivering us up to slaughter, by such as we took for Friends, our brethren of several Churches; and for whom with truth of affection we have even in the most difficult times done many Services: all which, and whatsoever else can be done against us, we shall reckon but as badges of our sincerity, and be no whit discouraged thereby from the discharge of our duties.

For the dis-satisfactions that be upon many good men's spirits, for that they are not ascertained whereunto all our motions tend, and in what they will center,

Though, we conceive, they may have received some general satisfaction from what we have formerly at several times propounded; yet since they were not disposed into such a form and condition as to become practicable; we have, with the best care and abilities God hath afforded us, cast the same into a Model and Platform, which we shall speedily present unto the view and consideration of all, as the *Standard* and ultimate scope of our Designs, that so (in case of approval) it may be subscribed and returned as agreed upon by the People. And thus far, we conceive, we may without offense or prejudice to Authority, proceed; and which we the rather do, because we know no better, and indeed no other way or means (but by such an Agreement) to remove (as much as may be) all disgusts and heart-burnings, and to settle the Commonwealth upon the fairest probabilities of a lasting Peace, and contentful Establishment.

The Agreement of the People which was presented by his Excellency and the Officers of the Army to the Right Honorable the Commons in Parliament, although in many things short (according to our apprehensions) of what is necessary for the good of the Commonwealth, and satisfaction of the People; particularly, in that it containeth no provision for the certain removal of notorious and generally complained of grievances: And although it hath some things of much hazard to the Public,—yet, had it been put in execution, we should scarcely have interrupted the proceedings thereof, since therein is contained many things of great and important concernment to. the Commonwealth. But seeing the time proposed therein for reducing the same into practice, is now past, and that likewise the generality of the people have not, or do not approve of the same, for the reasons (as we suppose) fore-mentioned: We have thought fit to revise it, making only such alterations therein as we conceive really necessary for the welfare, security and safety of the People, together with additional Provisions for the taking away of those Burdens and Grievances which may without real prejudice to the Management of public Affairs be removed.

And because it is essential to the nature of such an Agreement to take its rise from the People, we have therefore purposely declined the presentment thereof to the Parliament: and conceive it may speedily proceed to Subscription, and so to further practice, without any interruption to this Representative, until the season prefixed in the Agreement, for the assembling another: By whose immediate succession, without any interval, the Affairs of the Commonwealth may suffer no stop or intermission.

Lastly, We conceive we are much mistaken in being judged impatient, and over-violent in our motions for the public Good. To which we answer, That could we have had any assurance that what is desired should have otherwise, or by any have been done; and had not had some taste of the relinquishment of many good things that were promised, we should not have been so earnest and urgent for the doing thereof.

Though we know likewise it hath been very customary in such heretofore as never intended any freedom to the Nation, to except only against the season, and to protract the time so long, till they became sufficiently impowered to justify the total denial and refusal thereof. However, the main reason of our proceeding as we do, is, because we prefer the way of a settlement by an Agreement of the People before any other whatsoever.

And thus the world may clearly see what we are, and what we aim at: We are altogether ignorant, and do from our hearts abominate all designs and contrivances of dangerous consequence which we are said (but God knows, untruly) to be laboring withall. Peace and Freedom is our Design; by War we were never gainers, nor ever wish to be; and under bondage we have been hitherto sufferers. We desire, however, that what is past may be forgotten, provided the Commonwealth may have amends made it for the time to come. And this from our soul we desire.

Having no men's persons in hatred, and judging it needful that all other respects whatsoever are to give way to the good of the Commonwealth, and this is the very truth and inside of our hearts.

From the Tower,
April 14, 1649.

John Lilburne
William Walwyn
Thomas Prince
Richard Overton.

3. *THE TRUE LEVELLERS' STANDARD ADVANCED* *(1649) by William Everard, Gerrard Winstanley, et al*

In the beginning of time, the great Creator, Reason, made the earth to be a common treasury, to preserve beasts, birds, fishes, and man, the lord that was to govern this creation. For man had domination given to him over the beasts, birds, and fishes. But not one word was spoken in the beginning, that one branch of mankind should rule over another.

And the reason is this. Every single man, male and female, is a perfect creature of himself. And the same Spirit that made the globe dwells in man to govern the globe; so that the flesh of man, being subject to Reason, his Maker, hath him to be his teacher and ruler within himself, therefore needs not run abroad after any teacher and ruler without him. . . .

But since human flesh . . . began to delight himself in the objects of the creation more than in the Spirit Reason and

Righteousness, who manifests himself to be the indweller in the five senses . . . ; then he fell into blindness of mind and weakness of heart, and runs abroad for a teacher and ruler, and so selfish imaginations, taking possession of the five senses, and ruling as king in the room of Reason therein, and working with covetousness, did set up one man to teach and rule over another. And thereby the Spirit was killed, and man was brought into bondage and became a greater slave to such of his own kind than the beasts of the field were to him.

And hereupon the earth, which was made to be a common treasury of relief for all, both beasts and men, was hedged into enclosures by the teachers and rulers, and the others were made servants and slaves. And that earth that is within this creation made a common storehouse for all, is bought and sold and kept in the hands of a few; whereby the great Creator is mightily dishonored: as if he were a respecter of persons, delighting in the comfortable livelihood of some, and rejoicing in the miserable poverty and straits of others. From the beginning it was not so. . . .

But for the present state of the old world, that is running up like parchment in the fire and wearing away, we see proud imaginary flesh, which is the wise serpent, rises up in flesh and gets dominion in some to rule over others, and so forces one part of the creation, man, to be a slave to another. And thereby the Spirit is killed in both. The one looks upon himself as a teacher and ruler, and so is lifted up in pride over his fellow creature. The other looks upon himself as imperfect, and so is dejected in his spirit, and looks upon his fellow creature, of his own image, as a lord above him.

And thus Esau, the man of flesh, which is covetousness and pride, hath killed Jacob, the spirit of meekness, and righteous government in the light of reason, and rules over him. And so the earth that was made a common treasury for all to live comfortably upon, is become, through man's unrighteous actions one over another, to be a place wherein one torments another.

Now the great Creator, who is the Spirit Reason, suffered himself thus to be rejected and trodden under foot by the covetous, proud flesh, for a certain time limited. Therefore saith he: *The seed out of whom the creation did proceed, which is myself, shall bruise this serpent's head, and restore my creation again from this curse and bondage; and when I, the King of Righteousness, reigns in every man, I will be the blessing of the earth, and the joy of all nations.*

And . . . the earth hath been enclosed and given to the elder brother Esau, or man of flesh, and hath been bought and sold from one to another; and Jacob, or the younger brother, that is to succeed or come forth next, who is the universal spreading power of righteousness that gives liberty to the whole creation, is made a servant. And this elder son, or man of bondage, hath held the earth in bondage to himself, not by a meek law of righteousness, but by subtle selfish counsels, and by open and violent force. For wherefore is it that there is such wars and rumors of wars in the nations of the earth? And wherefore are men so mad to destroy one another? But only to uphold civil propriety of honor, dominion and riches one over another, which is the curse the creation groans under, waiting for deliverance.

But when once the earth becomes a common treasury again —as it must; for all the prophecies of scriptures and reason are circled here in this community, and mankind must have the law of righteousness once more writ in his heart, and all must be made of one heart and one mind—then this enmity in all lands will cease. For none shall dare to seek a dominion over others; neither shall any dare to kill another, nor desire more of the earth than another. For he that will rule over, imprison, oppress, and kill his fellow creatures under what pretense soever, is a destroyer of the creation and an actor of the curse, and walks contrary to the rule of righteousness: Do as you would have others do to you; and love your enemies, not in words, but in actions.

Therefore you powers of the earth, or Lord Esau, the elder brother, because you have appeared to rule the creation, first take notice that the power that sets you to work is selfish covetousness, and an aspiring pride to live in glory and ease over Jacob, the meek spirit; that is, the seed that lies hid in and among the poor common people, or younger brother, out of whom the blessing of deliverance is to rise and spring up to all nations. And Reason, the living King of Righteousness, doth only look on and lets thee alone, that whereas thou counts thyself an angel of light, thou shalt appear in the light of the Sun to be a devil . . . and the curse that the creation groans under. And the time is now come for thy downfall; and Jacob must rise, who is the universal spirit of love and righteousness that fills, and will fill, all the earth.

. . . .

Surely thou must not do this great work of advancing the creation out of bondage; for thou art lost extremely, and drowned in the sea of covetousness, pride, and hardness of heart. *The blessing shall rise out of the dust which thou treadest under foot, even the poor despised people, and they shall hold up salvation to this land, and to all lands, and thou shalt be ashamed.* . . .

The work we are going about is this: to dig up George's Hill and the waste ground thereabouts, and to sow corn, and to eat our bread together by the sweat of our brows.

And the first reason is this. That we may work in righteousness, and lay the foundation of making the earth a common treasury for all, both rich and poor. That every one that is born in the land may be fed by the earth, his mother that brought him forth, according to the reason that rules in the creation, not enclosing any part into any particular hand, but all as one man working together, and feeding together as sons of one father, members of one family; not one lording over another, but all looking upon each other as equals in the creation. So that our Maker may be glorified in the work of his own hands, and that every one may see he is no respecter of persons, but equally loves his whole creation, and hates nothing but the serpent. Which is covetousness, branching forth into selfish imagination, pride, envy, hypocrisy, uncleanness, all seeking the ease and honor of flesh, and fighting against the Spirit Reason that made the creation. For that is the corruption, the curse, the devil, the father of lies, death and bondage—that serpent and dragon that the creation is to be delivered from.

And we are moved hereunto for that reason, and others which hath been showed us, both by vision, voice, and revelation. For it is showed us, that so long as we or any other doth own the earth to be the peculiar interest of lords and landlords, and not common to others as well as them, we own the curse that holds the creation under bondage. And so long as we or any other doth own landlords and tenants, for one to call the land his, or another to hire it of him, or for one to give hire, and for another to work for hire; this is to dishonor the work of creation—as if the righteous Creator should have respect to persons, and therefore made the earth for some, and not for all. . . .

And that this civil propriety is the curse, is manifest thus. Those that buy and sell land and are landlords, have got it either by oppression or murder or theft; and all landlords live in the breach of the Seventh [sic] and Eighth Commandments, *Thou shalt not steal, nor kill.*

First by their oppression. They have, by their subtle, imaginary, and covetous wit, got the plain-hearted poor, or younger brethren, to work for them for small wages, and by their work have got a great increase; for the poor by their labor lifts up tyrants to rule over them. Or else by their covetous wit, they have outreached the plain-hearted in buying and selling, and thereby enriched themselves but impoverished others. Or else by their subtle wit, having been alifted up into places of trust, they have enforced people to pay money for a public use, but have divided much of it into their private purses, and so have got it by oppression.

Then, secondly, for murder. They have by subtle wit and power pretended to preserve a people in safety by the power of the sword. And what by large pay, much free-quarter, and other booties which they call their own, they get much moneys, and with this they buy land and become landlords. And if once landlords, then they rise to be justices, rulers, and state governors, as experience shows. But all this is but a bloody and subtle thievery, countenanced by a law that covetousness made; and is a breach of the Seventh [sic] Commandment, *Thou shalt not kill.*

And likewise, thirdly, a breach of the Eighth Commandment, *Thou shalt not steal.* But these landlords have thus stolen the earth from their fellow creatures, that have an equal share with them by the law of reason and creation, as well as they.

And such as these rise up to be rich in the objects of the earth. Then, by their plausible words of flattery to the plain-hearted people, whom they deceive, and that lies under confusion and blindness, they are lifted up to be teachers, rulers, and lawmakers over them that lifted them up; as if the earth were made peculiarly for them, and not for others' weal. If you cast your eye a little backward, you shall see that this outward teaching and ruling power is the Babylonish yoke laid upon Israel of old, under Nebuchadnezzar. And so successively from that time the conquering enemy have still laid these yokes upon Israel, to keep Jacob down. And the last enslaving conquest which the enemy got over Israel, was the Norman over England. And from that time kings, lords, judges, justices, bailiffs, and the violent bitter people that are freeholders, are and have been successively: the Norman bastard William himself, his colonels, captains, inferior officers, and common soldiers, who still are from that time to this day in pursuit of that victory, imprisoning, robbing, and killing the poor enslaved English Israelites.

And this appears clear. For when any trustee or state officer is to be chosen, the freeholders or landlords must be the choosers, who are the Norman common soldiers spread abroad in the land. And who must be chosen but some very rich man who is the successor of the Norman colonels or high officers? And to what end have they been thus chosen but to establish that Norman power the more forcibly over the enslaved English, and to beat them down again whereas they gather heart to seek for liberty? For what are all those binding and restraining laws that have been made from one age to another since that conquest, and are still upheld by fury over the people? I say, what are they but the cords, bands, manacles, and yokes that the enslaved English, like Newgate prisoners, wear upon their hands and legs as they walk the streets; by which those Norman oppressors, and these their successors from age to age, have enslaved the poor people by, killed their younger brother, and would not suffer Jacob to arise? . . .

It is showed us, that all the prophecies, visions and revelations of scriptures, of Prophets and Apostles, concerning the calling of the Jews, the restoration of Israel, and making of that people the inheritors of the whole earth, doth all seat themselves in this work of making the earth a common treasury.

. . . .

And when the Son of Man was gone from the Apostles, his Spirit descended upon the Apostles and Brethren as they were waiting at Jerusalem; and the rich men sold their possessions and gave part to the poor, and no man said that aught that he possessed was his own, for they had all things common (Acts 4. 32).

Now this community was suppressed by covetous, proud flesh, which was the powers that ruled the world. And the righteous Father suffered himself thus to be suppressed for a time, times and dividing of time, or for forty-two months, or for three days and an half, which are all but one and the same term of time. And the world is now come to the half day; and the Spirit of Christ, which is the Spirit of universal community and freedom, is risen, and is rising, and will rise higher and higher, till those pure waters of Shiloa, the well-springs of life and liberty to the whole creation, do overrun . . . those banks of bondage, curse, and slavery. . . .

Another voice that was heard was this: *Israel shall neither take hire nor give hire.*

And if so, then certainly none shall say, 'This is my land; work for me and I'll give you wages.' For the earth is the Lord's; that is man's, who is lord of the creation, in every branch of mankind. For as divers members of our human bodies make but one body perfect, so every particular man is but a member or branch of mankind; and mankind, living in the light and obedience to Reason, the King of Righteousness, is thereby made a fit and complete lord of the creation. And the whole earth is this Lord's man, subject to the Spirit, and not the inheritance of covetous, proud flesh that is selfish, and enmity to the Spirit. . . .

That which does encourage us to go on in this work is this. We find the streaming out of love in our hearts towards all, to enemies as well as friends. We would have none live in beggary, poverty, or sorrow, but that every one might enjoy the benefit of his creation. We have peace in our hearts, and quiet rejoicing in our work, and [are] filled with sweet content though we have but a dish of roots and bread for our food.

And we are assured that, in the strength of this Spirit that hath manifested himself to us, we shall not be startled, neither at prison nor death, while we are about his work. And we have been made to sit down and count what it may cost us in undertaking such a work. And we know the full sum, and are resolved to give all that we have to buy this pearl which we see in the field.

For by this work, we are assured, and reason makes it appear to others, that bondage shall be removed, tears wiped away, and all poor people by their righteous labors shall be relieved and freed from poverty and straits. For in this work of restoration there will be no beggar in Israel. For surely, if there was no beggar in literal Israel, there shall be no beggar in spiritual Israel, the antitype, much more. . . .

V

THE "ROYAL MARTYR"

There is no doubt but that the trial and execution of Charles I was the most famous, and to some, infamous, act of the twenty years from 1640–60. Kings, and even one queen (Mary of Scotland), had been put to death before in England, but death always had come after the title of king had been stripped away. Charles was considered a traitor to his people, not only as a man but also as a king. Neither the trial nor the consequences of the execution were quite what the regicides had hoped for, however.

Charles steadfastly refused to recognize the jurisdiction of the High Court of Justice [2] and would not address himself to the charge against him [1]. Of the 135 men nominated to sit on the court, a few were volunteers and a large number were forced into service. For most of them this trial was not only novel but terrifying. Back in 1640–41, parliament had sought to redress the nation's wrongs by forcing the king to govern in accord with the fundamental laws of the land. This trial of the king could in no way be justified in the light of those same fundamental laws. This was an appeal to a higher law than the laws of England. It was also revolution.

The extent of the break from English legal traditions is attested to by the fact that very few lawyers agreed to sit on the court, and none of them were prominent members of the profession. Out of 135 originally nominated for the court only about seventy to seventy-five attended the average session. The sentence [3] of the court must not have reflected the views even of this number, since only fifty-nine finally signed the death warrant [4]. Of course fear of ultimate retribution from a royalist reaction may have accounted for some of the dropouts.

From all accounts Charles's last days were a credit to his memory. In his own way he sought to get revenge on those who tried him. In his last recorded remarks before the ax fell he said that he would die to uphold the laws and the rights of all Englishmen. The upholder of divine right monarchy was casting himself in the role of a martyr for the liberties of his people. The performance was highly successful. From Cromwell on down, all agreed that if a free election had been held after the execution, the royalists would have won. The feelings of shock and revulsion that spread through England and onto the continent were not to last, however. Both at home and abroad there was soon accommodation with Cromwell and the new facts of life.

Yet the myth of the martyred king was to persist and was given great encouragement with the publication of *Eikon Basilike*[1] [8]. Even though England accepted Cromwell until his death in 1658, there always lurked beneath the surface a quiescent, but potentially powerful, stream of loyalty to monarchy and to the pretender—the exiled youth, Charles II.

A tidal wave of horror swept through the chancelleries of Europe. However, as the letters from Charles Parker [6] and the ever-observant Venetian Ambassadors [5, 7] show, Cromwell hoped to effect an amicable relationship with the Dutch, and Spain and France had little choice but to face facts and accept the Commonwealth as the heir of Charles I. Ironically, it was to be Protestant Holland, which so many Puritans wanted England to emulate, which alone had tried to intercede on the king's behalf and against which Cromwell would go to war.

---

[1] *Eikon Basilike* ("The Royal Image") began to circulate the day the king was executed. The true authorship is unknown, although at the time it was thought to be the work of the king himself. John Gauden, a priest appointed to a bishopric by Charles II, later claimed to be the author. It circulated widely, without the censor's approval, and went through thirty printings within a year. See Wedgwood, *A Coffin for King Charles*.

1. THE CHARGE AGAINST THE KING
[20 January 1649]

That the said Charles Stuart, being admitted King of England, and therein trusted with a limited power to govern by and according to the laws of the land, and not otherwise; and by his trust, oath, and office, being obliged to use the power committed to him for the good and benefit of the people, and for the preservation of their rights and liberties; yet, nevertheless, out of a wicked design to erect and uphold in himself an unlimited and tyrannical power to rule according to his will, and to overthrow the rights and liberties of the people, yea, to take away and make void the foundations thereof, and of all redress and remedy of misgovernment, which by the fundamental constitutions of this kingdom were reserved on the people's behalf in the right and power of frequent and successive Parliaments, or national meetings in Council; he, the said Charles Stuart, for accomplishment of such his designs, and for the protecting of himself and his adherents in his and their wicked practices, to the same ends hath traitorously and maliciously levied war against the present Parliament, and the people therein represented, particularly upon or about the 30th day of June, in the year of our Lord 1642, at Beverley, in the County of York; and upon or about the 24th day of August in the same year, at the County of the Town of Nottingham, where and when he set up his standard of war; and also on or about the 23rd day of October in the same year, at Edgehill or Keynton-field, in the County of Warwick; and upon or about the 30th day of November in the same year, at Brentford, in the County of Middlesex; and upon or about the 30th day of August, in the year of our Lord 1643, at the Caversham Bridge, near Reading, in the County of Berks; and upon or about the 30th day of October in the year last mentioned, at or upon the City of Gloucester; and upon or about the 30th day of November in the year last mentioned, at Newbury, in the County of Berks; and upon or about the 31st day of July, in the year of our Lord 1644, at Cropredy

Bridge, in the County of Oxon; and upon or about the 30th day of September in the last year mentioned, at Bodmin and other places near adjacent, in the County of Cornwall; and upon or about the 30th day of November in the year last mentioned, at Newbury aforesaid; and upon or about the 8th day of June, in the year of our Lord 1645, at the Town of Leicester; and also upon the 14th day of the same month in the same year, at Naseby-field, in the County of Northampton. At which several times and places, or most of them, and at many other places in this land, at several other times within the years aforementioned, and in the year of our Lord 1646, he, the said Charles Stuart, hath caused and procured many thousands of the free people of this nation to be slain; and by divisions, parties, and insurrections within this land, by invasions-from foreign parts, endeavored and procured by him, and by many other evil ways and means, he, the said Charles Stuart, hath not only maintained and carried on the said war both by land and sea, during the years beforementioned, but also hath renewed, or caused to be renewed, the said war against the Parliament and good people of this nation in this present year 1648, in the Counties of Kent, Essex, Surrey, Sussex, Middlesex, and many other Counties and places in England and Wales, and also by sea. And particularly he, the said Charles Stuart, hath for that purpose given commission to his son the Prince, and others, whereby, besides multitudes of other persons, many such as were by the Parliament entrusted and employed for the safety of the nation (being by him or his agents corrupted to the betraying of their trust, and revolting from the Parliament), have had entertainment and commission for the continuing and renewing of war and hostility against the said Parliament and people as aforesaid. By which cruel and unnatural wars, by him, the said Charles Stuart, levied, continued, and renewed as aforesaid, much innocent blood of the free people of this nation hath been spilt, many families have been undone, the public treasure wasted and exhausted, trade obstructed and miserably decayed, vast expense and damage to the nation incurred, and many parts of this land spoiled, some of them even to desolation. And for further prosecution of his said evil designs, he, the said

Charles Stuart, doth still continue his commissions to the said Prince, and other rebels and revolters, both English and foreigners, and to the Earl of Ormond, and the Irish rebels and revolters associated with him; from whom further invasions upon this land are threatened, upon the procurement, and on the behalf of the said Charles Stuart.

All which wicked designs, wars, and evil practices of him, the said Charles Stuart, have been, and are carried on for the advancement and upholding of a personal interest of will, power, and pretended prerogative to himself and his family, against the public interest, common right, liberty, justice, and peace of the people of this nation, by and from whom he was entrusted as aforesaid.

By all which it appeareth that the said Charles Stuart hath been, and is the occasioner, author, and continuer of the said unnatural, cruel and bloody wars; and therein guilty of all the treasons, murders, rapines, burnings, spoils, desolations, damages and mischiefs to this nation, acted and committed in the said wars, or occasioned thereby.

2. THE KING'S REASONS FOR DECLINING THE JURISDICTION OF THE HIGH COURT OF JUSTICE
[21 January 1649]

Having already made my protestations, not only against the illegality of this pretended Court, but also, that no earthly power can justly call me (who am your King) in question as a delinquent, I would not any more open my mouth upon this occasion, more than to refer myself to what I have spoken, were I in this case alone concerned: but the duty I owe to God in the preservation of the true liberty of my people will not suffer me at this time to be silent: for, how can any free-born subject of England call life or anything he possesseth his own, if power without right daily make new, and abrogate the old fundamental laws of the land which I now take to be the present case? Wherefore when I came hither, I expected that you would have endeavored to have satisfied me concerning these grounds which hinder me to answer to your pretended impeachment. But since I see that nothing I can say will move you to it (though negatives are not so naturally proved as affirmatives) yet I will show you the reason why I am confident you cannot judge me, nor indeed the meanest man in England: for I will not (like you) without showing a reason, seek to impose a belief upon my subjects.

There is no proceeding just against any man, but what is warranted, either by God's laws or the municipal laws of the country where he lives. Now I am most confident this day's proceeding cannot be warranted by God's laws; for, on the contrary, the authority of obedience unto Kings is clearly warranted, and strictly commanded in both the Old and New Testament, which, if denied, I am ready instantly to prove.

And for the question now in hand, there it is said, that 'where the word of a King is, there is power; and who may say unto him, what dost thou?' Eccles. viii. 4. Then for the law of this land, I am no less confident, that no learned lawyer will affirm that an impeachment can lie against the King, they all going in his name: and one of their maxims is, that the King can do no wrong. Besides, the law upon which you ground your proceedings, must either be old or new: if old, show it; if new, tell what authority, warranted by the fundamental laws of the land, hath made it, and when. But how the House of Commons can erect a Court of Judicature, which was never one itself (as is well known to all lawyers) I leave to God and the world to judge. And it were full as strange, that they should pretend to make laws without King or Lords' House, to any that have heard speak of the laws of England.

And admitting, but not granting, that the people of England's commission could grant your pretended power, I see nothing you can show for that; for certainly you never asked the question of the tenth man in the kingdom, and in this way you manifestly wrong even the poorest ploughman, if you demand not his free consent; nor can you pretend any color for this your pretended commission, without the consent at least of the major part of every man in England of whatsoever quality or condition, which I am sure you never went about to seek, so far are you from having it. Thus you see that I speak not for my own right alone, as I am your

King, but also for the true liberty of all my subjects, which consists not in the power of government, but in living under such laws, such a government, as may give themselves the best assurance of their lives, and property of their goods; nor in this must or do I forget the privileges of both Houses of Parliament, which this day's proceedings do not only violate, but likewise occasion the greatest breach of their public faith that (I believe) ever was heard of, with which I am far from charging the two Houses; for all the pretended crimes laid against me bear date long before this Treaty at Newport, in which I having concluded as much as in me lay, and hopefully expecting the Houses' agreement thereunto, I was suddenly surprised and hurried from thence as a prisoner; upon which account I am against my will brought hither, where since I am come, I cannot but to my power defend the ancient laws and liberties of this kingdom, together with my own just right. Then for anything I can see, the higher House is totally excluded; and for the House of Commons, it is too well known that the major part of them are detained or deterred from sitting; so as if I had no other, this were sufficient for me to protest against the lawfulness of your pretended Court. Besides all this, the peace of the kingdom is not the least in my thoughts; and what hope of settlement is there, so long as power reigns without rule or law, changing the whole frame of that government under which this kingdom hath flourished for many hundred years? (nor will I say what will fall out in case this lawless, unjust proceeding against me do go on) and believe it, the Commons of England will not thank you for this change; for they will remember how happy they have been of late years under the reigns of Queen Elizabeth, the King my father, and myself, until the beginning of these unhappy troubles, and will have cause to doubt, that they shall never be so happy under any new: and by this time it will be too sensibly evident, that the arms I took up were only to defend the fundamental laws of this kingdom against those who have supposed my power hath totally changed the ancient government.

Thus, having showed you briefly the reasons why I cannot submit to your pretended authority, without violating the trust which I have from God for the welfare and liberty of my people, I expect from you either clear reasons to convince my judgment, showing me that I am in an error (and then truly I will answer) or that you will withdraw your proceedings.

This I intended to speak in Westminster Hall, on Monday, January 22, but against reason was hindered to show my reasons.

3. *THE SENTENCE OF THE HIGH COURT OF JUSTICE UPON THE KING* [27 *January* 1649]

Whereas the Commons of England assembled in Parliament, have by their late Act entitled an Act of the Commons of England assembled in Parliament, for erecting an High Court of Justice for the trying and judging of Charles Stuart, King of England, authorized and constituted us an High Court of Justice for the trying and judging of the said Charles Stuart for the crimes and treasons in the said Act mentioned; by virtue whereof the said Charles Stuart hath been three several times convented before this High Court, where the first day, being Saturday, the 20th of January instant, in pursuance of the said Act, a charge of high treason and other high crimes was, in the behalf of the people of England, exhibited against him, and read openly unto him, wherein he was charged, that he, the said Charles Stuart, being admitted King of England, and therein trusted with a limited power to govern by, and according to the law of the land, and not otherwise; and by his trust, oath, and office, being obliged to use the power committed to him for the good and benefit of the people, and for the preservation of their rights and liberties; yet, nevertheless, out of a wicked design to erect and uphold in himself an unlimited and tyrannical power to rule according to his will, and to overthrow the rights and liberties of the people, and to take away and make void the foundations thereof, and of all redress and remedy of misgovernment, which by the fundamental constitutions of this kingdom were reserved on the people's behalf in the right and power of frequent and successive Parliaments, or national meetings in Council; he, the said

Charles Stuart, for accomplishment of such his designs, and for the protecting of himself and his adherents in his and their wicked practices, to the same end hath traitorously and maliciously levied war against the present Parliament, and people therein represented, as with the circumstances of time and place is in the said charge more particularly set forth; and that he hath thereby caused and procured many thousands of the free people of this nation to be slain; and by divisions, parties, and insurrections within this land, by invasions from foreign parts, endeavored and procured by him, and by many other evil ways and means, he, the said Charles Stuart, hath not only maintained and carried on the said war both by sea and land, but also hath renewed, or caused to be renewed, the said war against the Parliament and good people of this nation in this present year 1649, in several counties and places in this kingdom in the charge specified; and that he hath for that purpose given his commission to his son the Prince, and others, whereby, besides multitudes of other persons, many such as were by the Parliament entrusted and employed for the safety of this nation, being by him or his agents corrupted to the betraying of their trust, and revolting from the Parliament, have had entertainment and commission for the continuing and renewing of the war and hostility against the said Parliament and people: and that by the said cruel and unnatural war so levied, continued and renewed, much innocent blood of the free people of this nation hath been spilt, many families undone, the public treasure wasted, trade obstructed and miserably decayed, vast expense and damage to the nation incurred, and many parts of the land spoiled, some of them even to desolation; and that he still continues his commission to his said son, and other rebels and revolters, both English and foreigners, and to the Earl of Ormond, and to the Irish rebels and revolters associated with him, from who further invasions of this land are threatened by his procurement and on his behalf; and that all the said wicked designs, wars, and evil practices of him, the said Charles Stuart, were still carried on for the advancement and upholding of the personal interest of will, power, and pretended prerogative to himself and his family, against the public interest, common right, liberty, justice, and peace of the people of this nation; and that he thereby hath been and is the occasioner, author, and continuer of the said unnatural, cruel, and bloody wars, and therein guilty of all the treasons, murders, rapines, burnings, spoils, desolations, damage, and mischief to this nation, acted and committed in the said wars, or occasioned thereby; whereupon the proceedings and judgment of this Court were prayed against him, as a tyrant, traitor, and murderer, and public enemy to the Commonwealth, as by the said charge more fully appeareth. To which charge, being read unto him as aforesaid, he, the said Charles Stuart, was required to give his answer; but he refused so to do, and upon Monday, the 22nd day of January instant, being again brought before this Court, and there required to answer directly to the said charge, he still refused so to do; whereupon his default and contumacy was entered; and the next day, being the third time brought before the Court, judgment was then prayed against him on the behalf of the people of England for his contumacy, and for the matters contained against him in the said charge, as taking the same for confessed, in regard of his refusing to answer thereto: yet notwithstanding this Court (not willing to take advantage of his contempt) did once more require him to answer to the said charge; but he again refused so to do; upon which his several defaults, this Court might justly have proceeded to judgment against him, both for his contumacy and the matters of the charge, taking the same for confessed as aforesaid.

Yet nevertheless this Court, for its own clearer information and further satisfaction, have thought fit to examine witnesses upon oath, and take notice of other evidences, touching the matters contained in the said charge, which accordingly they have done.

Now, therefore, upon serious and mature deliberation of the premises, and consideration had of the notoriety of the matters of fact charged upon him as aforesaid, this Court is in judgment and conscience satisfied that he, the said Charles Stuart, is guilty of levying war against the said Parliament and people, and maintaining and continuing the same; for which in the said charge he stands accused, and by the general course of his government, counsels, and practices, before and since this Parliament began (which have been and are notorious and public, and the effects whereof remain abundantly upon record) this Court is fully satisfied in their judgments and consciences, that he has been and is guilty of the wicked design and endeavors in the said charge set forth; and that the said war hath been levied, maintained, and continued by him as aforesaid, in prosecution, and for accomplishment of the said designs; and that he hath been and is the occasioner, author, and continuer of the said unnatural, cruel, and bloody wars, and therein guilty of high treason, and of the murders, rapines, burnings, spoils, desolations, damage, and mischief to this nation acted and committed in the said war, and occasioned thereby. For all which treasons and crimes this Court doth adjudge that he, the said Charles Stuart, as a tyrant, traitor, murderer, and public enemy to the good people of this nation, shall be put to death by the severing of his head from his body.

4. THE DEATH WARRANT OF CHARLES I
[29 January 1649]

At the High Court of Justice for the trying and judging of Charles Stuart, King of England, Jan. 29, Anno Domini 1649.

Whereas Charles Stuart, King of England, is, and standeth convicted, attainted, and condemned of high treason, and other high crimes; and sentence upon Saturday last was pronounced against him by this Court, to be put to death by the severing of his head from his body; of which sentence, execution yet remaineth to be done; these are therefore to will and require you to see the said sentence executed in the open street before Whitehall, upon the morrow, being the thirtieth day of this instant month of January, between the hours of ten in the morning and five in the afternoon of the same day, with full effect. And for so doing this shall be your sufficient warrant. And these are to require all officers, soldiers, and others, the good people of this nation of England, to be assisting unto you in this service.

To Col. Francis Hacker, Col. Huncks, and Lieut.-Col. Phayre, and to every of them.

Given under our hands and seals.

JOHN BRADSHAW[1]

THOMAS GREY[2]

OLIVER CROMWELL

&c. &c.

5. *Alvise Contarini, VENETIAN AMBASSADOR AT MUNSTER, TO THE DOGE AND SENATE, 26 February 1649*

The poor king of England has at last lost both crown and life by the hand of the executioner, like a common criminal, in London, before all the people, without anyone speaking in his favor and by the judicial sentence of his own subjects. The accompanying narrative gives the particulars. History affords no example of the like. It is a shame to all contemporary sovereigns, who for the sake of revenge against each other about trifles have allowed themselves to be confronted by so imposing a spectacle, of the worst possible example.

The Prince of Wales, at the Hague, immediately assumed the royal title, although the kingdom has pronounced him ineligible, and denounces as guilty of treason anyone who calls himself king of England. The States [General] sent their condolences by a deputy from each province. In reply the king merely said that his sole comfort amid so many disasters was to find himself among them, through whose help he looked for his restoration, under God. They at once recalled the Ambassador Pauw, and some wished to recall the ordinary

[1] John Bradshaw (1602–59) was a lawyer and a radical. He had worked closely with both William Prynne and John Lilburne, and was chosen president of the parliamentary commission to try the king, since he was one of the few lawyers willing to serve. He was not a member of the House of Commons. Many thought his treatment of the king brutal. By 1656 he was an opponent of Cromwell.

[2] Thomas Grey (1623–57) [Lord Grey of Groby] was a member of the Long Parliament and an army officer, who had been active in Pride's Purge. He later joined the Fifth Monarchists and was imprisoned. After his release he went into retirement.

Joachimi[1] as well, so as not to give any sanction to their proceedings, but on second thoughts, as the ambassadors of Spain, France, Portugal and others remain, they have ordered Joachimi to do the same, especially as the Commonwealth (*commune*), as the English government now styles itself, has informed the States that all their merchants and goods will be treated over there like the native English, and that they mean to form a government resembling that of the Provinces [Dutch] in every respect, both ecclesiastical and civil, a thing easier said than done.

The States were to compliment the new king on his accession, but they are not yet agreed among themselves what to call him. Meanwhile he is drawing up letters to acquaint all the powers of Europe with the tragedy, and to ask for help. The Grand Chancellor of Denmark, Ullufelde, is being sent to Holland, France and Spain, to support his interests, as he is Denmark's cousin. All commiserate his misfortune and his innocence, although those who unite to avenge it may be few in number.

6. *LETTER TO LORD HATTON FROM CHARLES PARKER IN HOLLAND, 9 March 1649*

The very relation . . . of that monstrous fact in England upon the person of the King struck one woman dead upon the first hearing it, and another lies yet so ill that it is thought she will not recover. The States General came together in one body to our King both to condole his Father's death and to congratulate his succession. And it was done after they had been informed from their ambassadors in England that those bloody reigning villains had offered to make with them a league offensive and defensive, to make those of Holland as free in England as the English themselves, and that they make them their absolute pattern both in point of State and Church.

[1] Adriaen Pauw and Albert Joachimi were sent to England in January 1649 at the request of the Prince of Wales to intercede on behalf of Charles I. This was the only foreign help the king received.

7. *Michiel Morosini,* VENETIAN AMBASSADOR IN FRANCE, TO THE DOGE AND SENATE, *8 June 1649*

Fresh orders have been issued for the reduction of Bordeaux. This decision is generally condemned and it might lead the people there to appeal to England, who would not need much persuasion owing to the natural aversion they feel for the government here and the detestation felt here over the barbarous death of the king their master, which they know to be concealed, and to be only waiting for a favorable opportunity to break out and avenge him. To speak frankly, they discuss that unhappy accident here with so much passion that if God grants peace one day, as is so ardently desired, it seems likely that they would in a moment divert all their forces for the destruction of that barbarous people. It is possible it is this contingency that disputes with your Serenity for the assistance which is so necessary, while there would always be time for vengeance on England.

8. *EIKON BASILIKE*

10. *Upon their seizing the King's Magazines, Forts, Navy, and Militia.*

How untruly I am Charged with the first raising of an Army, and beginning this Civil War, the eyes that only pity Me, and the Loyal hearts that durst only pray for Me, at first, might witness, which yet appear not so many on My side, as there were men in Arms listed against Me; My unpreparedness for a War may well dishearten those that would help Me; while it argues (truly) My unwillingness to fight; yet it testifies for Me, that I am set on the defensive part; having so little hopes or power to offend others, that I have none to defend Myself, or to preserve what is Mine own from their propriation.

No man can doubt but they prevented Me in their purposes, as well as their injuries, who are so much beforehand in their preparations against Me, and surprisals of My strength. Such as are not for Them, yet dare not be for Me; so overawed is their Loyalty by the others' numbers and terrors. I believe My Innocency, and unpreparedness to assert My Rights and Honor, makes Me the more guilty in their esteem; who would not so easily have declared a War against Me, if I had first assaulted them.

They knew My chiefest Arms left Me, were those only, which the Ancient Christians were wont to use against their Persecutors, Prayers and Tears. These may serve a good man's turn, if not to Conquer as a Soldier, yet to suffer as a Martyr.

Their preventing of Me, and surprising my Castles, Forts, Arms, and Navy, with the Militia, is so far best for me, That it may drive me from putting any trust in the arm of flesh, and wholly to cast myself into the protection of the living God, who can save by few, or none, as well as by many.

He that made the greedy Ravens to be *Elias'* [Elijah's] Caterers, and bring him food, may also make their surprisal of outward force and defense, an opportunity to show me the special support of his power and protection.

I thank God I reckon not now the want of the *Militia* so much in reference to My own protection as My People's.

Their many and sore oppressions grieve Me, I am above My own, what I want in the hands of Force and Power, I have in the wings of Faith and Prayer.

But this is the strange method these men will needs take to resolve their riddle of Making Me a glorious King, by taking away my Kingly power: Thus I shall become a support to My Friends, and a Terror to My Enemies by being unable to succor the one, or suppress the other.

For thus have they designed, and proposed to Me, the new modeling of Sovereignty and Kingship, as without any reality of power, or without any necessity of subjection and obedience: That the Majesty of the Kings of *England* might hereafter, hang like *Mahomet's* Tomb, by a magnetic Charm, between the Power and Privileges of the two Houses, in an airy imagination of Regality.

But I believe the surfeit of too much Power, which some men have greedily seized on, and now seek wholly to devour, will ere long make the Commonwealth sick both of it and them, since they cannot well digest it; Sovereign Power in Subjects seldom agreeing with the stomachs of fellow Subjects.

Yet I have even in this point of the constant *Militia* sought, by satisfying their fears, and importunities, both to secure My Friends, and overcome Mine Enemies, to gain the peace of all, by depriving Myself of a sole power to help, or hurt any: yielding the *Militia* (which is My undoubted Right no less than the Crown) to be disposed of as the two Houses shall think fit, during My time.

So willing am I to bury all Jealousies in them, of Me, and to live above all Jealousies of them, as to Myself; I desire not to be safer than I wish them and My People; If I had the sole actual disposing of the *Militia*, I could not protect My People, further than they protected Me, and themselves: so that the use of the *Militia* is mutual. I would but defend Myself so far, as to be able to defend My good Subjects from those men's violence and fraud, who conscious to their own evil merits and designs, will needs persuade the world, that none but Wolves are fit to be trusted with the custody of the Shepherd and his Flock. Miserable experience hath taught My Subjects, since Power hath been wrested from Me, and employed against Me & Them! that neither can be safe if both be not in such a way as the Law hath entrusted the public safety and welfare.

Yet even this Concession of Mine as to the exercise of the *Militia*, so vast and large, is not satisfactory to some men; which seem to be Enemies not to Me only, but to all Monarchy; and are resolved to transmit to posterity such Jealousies of the Crown, as they should never permit it to enjoy its just and necessary Rights, in point of Power; to which (at last) all Law is resolved, while thereby it is best protected.

But here Honor and Justice due to My Successors, forbid Me to yield to such a total alienation of that power from them, which civility & duty (no less than justice and honor) should have forbade them to have asked of Me.

For, although I can be content to Eclipse My own beams, to satisfy their fears; who think they must needs be scorched or blinded, if I should shine in the full luster of Kingly Power, wherewith God and the Laws have invested Me: yet

I will never consent to put out the Sun of Sovereignty to all Posterity, and succeeding Kings; whose just recovery of their Rights from unjust usurpations and extortions, shall never be prejudiced or obstructed by any Act of Mine, which indeed would not be more injurious to succeeding Kings, than to My Subjects; whom I desire to leave in a condition not wholly desperate for the future; so as by a Law to be ever subjected to those many factious distractions, which must needs follow the many-headed *Hydra* of Government: which as it makes a show to the People to have more eyes to foresee; so they will find it hath more mouths too, which much be satisfied: and (at best) it hath rather a monstrosity, than anything of perfection, beyond that of right Monarchy; where counsel may be in many as the senses, but the Supreme Power can be but in One as the Head.

Happily where men have tried the horrors and malignant influence which will certainly follow My enforced darkness and Eclipse (occasioned by the interposition and shadow of that body, which as the Moon receiveth its chiefest light from Me), they will at length more esteem and welcome the restored glory and blessing of the Sun's light.

And if at present I may seem by My receding so much from the use of My Right in the Power of the *Militia*, to come short of the discharge of that trust to which I am sworn for My People's protection; I conceive those men are guilty of the enforced perjury (if so it may seem) who compel Me to take this new and strange way of discharging My trust, by seeming to desert it; of protecting My Subjects by exposing Myself to danger or dishonor, for their safety and quiet.

Which in the conflicts of Civil War and advantages of Power cannot be effected but by some side yielding; to which the greatest love of the public Peace, and the firmest assurance of God's protection (arising from a good conscience) doth more invite Me, than can be expected from other men's fears; which arising from the injustice of their actions (though never so successful) yet dare not adventure their Authors upon any other way of safety than that of the Sword and *Militia*; which yet are but weak defenses against the strokes of divine vengeance, which will overtake; or of men's own Consciences, which always attend injurious perpetrations.

For Myself, I do not think that I can want anything which providential necessity is pleased to take from Me, in order to My People's tranquillity and God's glory, whose protection is sufficient for Me; and he is able by his being with Me, abundantly to compensate to Me, as he did to *Job*, what ever honor, power, or liberty the Chaldeans, the Sabeans, or the Devil himself can deprive Me of.

Although they take from me all defense of Arms and *Militia*, all refuge by land, of Forts, and Castles, all flight by Sea in my Ships, and Navy; yea, though they study to rob me of the Hearts of my Subjects, the greatest Treasure and best ammunition of a King, yet cannot they deprive me of my own innocency, or God's mercy, nor obstruct my way to Heaven.

27. To the Prince of Wales

Son, if these papers, with some others, wherein I have set down the private reflections of My Conscience, and My most impartial thoughts, touching the chief passages, which have been most remarkable, or disputed in My late troubles, come to your hands, to whom they are chiefly designed; they may be so far useful to you, as to state your judgment aright in what hath passed; whereof, a pious is the best use can be made; and they may also give you some directions, how to remedy the present distempers, and prevent (if God will) the like for time to come.

It is some kind of deceiving and lessening the injury of My long restraint, when I find My leisure and solitude have produced something worthy of Myself, and useful to you; That neither you, nor any other, may hereafter measure My Cause by the Success; nor My Judgment of things by My misfortunes; which I count the greater by far, because they have so far lighted upon you, and some others, whom I have most cause to love as well as Myself; and of whose unmerited sufferings I have a greater sense than of Mine own.

But this advantage of wisdom you have above most Princes; that you have begun, and now spent some years of discretion, in the experience of troubles, and exercise of patience, wherein Piety, and all Virtues, both Moral and Political, are commonly better planted to a thriving (as trees set in winter) than in the warmth, and serenity of times; or amidst those delights, which usually attend Princes' Courts in times of peace and plenty; which are prone, either to root up all plants of true Virtue and Honor; or to be contented only with some leaves, and withering formalities of them, without any real fruits, such as tend to the Public good; for which Princes should always remember they are born and by providence designed.

The evidence of which different education the holy Writ affords us in the contemplation of *David* and *Rehoboam:* The one prepared, by many afflictions for a flourishing Kingdom, the other softened by the unparalleled prosperity of *Solomon's* Court; and so corrupted to the great diminution, both for Peace, Honor, and Kingdom, by those flatteries, which are as unseparable from prosperous Princes, as Flies are from fruit in summer; whom adversity, like cold weather, drives away.

I had rather you should be *Charles le Bow*, than *le Grand*, good, than great; I hope God hath designed you to be both, having so early put you into that exercise of his Graces, and gifts bestowed upon you, which may best weed out all vicious inclinations, and dispose you to those Princely endowments, and employments, which will most gain the love, and intend the welfare of those, over whom God shall place you.

With God I would have you begin and end, who is King of Kings; the Sovereign disposer of the Kingdoms of the world, who pulleth down one, and setteth up another.

The best Government, and highest Sovereignty you can attain to is, to be subject to him, that the Scepter of his Word and Spirit may rule in your heart.

The true glory of Princes consists in advancing God's Glory in the maintenance of true Religion, and the Church's good: Also in the dispensation of civil Power, with Justice and Honor to the Public Peace.

Piety will make you prosperous; at least it will keep you from being miserable; nor is he much a loser, that loseth all, yet saveth his own soul at last.

To which Center of true Happiness God, I trust, hath and

will graciously direct all these black lines of Affliction, which he hath been pleased to draw on me, and by which he hath (I hope) drawn me nearer to himself. You have already tasted of that cup whereof I have liberally drank, which I look upon as God's Physic, having that in healthfulness which it wants in pleasure.

Above all, I would have you, as I hope you are already; well-grounded and settled in your Religion: The best profession of which, I have ever esteemed that of the Church of *England*, in which you have been educated; yet I would have your own Judgment and Reason now seal to that sacred bond which education hath written, that it may be judiciously your own Religion, and not other men's custom or tradition, which you profess.

In this I charge you to persevere, as coming nearest to God's Word for Doctrine, and to the primitive examples for Government, with some little amendment, which I have otherwhere expressed, and often offered, though in vain. Your fixation in matters of Religion will not be not more necessary for your souls than your Kingdom's peace, when God shall bring you to them.

For I have observed, that the Devil of Rebellion, doth commonly turn himself into an Angel of Reformation; and the old Serpent can pretend new Lights: When some men's Consciences accuse them for Sedition and Faction, they stop its mouth with the name and noise of Religion; when Piety pleads for peace and patience, they cry out Zeal.

So that, unless in this point You be well settled, you shall never want temptations to destroy you and yours, under pretensions of reforming matters of Religion; for that seems, even to worst men, as the best and most auspicious beginning of their worst designs.

Where, besides the Novelty which is taking enough with the Vulgar, every one hath an affectation, by seeming forward to an outward Reformation of Religion, to be thought zealous; hoping to cover those irreligious deformities, whereto they are conscious by a severity of censuring other men's opinions or actions.

Take heed of abetting any Factions, or applying to any public Discriminations in matters of Religion, contrary to what is in your Judgment, and the Church well settled; your partial adhering, as head, to any one side, gains you not so great advantages in some men's hearts (who are prone to be of their King's Religion) as it loseth you in others; who think themselves, and their profession first despised, then persecuted by you: Take such a course as may either with calmness & charity quite remove the seeming differences and offenses by impartiality, or so order affairs in point of Power that you shall not need to fear or flatter any Faction. For if ever you stand in need of them, or must stand to their courtesy, you are undone: The Serpent will devour the Dove: you may never expect less of loyalty, justice, or humanity, than from those, who engage into religious Rebellion; Their interest is always made God's; under the colors of Piety, ambitious policies march, not only with greatest security, but applause, as to the populacy; you may hear from them *Jacob's* voice, but you shall feel they have *Esau's* hands.

Nothing seemed less considerable than the Presbyterian Faction in *England*, for many years; so compliant they were to public order: nor indeed was their Party great either in Church, or State, as to men's judgments: But as soon as discontents drove men into Sidings (as ill humors fall to the disaffected mart, which causes inflammations) so did all, at first, who affected any novelties, adhere to that Side, as the most remarkable and specious note of difference (than) in point of Religion.

All the lesser Factions at first were officious Servants to Presbytery their great Master: till time and military success discovering to each their peculiar advantages, invited them to part stakes, and leaving the joint stock of uniform Religion, pretended each to drive for their Party the trade of profits and preferments, to the breaking and undoing not only of the Church and State, but even of Presbytery itself, which seemed and hoped at first to have engrossed all.

Let nothing seem little or despicable to you in matters which concern Religion and the Church's peace, so as to neglect a speedy reforming and effectual suppressing Errors & Schisms, which seem at first but as a handbreadth, by seditious Spirits, as by strong winds are soon made to cover and darken the whole Heaven.

When you have done justice to God, your own soul and his Church, in the profession and preservation both of truth and unity in Religion: the next main hinge on which your prosperity will depend, and move, is, that of civil Justice, wherein the settled Laws of these Kingdoms, to which you are rightly Heir, are the most excellent rules you can govern by; which by an admirable temperament give very much to Subjects' industry, liberty, and happiness; and yet reserve enough to the Majesty and prerogative of any King, who owns his People as Subjects, not as Slaves; whose subjection, as it preserves their property, peace, and safety, so it will never diminish your Rights, nor their ingenious Liberties; which consists in the enjoyment of the fruits of their industry, and the benefit of those Laws to which themselves have consented.

Never charge your Head with such a Crown, as shall by its heaviness oppress the whole body, the weakness of whose parts cannot return anything of strength, honor, or safety, to the Head, but a necessary debilitation and ruin.

Your Prerogative is best shown, and exercised in remitting, rather than exacting the rigor of the Laws; there being nothing worse than legal Tyranny.

In these two points, the preservation of established Religion, and Laws, I may (without vanity) turn the reproach of My sufferings, as to the world's censure, into the honor of a kind of Martyrdom, as to the testimony of My own Conscience; The Troublers of My Kingdoms having nothing else to object against Me but this, That I prefer Religion, and Laws established before those alterations they propounded.

And so indeed I do, and ever shall, till I am convinced by better Arguments, than what hitherto have been chiefly used towards Me, Tumults, Armies, and Prisons.

I cannot yet learn that lesson, nor I hope ever will you, That it is safe for a King to gratify any Faction with the perturbation of the Laws, in which is wrapt up the public Interest, and the good of the Community.

How God will deal with Me, as to the removal of these pressures, & indignities, which his justice by the very unjust hands of some of My Subjects, hath been pleased to lay upon Me, I cannot tell: nor am I much solicitous what wrong I suffer from men, while I retain in My soul, what I believe is right before God.

I have offered all for Reformation and Safety, that in Reason, Honor, and Conscience I can; reserving only what I cannot consent unto, without an irreparable injury to My own Soul, the Church, and My People, and to You also, as the next and undoubted Heir of My Kingdoms.

To which if the divine Providence, to whom no difficulties are insuperable, shall in his due time after My decease bring You, as I hope he will; My counsel and charge to You, is, That You seriously consider the former, real, or objected miscarriages, which might occasion My troubles, that You may avoid them.

Never repose so much upon any man's single counsel, fidelity and discretion, in managing affairs of the first magnitude (that is, matters of Religion and Justice) as to create in Yourself, or others, a diffidence of Your own judgment, which is likely to be always more constant & impartial to the interests of Your Crown and Kingdom than any man's.

Next, beware of exasperating any Factions by the crossness, and asperity of some men's passions, humors, or private opinions, imployed by You, grounded only upon the differences in lesser matters, which are but the skirts and suburbs of Religion.

Wherein a charitable connivance and Christian toleration often dissipates their strength, whom rougher opposition fortifies; and puts the despised and oppressed Party, into such Combinations, as may most enable them to get a full revenge on those they count their Persecutors, who are commonly assisted by that vulgar commiseration, which attends all, that are said to suffer under the notion of Religion.

Provided the differences amount not to an insolent opposition of Laws, and Government, or Religion established, as to the essentials of them, such motions and minings are intolerable.

Always keep up solid piety, and those fundamental Truths (which mend both hearts and lives of men) with impartial favor and justice.

Take heed that outward circumstances and formalities of Religion devour not all, or the best encouragements of learning, industry, and piety; but with an equal eye, and impartial hand, distribute favors and rewards to all men, as you find them for their real goodness both in abilities and fidelity worthy and capable of them.

This will be sure to gain You the hearts of the best, and the most too; who, though they be not good themselves, yet are glad to see the severer ways of virtue at any time sweetened by temporal rewards.

I have, You see, conflicted with different and opposite Factions (for so I must needs call and count all those, that act not in any conformity to the Laws established, in Church and State); no sooner have they by force subdued what they counted their Common Enemy (that is, all those that adhered to the Laws, and to Me), and are secured from that fear, but they are divided to so high a rivalry, as sets them more at defiance against each other, than against their first Antagonists.

Time will dissipate all factions, when once the rough horns of private men's covetous and ambitious designs, shall discover themselves; which were at first wrapt up & hidden under the soft and smooth pretensions of Religion, Reformation, and Liberty: As the Wolf is not less cruel, so he will be more justly hated, when he shall appear no better than a Wolf under Sheep's clothing.

But as for the seduced Train of the Vulgar, who in their simplicity follow those disguises; My charge and counsel to You, is That as You need no palliations for any designs (as other men), so that you study really to exceed (in true and constant demonstrations of goodness, piety, and virtue, towards the People) even all those men, that make the greatest noise and ostentations of Religion; so You shall neither fear any detection (as they do, who have but the face and mask of goodness), nor shall You frustrate the just expectations of Your People; who cannot in Reason promise themselves so much good from any Subject's novelties, as from the virtuous constancy of their King.

When these mountains of congealed factions shall by the sunshine of God's mercy, and the splendor of Your virtues be thawed and dissipated; and the abused Vulgar shall have learned, that none are greater Oppressors of their Estates,

Liberties, and Consciences, than those men, that entitle themselves, The Patrons and Vindicators of them, only to usurp power over them; Let then no passion betray You to any study of revenge upon those, whose own sin and folly will sufficiently punish them in due time.

But as soon as the forked arrow of factious emulations is drawn out, use all princely arts, and clemency to heal the wounds; that the smart of the cure may not equal the anguish of the hurt.

I have offered Acts of Indemnity, and Oblivion, to so great a latitude, as may include all, that can but suspect themselves to be any way obnoxious to the Laws; and which might serve to exclude all future Jealousies and insecurities.

I would have You always propense to the same way, when ever it shall be desired and accepted, let it be granted, not only as an Act of State-policy and necessity, but of Christian charity and choice.

It is all I have now left Me, a power to forgive those, that have deprived Me of all; and I thank God, I have a heart to do it; and joy as much in this grace, which God hath given Me, as in all My former enjoyments; for this is a greater argument of God's love to Me, than any prosperity can be.

Be confident (as I am) that the most of all sides, who have done amiss, have done so, not out of malice, but misinformation, or mis-apprehension of things.

None will be more loyal and faithful to Me and You, than those Subjects, who sensible of their Errors, and our Injuries, will feel in their own Souls most vehement motives to repentance; and earnest desires to make some reparations for their former defects.

As Your quality sets You beyond any Duel with any Subject; so the nobleness of Your mind must raise You above the meditating any revenge, or executing Your anger upon the many.

The more conscious You shall be to Your own merits, upon Your People, the more prone You will be to expect all love and loyalty from them; and to inflict no punishment upon them for former miscarriages: You will have more inward complacency in pardoning one, than in punishing a thousand.

This I write to you, not despairing of God's mercy, and

my Subjects' affections towards You; both which, I hope You will study to deserve, yet We cannot merit of God, but by his own mercy.

If God shall see fit to restore Me, and You after Me, to those enjoyments, which the Laws have assigned to Us; and no Subjects without an high degree of guilt and sin can divest Us of; then may I have better opportunity, when I shall be so happy to see You in peace, to let You more fully understand the things that belong to God's glory, Your own honor, and the Kingdom's peace.

But if You never see My face again, and God will have Me buried in such a barbarous Imprisonment & obscurity (which the perfecting some men's designs require), wherein few hearts that love me are permitted to exchange a word, or a look with Me; I do require and entreat You as your Father, and your KING, that You never suffer Your heart to receive the least check against, or disaffection from the true Religion established in the Church of *England*.

I tell You I have tried it, and after much search, and many disputes, have concluded it to be the best in the world; not only in the Community, as Christian, but also in the special notion, as Reformed; keeping the middle way between the pomp of superstitious Tyranny, and the meanness of fantastic Anarchy.

Not but that (the draught being excellent as to the main, both for Doctrine and Government, in the Church of *England*) some lines, as in very good figures, may happily need some sweetening, or polishing; which might here have easily been done by a safe and gentle hand; if some men's precipitancy had not violently demanded such rude alterations, as would have quite destroyed all the beauty and proportions of the whole.

The scandal of the late Troubles, which some may object, and urge to You against the Protestant Religion established in *England*, is easily answered to them, or Your own thoughts in this, That scarce any one who hath been a Beginner, or an active Prosecutor of this late War against the Church, the Laws, and Me, either was, or is a true Lover, Embracer, or Practicer of the Protestant Religion, established in *England*:

which neither gives such rules, nor ever before set such examples.

'Tis true, some heretofore had the boldness to present threatening Petitions to their Princes and Parliaments, which others of the same Faction (but of worse Spirits) have now put in execution: but let not counterfeit and disorderly Zeal abate Your value and esteem of true piety, both of them are to be known by their fruits; the sweetness of the Wine & Fig-tree is not to be despised, though the Brambles and Thorns should pretend to bear Figs and Grapes, thereby to rule over the Trees.

Nor would I have You to entertain any aversation, or dislike of Parliaments; which in their right constitution with Freedom and Honor, will never injure or diminish Your greatness, but will rather be as interchangings of love, loyalty, and confidence, between a Prince, and his People.

Nor would the events of this black Parliament have been other than such (however much biased by Factions in the Elections) if it had been preserved from the insolencies of popular dictates, and tumultuary impressions: The sad effects of which will no doubt, make all Parliaments after this more cautious to preserve that Freedom, and Honor, which belongs to such Assemblies (when once they have fully shaken off this yoke of Vulgar encroachment) since the public interest consists in the mutual and common good both of Prince and People.

Nothing can be more happy for all, than in fair, grave, and Honorable ways to contribute their Counsels in Common, enacting all things by public consent; without tyranny or Tumults. We must not starve ourselves, because some men have surfeited of wholesome food.

And if neither I, nor You, be ever restored to Our Rights, but God in his severest justice, will punish My Subjects with continuance in their sin, and suffer them to be deluded with the prosperity of their wickedness; I hope God will give Me, and You, that grace, which will teach and enable Us, to want, as well as to wear a Crown, which is not worth taking up, or enjoying upon sordid, dishonorable, and irreligious terms.

Keep You to true principles of piety, virtue, and honor, You shall never want a Kingdom.

A principal point of Your honor will consist in Your deferring all respect, love, and protection to Your Mother, My Wife; who hath many ways deserved well of Me, and chiefly in this, that (having been a means to bless Me with so many hopeful Children all which, with their Mother, I recommend to Your love, and care); She hath been content with incomparable magnanimity and patience to suffer both for, and with Me, and You.

My prayer to God Almighty is (whatever becomes of Me, who am, I thank God, wrapt up and fortified in My own Innocency, and his Grace) that he would be pleased to make You an Anchor, or Harbor rather, to these tossed and weather-beaten Kingdoms; a Repairer by Your wisdom, justice, piety, and valor, of what, the folly and wickedness of some men have so far ruined, as to leave nothing entire in Church or State; to the Crown, the Nobility, the Clergy, or the Commons; either as to Laws, Liberties, Estates, Order, Honor, Conscience, or lives.

When they have destroyed Me (for I know not how far God may permit the malice and cruelty of My Enemies to proceed, and such apprehensions some men's words and actions have already given Me), as I doubt not but My blood will cry aloud for vengeance to heaven; so I beseech God not to pour out his wrath upon the generality of the People, who have either deserted Me, or engaged against Me, through the artifice and hypocrisy of their Leaders, whose inward horror will be their first Tormenter, nor will they escape exemplary judgments.

For those that loved Me, I pray God, they may have no miss of Me, when I am gone; so much I wish and hope, that all good Subjects may be satisfied with the blessings of Your presence and virtues.

For those that repent of any defects in their duty toward Me, as I freely forgive them in the word of a Christian KING, so I believe You will find them truly Zealous, to repay with interest that loyalty and love to You, which was due to Me.

In sum, what good I intended, do You perform; when God shall give You power: much good I have offered, more I purposed to Church & State, if times had been capable of it.

The deception will soon vanish, and the Vizards will fall

off apace; This mask of Religion on the face of Rebellion (for so it now plainly appears, since My Restraint and cruel usage, that they sought not for Me, as was pretended) will not long serve to hide some men's deformities.

Happy times, I hope, attend You, wherein Your Subjects (by their miseries) will have learned, That Religion to their God, and Loyalty to their King, cannot be parted without both their sin and their infelicity.

I pray God bless You, and establish Your Kingdoms in righteousness, Your Soul in true Religion, and Your honor in the love of God and Your people.

And if God will have disloyalty perfected by My destruction; let My memory ever, with My name, live in you; as of Your Father, that loves You: and once a KING of three flourishing Kingdoms; whom God thought fit to honor, not only with the Scepter and Government of them, but also with the suffering many indignities, and an untimely death for them; while I studied to preserve the rights of the Church, the power of the Laws, the honor of My Crown, the privilege of Parliaments, the liberties of My People, and my own Conscience, which, I thank God, is dearer to Me than a thousand Kingdoms.

I know God can, I hope he yet will restore Me to My Rights. I cannot despair either of his mercy, or of My People's love and pity.

At worst, I trust I shall but go before You to a better Kingdom, which God hath prepared for Me, and Me for it, through My Saviour Jesus Christ, to whose mercies I commend You and all Mine.

Farewell, till We meet, if not on Earth, yet in Heaven.

THE COMMONWEALTH

A. PAPER CONSTITUTIONS

Inability to find a permanent and stable constitutional settlement was the great tragedy of the Revolution. With the end of the first civil war, both officers and men in the army brought forth comprehensive paper constitutions. The Levellers presented "The Agreement of the People," first in October 1647 and again in January 1649 [3].[1] The "Letter to the Free-born People of England" [2] was published in support of the first version of "The Agreement." Among the signatories was Robert Everard (often called Buff Coat) who played a conspicuous part in the debates in the army between the officers and men. The officers led by Henry Ireton, Cromwell's son-in-law, countered the plans of the Levellers by issuing "The Heads of the Proposals" [1]. The Agreement called for a republic, the supremacy of parliament, annual elections, and a franchise akin to universal manhood suffrage. To Cromwell and his fellow officers the adoption of this constitution would reduce England to anarchy.

In "The Heads of the Proposals," Ireton called for a limited monarchy and a strong parliament, but the franchise was to be limited to those who paid rates [real estate taxes]. Of course neither constitution was adopted, and so the execution of the king and the abolition of monarchy left England with only the Rump and the common law courts remaining from the old constitution. There was no constitutional executive,

[1] The second or longer "Agreement" is presented here. It is more moderate than the earlier version, and in the end was opposed by the Levellers.

and, by 1649, the Rump was merely the shadow of the Long Parliament elected nine years earlier in totally different circumstances. Its claims that all the former powers of the crown had now devolved upon it and that it alone embodied the sovereign powers of the state proved unacceptable to the Levellers and, in time, to Cromwell and the officers. But not until 1653 would another constitution be drawn up—"The Instrument of Government."

Thus the Commonwealth of England began its career on an unsure foundation, with all elements of the army and society vying for the right to determine the final settlement. In a desperate attempt to exert its authority the Rump required all men over the age of eighteen to take the "Engagement" [4] in place of the oath to the Solemn League and Covenant. Fairfax himself was among the first who refused to take it. From this point on the Rump lived at the sufferance of Cromwell and the army.

1. THE HEADS OF THE PROPOSALS, OFFERED BY THE ARMY [1 August 1647]

The Heads of the Proposals agreed upon by his Excellency Sir Thomas Fairfax and the Council of the Army, to be tendered to the Commissioners of Parliament residing with the Army, and with them to be treated on by the Commissioners of the Army: containing the particulars of their desires in pursuance of their former declarations and papers, in order to the clearing and securing of the rights and liberties of the kingdom, and the settling a just and lasting peace. To which are added some further particular desires (for the removing and redressing of divers pressing grievances), being also comprised in or necessary pursuance of their former representations and papers appointed to be treated upon.

I. That (things hereafter proposed, being provided for by this Parliament) a certain period may (by Act of Parliament) be set for the ending of this Parliament (such period to be put within a year at most), and in the same Act provision to be made for the succession and constitution of Parliaments in future, as followeth:

1. That Parliaments may biennially be called and meet at a certain day, with such provision for the certainty thereof, as in the late Act was made for triennial Parliaments; and what further or other provision shall be found needful by the Parliament to reduce it to more certainty; and upon the passing of this, the said Act for triennial Parliaments to be repealed.

2. Each biennial Parliament to sit 120 days certain (unless adjourned or dissolved sooner by their own consent), afterwards to be adjournable or dissolvable by the King, and no Parliament to sit past 240 days from their first meeting, or some other limited number of days now to be agreed on; upon the expiration whereof each Parliament to dissolve of course, if not otherwise dissolved sooner.

3. The King, upon advice of the Council of State, in the intervals between biennial Parliaments, to call a Parliament extraordinary, provided it meet above 70 days before the next biennial day, and be dissolved at least 60 days before the same; so as the course of biennial elections may never be interrupted.

4. That this Parliament and each succeeding biennial Parliament, at or before adjournment or dissolution thereof, may appoint Committees to continue during the interval for such purposes as are in any of these Proposals referred to such Committees.

5. That the elections of the Commons for succeeding Parliaments may be distributed to all counties, or other parts or divisions of the kingdom, according to some rule of equality or proportion, so as all counties may have a number of Parliament members allowed to their choice, proportionable to the respective rates they bear in the common charges and burdens of the kingdom, according to some other rule of equality or proportion, to render the House of Commons (as near as may be) an equal representative of the whole; and in order thereunto, that a present consideration be had to take off the elections of burgesses for poor decayed or inconsiderable towns, and to give some present addition to the number of Parliament members for great counties that have

now less than their due proportion, to bring all (at present), as near as may be, to such a rule of proportion as aforesaid.

6. That effectual provision be made for future freedom of elections, and certainty of due returns.

7. That the House of Commons alone have the power from time to time to set down further orders and rules for the ends expressed in the two last preceding articles, so as to reduce the elections of members for that House to more and more perfection of equality in the distribution, freedom in the election, order in the proceeding thereto, and certainty in the returns, with orders and rules (in that case) to be in laws.

8. That there be a liberty for entering dissents in the House of Commons, with provision that no member be censurable for ought said or voted in the House further than to exclusion from that trust; and that only by the judgment of the House itself.

9. That the judicial power, or power of final judgment in the Lords and Commons (and their power of exposition and application of law, without further appeal), may be cleared; and that no officer of justice, minister of state, or other person adjudged by them, may be capable of protection or pardon from the King without their advice or consent.

10. That the right and liberty of the Commons of England may be cleared and vindicated as to a due exemption from any judgment, trial or other proceeding against them by the House of Peers, without the concurring judgment of the House of Commons: as also from any other judgment, sentence or proceeding against them, other than by their equals, or according to the law of the land.

11. The same Act to provide that grand jurymen may be chosen by and for several parts or divisions of each county respectively, in some equal way (and not to remain as now, at the discretion of an Under-Sheriff to be put on or off), and that such grand jurymen for their respective counties, may at each Assize present the name of persons to be made Justices of the Peace from time to time, as the county hath need for any to be added to the Commission, and at the Summer Assize to present the names of three persons, out of whom the King may prick one to be Sheriff for the next year.

II. For the future security of Parliament and the militia

in general, in order thereunto, that it be provided by Act of Parliament:

1. That the power of the militia by sea and land, during the space of ten years next ensuing, shall be ordered and disposed by the Lords and Commons assembled, and to be assembled in the Parliament or Parliaments of England, by such persons as they shall nominate and appoint for that purpose from time to time during the said space.

2. That the said power shall not be ordered, disposed or exercised by the King's Majesty that now is, or by any person or persons by any authority derived from him, during the said space, or at any time hereafter by His said Majesty, without the advice and consent of the said Lords and Commons, or of such Committees or Council in the intervals of Parliament as they shall appoint.

3. That during the same space of ten years the said Lords and Commons may by Bill or Ordinance raise and dispose of what moneys and for what forces they shall from time to time find necessary; as also for payment of the public debts and damages, and for all other the public uses of the kingdom.

4. And to the end the temporary security intended by the three particulars last precedent may be the better assured, it may therefore be provided,

That no subjects that have been in hostility against the Parliament in the late war, shall be capable of bearing any office of power or public trust in the Commonwealth during the space of five years, without the consent of Parliament or of the Council of State; or to sit as members or assistants of either House of Parliament, until the second biennial Parliament be passed.

III. For the present form of disposing the militia in order to the peace and safety of this kingdom and the service of Ireland:

1. That there be Commissioners for the Admiralty, with the Vice-Admiral and Rear-Admiral, now to be agreed on, with power for the forming, regulating, appointing of officers and providing for the Navy, and for ordering the same to, and in the ordinary service of the Kingdom; and that there be a sufficient provision and establishment for pay and maintenance thereof.

2. That there be a General for command of the land forces that are to be in pay both in England, Ireland and Wales, both for field and garrison.

3. That there be Commissioners in the several counties for the standing militia of the respective counties (consisting of trained bands and auxiliaries not in pay), with power for the proportioning, forming, regulating, training and disciplining of them.

4. That there be a Council of State, with power to superintend and direct the several and particular powers of the militia last mentioned, for the peace and safety of this kingdom, and of Ireland.

5. That the same Council may have power as the King's Privy Council, for and in all foreign negotiations; provided that the making of war or peace with any other kingdom or state shall not be without the advice and consent of Parliament.

6. That the said power of the Council of State be put into the hands of trusty and able persons now to be agreed on, and the same persons to continue in that power (*si bene se gesserint*) for the certain term not exceeding seven years.

7. That there be a sufficient establishment now provided for the salary forces both in England and Ireland, the establishment to continue until two months after the meeting of the first biennial Parliament.

IV. That an Act be passed for disposing the great offices for ten years by the Lords and Commons in Parliament; or by such Committees as they shall appoint for that purpose in the intervals (with submission to the approbation of the next Parliament), and after ten years they to nominate three, and the King out of that number to appoint one for the succession upon any vacancy.

V. That an Act be passed for restraining of any Peers made since the 21st day of May, 1642, or to be hereafter made, from having any power to sit or vote in Parliament without consent of both Houses.

VI. That an Act be passed for recalling and making void all declarations and other proceedings against the Parliament, or against any that have acted by or under their authority in the late war, or in relation to it; and that the Ordinances for indemnity may be confirmed.

VII. That an Act be passed for making void all grants, &c. under the Great Seal, that was conveyed away from the Parliament, since the time that it was so conveyed away (except as in the Parliament's propositions), and for making those valid that have been or shall be passed under the Great Seal, made by the authority of both Houses of Parliament.

VIII. That an Act be passed for confirmation of the Treaties between the two kingdoms of England and Scotland, and for appointing conservators of the peace between them.

IX. That the Ordinance for taking away the Court of Wards and Liveries be confirmed by Act of Parliament; provided His Majesty's revenue be not damnified therein, nor those that last held offices in the same left without reparation some other way.

X. An Act to declare void the cessation of Ireland, &c., and to leave the prosecution of that war to the Lords and Commons in the Parliament of England.

XI. An Act to be passed to take away all coercive power, authority, and jurisdiction of Bishops and all other Ecclesiastical Officers whatsoever, extending to any civil penalties upon any: and to repeal all laws whereby the civil magistracy hath been, or is bound, upon any ecclesiastical censure to proceed (*ex officio*) unto any civil penalties against any persons so censured.

XII. That there be a repeal of all Acts or clauses in any Act enjoining the use of the Book of Common Prayer, and imposing any penalties for neglect thereof; as also of all Acts or clauses of any Act, imposing any penalty for not coming to church, or for meetings elsewhere for prayer or other religious duties, exercises or ordinances, and some other provision to be made for discovering of Papists and Popish recusants, and for disabling of them, and of all Jesuits or priests from disturbing the State.

XIII. That the taking of the Covenant be not enforced upon any, nor any penalties imposed on the refusers, whereby men might be restrained to take it against their judgments or consciences; but all Orders and Ordinances tending to that purpose to be repealed.

XIV. That (the things here before proposed being provided, for settling and securing the rights, liberties, peace and safety of the kingdom) His Majesty's person, his Queen, and royal issue, may be restored to a condition of safety, honor and freedom in this nation, without diminution to their personal rights, or further limitation to the exercise of the regal power than according to the particulars foregoing.

XV. For the matter of composition:

1. That a less number out of the persons excepted in the two first qualifications (not exceeding five for the English) being nominated particularly by the Parliament, who (together with the persons in the Irish Rebellion, included in the third qualification) may be reserved to the further judgment of the Parliament as they shall find cause, all other excepted persons may be remitted from the exception, and admitted to composition.

2. That the rates of all future compositions may be lessened and limited, not to exceed the several proportions hereafter expressed respectively. That is to say,

(1) For all persons formerly excepted, not above a third part.

(2) For the late members of Parliament under the first branch of the fourth qualification in the Propositions, a fourth part.

(3) For other members of Parliament in the second and third branches of the same qualification, a sixth part.

(4) For the persons nominated in the said fourth qualification, and those included in the tenth qualification, an eighth part.

(5) For all others included in the sixth qualification, a tenth part: and that real debts either upon record, or proved by witnesses, be considered and abated in the valuation of their estates in all the cases aforesaid.

3. That those who shall hereafter come to compound, may not have the Covenant put upon them as a condition without which they may not compound, but in case they shall not willingly take it, they may pass their compositions without it.

4. That the persons and estates of all English not worth £200 in land or goods, be at liberty and discharged: and that

the King's menial servants that never took up arms, but only attended his person according to their offices, may be freed from composition, or to pay (at most) but the proportion of one year's revenue, or a twentieth part.

5. That in order to the making and perfecting of compositions at the rates aforesaid, the rents, revenues, and other duties and profits of all sequestered estates whatsoever (except the estates of such persons who shall be continued under exception as before), be from henceforth suspended and detained in the hands of the respective tenants, occupants and others from whom they are due, for the space of six months following.

6. That the faith of the army, or other forces of the Parliament given in articles upon surrenders to any of the King's party, may be fully made good; and where any breach thereof shall appear to have been made, full reparation and satisfaction may be given to the parties injured, and the persons offending (being found out) may be compelled thereto.

XVI. That there may be a general Act of Oblivion to extend unto all (except the persons to be continued in exception as before), to absolve from all trespasses, misdemeanors, &c. done in prosecution of the war; and from all trouble or prejudice for or concerning the same (after their compositions past), and to restore them to all privileges, &c. belonging to other subjects, provided as in the fourth particular under the second general head aforegoing concerning security.

And whereas there have been of late strong endeavors and practices of a factious and desperate party to embroil this kingdom in a new war, and for that purpose to induce the King, the Queen, and the Prince to declare for the said party, and also to excite and stir up all those of the King's late party to appear and engage for the same, which attempts and designs, many of the King's party (out of their desires to avoid further misery to the kingdom) have contributed their endeavors to prevent (as for divers of them we have had particular assurance): we do therefore desire, that such of the King's party who shall appear to have expressed, and shall hereafter express, that way their good affections to the peace and welfare of the kingdom, and to hinder the embroiling of the same in a new war, may be freed and exempted from compositions, or to pay but one year's revenue, or a twentieth part.

These particulars aforegoing are the heads of such Proposals as we have agreed on to tender in order to the settling of the peace of this kingdom, leaving the terms of peace for the kingdom of Scotland to stand as in the late Propositions of both kingdoms, until that kingdom shall agree to any alteration.

Next to the Proposals aforesaid for the present settling of a peace, we shall desire that no time may be lost by the Parliament for despatch of other things tending to the welfare, ease and just satisfaction of the kingdom, and in special manner:

I. That the just and necessary liberty of the people to represent their grievances and desires by way of petition, may be cleared and vindicated, according to the fifth head in the late representation or Declaration of the army sent from St. Albans.

II. That (in pursuance of the same head in the said Declaration) the common grievances of this people may be speedily considered of, and effectually redressed, and in particular,

1. That the excise may be taken off from such commodities, whereon the poor people of the land do ordinarily live, and a certain time to be limited for taking off the whole.

2. That the oppressions and encroachments of forest laws may be prevented for the future.

3. All monopolies (old or new) and restraints to the freedom of trade to be taken off.

4. That a course may be taken, and Commissioners appointed to remedy and rectify the inequality of rates lying upon several counties, and several parts of each county in respect of others, and to settle the proportion of land rates to more equality throughout the kingdom; in order to which we shall offer some further particulars, which we hope may be useful.

5. The present unequal troublesome and contentious way of ministers' maintenance by tithes to be considered of, and some remedy applied.

6. That the rules and course of law, and the officers of it,

may be so reduced and reformed, as that all suits and questions of right may be more clear and certain in the issues, and not so tedious nor chargeable in the proceedings as now; in order to which we shall offer some further particulars hereafter.

7. That prisoners for debt or other creditors (who have estates to discharge them) may not by embracing imprisonment, or any other ways, have advantage to defraud their creditors, but that the estates of all men may be some way made liable to their debts (as well as tradesmen are by commissions of bankrupt), whether they be imprisoned for it or not; and that such prisoners for debt, who have not wherewith to pay, or at least do yield up what they have to their creditors, may be freed from imprisonment or some way provided for, so as neither they nor their families may perish by imprisonment.

8. Some provision to be made, that none may be compelled by penalty or otherwise to answer unto questions tending to the accusing of themselves or their nearest relations in criminal causes; and no man's life to be taken away under two witnesses.

9. That consideration may be had of all Statutes, and the laws or customs of Corporations, imposing any oaths either to repeal, or else to qualify and provide against the same, so far as they may extend or be construed to the molestation or ensnaring of religious and peaceable people, merely for nonconformity in religion.

III. That according to the sixth head in the Declaration of the army, the large power given to Committees or Deputy-Lieutenants during the late times of war and distraction, may be speedily taken into consideration to be recalled and made void, and that such powers of that nature as shall appear necessary to be continued, may be put into a regulated way, and left to as little arbitrariness as the statute and necessity of the things (wherein they are conversant) will bear.

IV. That (according to the seventh head in the said Declaration) an effectual course may be taken that the kingdom may be righted, and satisfied in point of accounts for the vast sums that have been levied.

V. That provision may be made for payment of arrears to

the army, and the rest of the soldiers of the kingdom who have concurred with the army in the late desires and proceedings thereof; and in the next place for payment of the public debts and damages of the kingdom; and that to be performed, first to such persons whose debt or damages (upon the public account) are great, and their estates small, so as they are thereby reduced to a difficulty of subsistence: in order to all which, and to the fourth particular last proceeding, we shall speedily offer some further particulars (in the nature of rules), which we hope will be of good use towards public satisfaction.

1 *August* 1647.

> Signed by the appointment of His Excellency Sir Thomas Fairfax and the Council of War.
>
> J. RUSHWORTH.

2. *LETTER TO THE FREE-BORN PEOPLE OF ENG-LAND* [1647]

For the noble and highly honored the free-born people of England, in their respective counties and divisions, these.

Dear Countrymen, and Fellow Commoners,

For your sakes, our friends, estates, and lives have not been dear to us. For your safety and freedom we have cheerfully endured hard labors and run most desperate hazards, and in comparison to your peace and freedom we neither do, nor ever shall, value our dearest blood. And we profess, our bowels are and have been troubled, and our hearts pained within us, in seeing and considering that you have been so long bereaved of these fruits and ends of all our labors and hazards. We cannot but sympathize with you in your miseries and oppressions. . . . And therefore upon most serious considerations that your principal right, most essential to your well-being, is the clearness, certainty, sufficiency, and freedom of your power in your representatives in Parliament, and considering that the original of most of your oppressions and miseries hath been either from the obscurity and doubtfulness of the power you have committed to your representatives in your elections or from the want of courage in those whom you have betrusted to claim and exercise their power, which might probably proceed from their uncertainty of your assistance and maintenance of their power . . . , and further minding the only effectual means to settle a just and lasting peace, to obtain remedy for all your grievances, and to prevent future oppressions, is the making clear and secure the power that you betrust to your representatives in Parliament, that they may know their trust, in the faithful execution whereof you will assist them: upon all these grounds, we propound your joining with us in the Agreement herewith sent unto you; that by virtue thereof we may have Parliaments certainly called, and have the time of their sitting and ending certain, and their power or trust clear and unquestionable, that hereafter they may remove your burdens and secure your rights, without oppositions or obstructions, and that the foundations of your peace may be so free from uncertainty that there may be no grounds for future quarrels or contentions to occasion war and bloodshed. And we desire you would consider that, as these things wherein we offer to agree with you are the fruits and ends of the victories which God hath given us, so the settlement of these are the most absolute means to preserve you and your posterity from slavery, oppression, distraction, and trouble. By this, those whom yourselves shall choose shall have power to restore you to, and secure you in, all your rights; and they shall be in a capacity to taste of subjection as well as rule, and so shall be equally concerned with yourselves in all they do. For they must equally suffer with you under any common burdens, and partake with you in any freedoms; and by this they shall be disabled to defraud or wrong you when the laws shall bind all alike, without privilege or exemption. And by this your consciences shall be free from tyranny and oppression, and those occasions of endless strifes and bloody wars shall be perfectly removed without controversy. By your joining with us in this Agreement, all your particular and common grievances will be redressed forthwith without delay: the Parliament must then make your relief and common good their only study.

Now because we are earnestly desirous of the peace and good of all our countrymen, even of those that have opposed us, and would to our utmost possibility provide for perfect peace and freedom, and prevent all suits, debates, and contentions that may happen amongst you in relation to the late war; we have therefore inserted it into this Agreement that no person shall be questionable for anything done in relation to the late public differences, after the dissolution of this present Parliament, further than in execution of their judgment; that thereby all may be secure from all sufferings for what they have done, and not liable hereafter to be troubled or punished by the judgment of another Parliament, which may be to their ruin unless this Agreement be joined in, whereby any Acts of Indemnity or Oblivion shall be made unalterable, and you and your posterities be secure.

But if any shall inquire why we should desire to join in an Agreement with the people, to declare these to be our native rights, and not rather petition to the Parliament for them, the reason is evident. No Act of Parliament is, or can be, unalterable, and so cannot be sufficient security to save you or us harmless from what another Parliament may determine if it should be corrupted. And besides Parliaments are to receive the extent of their power and trust from those that betrust them, and therefore the people are to declare what their power and trust is; which is the intent of this Agreement. And it's to be observed, that though there hath formerly been many Acts of Parliament for the calling of Parliaments every year, yet you have been deprived of them, and enslaved through want of them. And therefore both necessity for your security in these freedoms that are essential to your well-being, and woeful experience of the manifold miseries and distractions that have been lengthened out since the war ended, through want of such a settlement, requires this Agreement. And when you and we shall be joined together therein, we shall readily join with you to petition the Parliament, as they are our fellow Commoners equally concerned to join with us.

And if any shall inquire why we undertake to offer this Agreement, we must profess we are sensible that you have been so often deceived with Declarations and Remonstrances, and fed with vain hopes, that you have sufficient reason to abandon all confidence in any persons whatsoever from whom you have no other security of their intending your freedom

than bare declaration. And therefore, as our consciences witness that in simplicity and integrity of heart we have proposed lately, in *The Case of the Army Stated*, your freedom
and deliverance from slavery, oppression, and all burdens, so
we desire to give you satisfying assurance thereof by this
Agreement, whereby the foundations of your freedoms provided in *The Case, &c.*, shall be settled unalterably. . . .

And though the malice of our enemies, and such as they
delude, would blast us by scandals, aspersing us with designs
of anarchy and community; yet we hope the righteous God
will not only by this our present desire of settling an equal,
just government, but also by directing us unto all righteous
undertakings simply for public good, make our uprightness
and faithfulness to the interest of all our countrymen shine
forth so clearly that malice itself shall be silenced and confounded. We question not but the longing expectation of a
firm peace will incite you to the most speedy joining in this
Agreement: in the prosecution whereof, or of anything that
you shall desire for public good, you may be confident you
shall never want the assistance of

Your most faithful fellow Commoners, now in arms for
your service. . . .

3. THE AGREEMENT OF THE PEOPLE
[15 January 1649]

An Agreement of the People of England, and the places
therewith incorporated, for a secure and present peace,
upon grounds of common right, freedom and safety.

Having, by our late labors and hazards, made it appear to
the world at how high a rate we value our just freedom, and
God having so far owned our cause as to deliver the enemies
thereof into our hands, we do now hold ourselves bound, in
mutual duty to each other, to take the best care we can for
the future, to avoid both the danger of returning into a slav-
ish condition and the chargeable remedy of another war: for
as it cannot be imagined that so many of our countrymen
would have opposed us in this quarrel if they had understood

their own good, so may we hopefully promise to ourselves, that when our common rights and liberties shall be cleared, their endeavors will be disappointed that seek to make themselves our masters. Since therefore our former oppressions and not-yet-ended troubles have been occasioned either by want of frequent national meetings in council, or by the undue or unequal constitution thereof, or by rendering those meetings ineffectual, we are fully agreed and resolved, God willing, to provide, that hereafter our Representatives be neither left to an uncertainty for times nor be unequally constituted, nor made useless to the ends for which they are intended. In order whereunto we declare and agree,

First, that, to prevent the many inconveniences apparently arising from the long continuance of the same persons in supreme authority, this present Parliament end and dissolve upon, or before, the last day of April, 1649.

Secondly, that the people of England (being at this day very unequally distributed by counties, cities, and boroughs, for the election of their Representatives) be indifferently proportioned; and, to this end, that the Representative of the whole nation shall consist of 400 persons, or not above; and in each county, and the places thereto subjoined, there shall be chosen, to make up the said Representative at all times, the several numbers here mentioned, viz.

KENT, with the Boroughs, Towns, and Parishes therein, except such as are hereunder particularly named	10
Canterbury, with the Suburbs adjoining and Liberties thereof	2
Rochester, with the Parishes of Chatham and Stroud	1
The Cinque Ports in Kent and Sussex, viz. Dover, Romney, Hythe, Sandwich, Hastings, with the Towns of Rye and Winchelsea	3
SUSSEX, with the Boroughs, Towns, and Parishes therein, except Chichester	8
Chichester, with the Suburbs and Liberties thereof	1
SOUTHAMPTON COUNTY, with the Boroughs, Towns, and Parishes therein, except such as are hereunder named	8
Winchester, with the Suburbs and Liberties thereof	1
Southampton Town and the County thereof	1
DORSETSHIRE, with the Boroughs, Towns, and Parishes therein, except Dorchester	7
Dorchester	1

DEVONSHIRE, with the Boroughs, Towns, and Parishes therein, except such as are hereunder particularly named 12
   Exeter 2
   Plymouth 2
   Barnstaple 1
CORNWALL, with the Boroughs, Towns, and Parishes therein 8
SOMERSETSHIRE, with the Boroughs, Towns, and Parishes therein, except such as are hereunder named 8
   Bristol 3
   Taunton-Dean 1
WILTSHIRE, with the Boroughs, Towns, and Parishes therein, except Salisbury 7
   Salisbury 1
BERKSHIRE, with the Boroughs, Towns, and Parishes therein, except Reading 5
   Reading 1
SURREY, with the Boroughs, Towns, and Parishes therein, except Southwark 5
   Southwark 2
MIDDLESEX, with the Boroughs, Towns, and Parishes therein, except such as are hereunder named 4
   London 8
   Westminster and the Duchy 2
HERTFORDSHIRE, with the Boroughs, Towns, and Parishes therein 6
BUCKINGHAMSHIRE, with the Boroughs, Towns, and Parishes therein 6
OXFORDSHIRE, with the Boroughs, Towns, and Parishes therein, except such as are hereunder named 4
   Oxford City 2
   Oxford University 2
GLOUCESTERSHIRE, with the Boroughs, Towns, and Parishes therein, except Gloucester 7
   Gloucester 2
HEREFORDSHIRE, with the Boroughs, Towns, and Parishes therein, except Hereford 4
   Hereford 1
WORCESTERSHIRE, with the Boroughs, Towns, and Parishes therein, except Worcester 4
   Worcester 2
WARWICKSHIRE, with the Boroughs, Towns, and Parishes therein, except Coventry 5
   Coventry 2
NORTHAMPTONSHIRE, with the Boroughs, Towns, and Parishes therein, except Northampton 5
   Northampton 1
BEDFORDSHIRE, with the Boroughs, Towns, and Parishes therein 4
CAMBRIDGESHIRE, with the Boroughs, Towns, and Parishes therein, except such as are hereunder particularly named 4

Cambridge University	2
Cambridge Town	2
Essex, with the Boroughs, Towns, and Parishes therein, except Colchester	11
Colchester	2
Suffolk, with the Boroughs, Towns, and Parishes therein, except such as are hereafter named	10
Ipswich	2
St. Edmund's Bury	1
Norfolk, with the Boroughs, Towns, and Parishes therein, except such as are hereunder named	9
Norwich	3
Lynn	1
Yarmouth	1
Lincolnshire, with the Boroughs, Towns, and Parishes therein, except the City of Lincoln and the Town of Boston	11
Lincoln	1
Boston	1
Rutlandshire, with the Boroughs, Towns, and Parishes therein	1
Huntingdonshire, with the Boroughs, Towns, and Parishes therein	3
Leicestershire, with the Boroughs, Towns, and Parishes therein, except Leicester	5
Leicester	1
Nottinghamshire, with the Boroughs, Towns, and Parishes therein, except Nottingham	4
Nottingham	1
Derbyshire, with the Boroughs, Towns, and Parishes therein, except Derby	5
Derby	1
Staffordshire, with the City of Lichfield, the Boroughs, Towns, and Parishes therein	6
Shropshire, with the Boroughs, Towns, and Parishes therein, except Shrewsbury	6
Shrewsbury	1
Cheshire, with the Boroughs, Towns, and Parishes therein, except Chester	5
Chester	2
Lancashire, with the Boroughs, Towns, and Parishes therein, except Manchester	6
Manchester and the Parish	1
Yorkshire, with the Boroughs, Towns, and Parishes therein, except such as are hereafter named	15
York City and the County thereof	3
Kingston upon Hull and the County thereof	1
Leeds Town and Parish	1

DURHAM COUNTY PALATINE, with the Boroughs, Towns, and
    Parishes therein, except Durham and Gateside   3
    Durham City   1
NORTHUMBERLAND, with the Boroughs, Towns, and Parishes
    therein, except such as are hereunder named   3
    Newcastle upon Tyne and the County thereof, with Gateside   2
    Berwick   1
CUMBERLAND, with the Boroughs, Towns, and Parishes therein   3
WESTMORELAND, with the Boroughs, Towns, and Parishes
    therein   2

WALES

ANGLESEA, with the Parishes therein   2
BRECKNOCK, with the Boroughs and Parishes therein   3
CARDIGAN, with the Boroughs and Parishes therein   3
CARMARTHEN, with the Boroughs and Parishes therein   3
CARNARVON, with the Boroughs and Parishes therein   2
DENBIGH, with the Boroughs and Parishes therein   2
FLINT, with the Boroughs and Parishes therein   1
MONMOUTH, with the Boroughs and Parishes therein   4
GLAMORGAN, with the Boroughs and Parishes therein   4
MERIONETH, with the Boroughs and Parishes therein   2
MONTGOMERY, with the Boroughs and Parishes therein   3
RADNOR, with the Boroughs and Parishes therein   2
PEMBROKE, with the Boroughs, Towns, and Parishes therein   4

Provided, that the first or second Representative may, if
they see cause, assign the remainder of the 400 representers,
not hereby assigned, or so many of them as they shall see
cause for, unto such counties as shall appear in this present
distribution to have less than their due proportion. Provided
also, that where any city or borough, to which one representer
or more is assigned, shall be found in a due proportion not
competent alone to elect a representer, or the number of
representers assigned thereto, it is left to future Representatives to assign such a number of parishes or villages near
adjoining to such city or borough, to be joined therewith in
the elections, or may make the same proportionable.

Thirdly. That the people do, of course, choose themselves
a Representative once in two years, and shall meet for that
purpose upon the first Thursday in every second May, by
eleven in the morning; and the Representatives so chosen to
meet upon the second Thursday in the June following, at the
usual place in Westminster, or such other place as, by the

foregoing Representative, or the Council of State in the interval, shall be, from time to time, appointed and published to the people, at the least twenty days before the time of election: and to continue their sessions there, or elsewhere, until the second Thursday in December following, unless they shall adjourn or dissolve themselves sooner; but not to continue longer. The election of the first Representative to be on the first Thursday in May, 1649; and that, and all future elections, to be according to the rules prescribed for the same purpose in this Agreement, viz. 1. That the electors in every division shall be natives or denizens of England; not persons receiving alms, but such as are assessed ordinarily towards the relief of the poor; no servants to, and receiving wages from, any particular person; and in all elections, except for the Universities, they shall be men of twenty-one years of age, or upwards, and housekeepers, dwelling within the division for which the election is: provided, that (until the end of seven years next ensuing the time herein limited for the end of this present Parliament) no person shall be admitted to, or have any hand or voice in, such elections, who hath adhered unto or assisted the King against the Parliament in any of the late wars or insurrections; or who shall make or join in, or abet, any forcible opposition against this Agreement. 2. That such persons, and such only, may be elected to be of the Representative, who, by the rule aforesaid, are to have voice in elections in one place or other. Provided, that of those none shall be eligible for the first or second Representative, who have not voluntarily assisted the Parliament against the King, either in person before the 14th of June, 1645, or else in money, plate, horse, or arms, lent upon the Propositions, before the end of May, 1643; or who have joined in, or abetted, the treasonable engagement in London, in 1647; or who declared or engaged themselves for a cessation of arms with the Scots that invaded this nation the last summer; or for compliance with the actors in any insurrections of the same summer; or with the Prince of Wales, or his accomplices, in the revolted fleet. Provided also, that such persons as, by the rules in the preceding Article, are not capable of electing until the end of seven years, shall not be capable to be elected until the end of fourteen years next ensuing. And we desire and

recommend it to all men, that, in all times, the persons to
be chosen for this great trust may be men of courage, fearing
God and hating covetousness; and that our Representatives
would make the best provisions for that end. 3. That whoever,
by the rules in the two preceding Articles, are incapable of
electing, or to be elected, shall presume to vote in, or be
present at, such election for the first or second Representative; or, being elected, shall presume to sit or vote in either
of the said Representatives, shall incur the pain of confiscation of the moiety of his estate, to the use of the public, in
case he have any visible estate to the value of £50, and if he
has not such an estate, then shall incur the pain of imprisonment for three months. And if any person shall forcibly oppose, molest or hinder the people, capable of electing as
aforesaid, in their quiet and free election of representers, for
the first Representative, then each person so offending shall
incur the penalty of confiscation of his whole estate, both real
and personal; and, if he has not an estate to the value of £50,
shall suffer imprisonment during one whole year without bail
or mainprize. Provided, that the offender in each such case be
convicted within three months next after the committing of
his offense, and the first Representative is to make further
provision for the avoiding of these evils in future elections.
4. That to the end all officers of state may be certainly accountable, and no faction made to maintain corrupt interests,
no member of a Council of State, nor any officer of any salary-
forces in army or garrison, nor any treasurer or receiver of
public money, shall, while such, be elected to be of a Representative: and in case any such election shall be, the same
to be void. And in case any lawyer shall be chosen into any
Representative or Council of State, then he shall be incapable
of practice as a lawyer during that trust. 5. For the more convenient election of Representatives, each county, wherein
more than three representers are to be chosen, with the town
corporate and cities, if there be any, lying within the compass
thereof, to which no representers are herein assigned, shall be
divided by a due proportion into so many, and such parts, as
each part may elect two, and no part above three representers.
For the setting forth of which divisions, and the ascertaining
of other circumstances hereafter expressed, so as to make the

elections less subject to confusion or mistake, in order to the
next Representative, Thomas Lord Grey of Groby, Sir John
Danvers, Sir Henry Holcroft, knights; Moses Wall, gentleman; Samuel Moyer, John Langley, Wm. Hawkins, Abraham
Babington, Daniel Taylor, Mark Hilsley, R[ichar]d Price, and
Col. John White, citizens of London, or any five or more of
them, are intrusted to nominate and appoint, under their
hands and seals, three or more fit persons in each county,
and in each city and borough, to which one representer or
more is assigned, to be as Commissioners for the ends aforesaid, in the respective counties, cities and boroughs; and, by
like writing under their hands and seals, shall certify into the
Parliament Records, before the 11th of February next, the
names of the Commissioners so appointed for the respective
counties, cities and boroughs, which Commissioners, or any
three or more of them, for the respective counties, cities and
boroughs, shall before the end of February next, by writing
under their hands and seals, appoint two fit and faithful persons, or more, in each hundred, lathe or wapentake, within
the respective counties, and in each ward within the City of
London, to take care for the orderly taking of all voluntary
subscriptions to this Agreement, by fit persons to be employed
for that purpose in every parish; who are to return the subscription so taken to the persons that employed them, keeping a transcript thereof to themselves; and those persons,
keeping like transcripts, to return the original subscriptions
to the respective Commissioners by whom they were appointed, at, or before, the 14th day of April next, to be regis-
tered and kept in the chief court within the respective cities
and boroughs. And the said Commissioners, or any three or
more of them, for the several counties, cities and boroughs,
respectively, shall, where more than three representers are to
be chosen, divide such counties, as also the City of London,
into so many, and such parts as are aforementioned, and shall
set forth the bounds of such divisions; and shall, in every
county, city and borough, where any representers are to be
chosen, and in every such division as aforesaid within the
City of London, and within the several counties so divided,
respectively, appoint one place certain wherein the people
shall meet for the choice of the representers; and some one

fit person, or more, inhabiting within each borough, city, county or division, respectively, to be present at the time and place of election, in the nature of Sheriffs, to regulate the elections; and by poll, or otherwise, clearly to distinguish and judge thereof, and to make return of the person or persons elected, as is hereafter expressed; and shall likewise, in writing under their hands and seals, make certificates of the several divisions, with the bounds thereof, by them set forth, and of the certain places of meeting, and persons, in the nature of Sheriff, appointed in them respectively as aforesaid; and cause such certificates to be returned into the Parliament Records before the end of April next; and before that time shall also cause the same to be published in every parish within the counties, cities and boroughs repectively; and shall in every such parish likewise nominate and appoint, by warrant under their hands and seals, one trusty person, or more, inhabiting therein, to make a true list of all the persons within their respective parishes, who, according to the rules aforegoing, are to have voice in the elections; and expressing who amongst them are, by the same rules, capable of being elected; and such list, with the said warrant, to bring in and return, at the time and place of election, unto the person appointed in the nature of Sheriff, as aforesaid, for that borough, city, county or division respectively; which person so appointed as Sheriff, being present at the time and place of election; or, in case of his absence, by the space of one hour after the time limited for the peoples' meeting, then any person present that is eligible, as aforesaid, whom the people then and there assembled shall choose for that end, shall receive and keep the said lists and admit the persons therein contained, or so many of them as are present, unto a free vote in the said election; and, having first caused this Agreement to be publicly read in the audience of the people, shall proceed unto, and regulate and keep peace and order in the elections; and, by poll or otherwise, openly distinguish and judge of the same; and thereof, by certificate or writing under the hands and seals of himself, and six or more of the electors, nominating the person or persons duly elected, shall make a true return into the Parliament Records within twenty-one days after the election, under pain for default thereof, or, for making any false return, to forfeit £100 to the public use; and also cause indentures to be made, and unchangeably sealed and delivered, between himself and six or more of the said electors, on the one part, and the persons, or each person, elected severally, on the other part, expressing their election of him as a representer of them according to this Agreement, and his acceptance of that trust, and his promise accordingly to perform the same with faithfulness, to the best of his understanding and ability, for the glory of God and good of the people. This course is to hold for the first Representative, which is to provide for the ascertaining of these circumstances in order to future Representatives.

Fourthly. That 150 members at least be always present in each sitting of the Representative, at the passing of any law or doing of any act whereby the people are to be bound; saving, that the number of sixty may make a House for debates or resolutions that are preparatory thereunto.

Fifthly. That the Representative shall, within twenty days after their first meeting, appoint a Council of State for the managing of public affairs, until the tenth day after the meeting of the next Representative, unless that next Representative think fit to put an end to that trust sooner. And the same Council to act and proceed therein, according to such instructions and limitations as the Representative shall give, and not otherwise.

Sixthly. That in each interval between biennial Representatives, the Council of State, in case of imminent danger or extreme necessity, may summon a Representative to be forthwith chosen, and to meet; so as the Session thereof continue not above eighty days; and so as it dissolve at least fifty days before the appointed time for the next biennial Representative; and upon the fiftieth day so preceding it shall dissolve of course, if not otherwise dissolved sooner.

Seventhly. That no member of any Representative be made either receiver, treasurer, or other officer, during that employment, saving to be a member of the Council of State.

Eighthly. That the Representatives have, and shall be understood to have, the supreme trust in order to the preservation and government of the whole; and that their power extend, without the consent or concurrence of any other person

or persons, to the erecting and abolishing of Courts of Justice
and public offices, and to the enacting, altering, repealing and
declaring of laws, and the highest and final judgment, concerning all natural or civil things, but not concerning things
spiritual or evangelical. Provided that, even in things natural
and civil, these six particulars next following are, and shall be,
understood to be excepted and reserved from our Representatives, viz. 1. We do not empower them to impress or
constrain any person to serve in foreign war, either by sea or
land, nor for any military service within the kingdom; save
that they may take order for the forming, training, and exercising of the people in a military way, to be in readiness for
resisting of foreign invasions, suppressing of sudden insurrections, or for assisting in execution of the laws; and may take
order for the employing and conducting of them for those
ends; provided, that, even in such cases, none be compellable
to go out of the county he lives in, if he procure another to
serve in his room. 2. That, after the time herein limited for
the commencement of the first Representative, none of the
people may be at any time questioned for any thing said or
done in relation to the late wars or public differences, otherwise than in execution or pursuance of the determinations of
the present House of Commons, against such as have adhered
to the King, or his interest, against the people; and saving
that accountants for public moneys received, shall remain
accountable for the same. 3. That no securities given, or to
be given, by the public faith of the nation, nor any engagements of the public faith for satisfaction of debts and damages, shall be made void or invalid by the next or any future
Representatives; except to such creditors as have, or shall
have, justly forfeited the same: and saving, that the next
Representative may confirm or make null, in part or in whole,
all gifts of lands, moneys, offices, or otherwise, made by the
present Parliament to any member or attendant of either
House. 4. That, in any laws hereafter to be made, no person,
by virtue of any tenure, grant, charter, patent, degree or
birth, shall be privileged from subjection thereto, or from being bound thereby, as well as others. 5. That the Representative may not give judgment upon any man's person or estate,

where no law hath before provided; save only in calling to account and punishing public officers for abusing or failing in their trust. 6. That no Representative may in any wise render up, or give, or take away, any of the foundations of common right, liberty, and safety contained in this Agreement, nor level men's estates, destroy property, or make all things common; and that, in all matters of such fundamental concernment, there shall be a liberty to particular members of the said Representatives to enter their dissents from the major vote.

Ninthly. Concerning religion, we agree as followeth:—1. It is intended that the Christian Religion be held forth and recommended as the public profession in this nation, which we desire may, by the grace of God, be reformed to the greatest purity in doctrine, worship and discipline, according to the Word of God; the instructing the people thereunto in a public way, so it be not compulsive; as also the maintaining of able teachers for that end, and for the confutation or discovering of heresy, error, and whatsoever is contrary to sound doctrine, is allowed to be provided for by our Representatives; the maintenance of which teachers may be out of a public treasury, and, we desire, not by tithes: provided, that Popery or Prelacy be not held forth as the public way or profession in this nation. 2. That, to the public profession so held forth, none be compelled by penalties or otherwise; but only may be endeavored to be won by sound doctrine, and the example of a good conversation. 3. That such as profess faith in God by Jesus Christ, however differing in judgment from the doctrine, worship or discipline publicly held forth, as aforesaid, shall not be restrained from, but shall be protected in, the profession of their faith and exercise of religion, according to their consciences, in any place except such as shall be set apart for the public worship; where we provide not for them, unless they have leave, so as they abuse not this liberty to the civil injury of others, or to actual disturbance of the public peace on their parts. Nevertheless, it is not intended to be hereby provided, that this liberty shall necessarily extend to Popery or Prelacy. 4. That all laws, ordinances, statutes, and clauses in any law, statute, or ordinance to the contrary of the liberty herein provided for, in the two particulars next preceding concerning religion, be, and are hereby, repealed and made void.

Tenthly. It is agreed, that whosoever shall, by force of arms, resist the orders of the next or any future Representative (except in case where such Representative shall evidently render up, or give, or take away the foundations of common right, liberty, and safety, contained in this Agreement), he shall forthwith, after his or their such resistance, lose the benefit and protection of the laws, and shall be punishable with death, as an enemy and traitor to the nation. Of the things expressed in this Agreement: the certain ending of this Parliament, as in the first Article; the equal or proportionable distribution of the number of the representers to be elected, as in the second; the certainty of the people's meeting to elect for Representatives biennial, and their freedom in elections; with the certainty of meeting, sitting and ending of Representatives so elected, which are provided for in the third Article; as also the qualifications of persons to elect or be elected, as in the first and second particulars under the third Article; also the certainty of a number for passing a law or preparatory debates, provided for in the fourth Article; the matter of the fifth Article, concerning the Council of State, and of the sixth, concerning the calling, sitting and ending of Representatives extraordinary; also the power of Representatives to be, as in the eighth Article, and limited, as in the six reserves next following the same: likewise the second and third Particulars under the ninth Article concerning religion, and the whole matter of the tenth Article; all these we do account and declare to be fundamental to our common right, liberty, and safety: and therefore do both agree thereunto, and resolve to maintain the same, as God shall enable us. The rest of the matters in this Agreement we account to be useful and good for the public; and the particular circumstances of numbers, times, and places, expressed in the several Articles, we account not fundamental; but we find them necessary to be here determined, for the making the Agreement certain and practicable, and do hold these most convenient that are here set down; and therefore do positively agree thereunto. By the appointment of his Excellency the Lord-General and his General Council of Officers.

JOHN RUSHWORTH, Sec.

4. THE ENGAGEMENT, A.D. 1650

I do declare and promise that I will be true and faithful to the commonwealth of England, as it is now established, without a king or House of Lords.

B. THE CALL FOR REFORM

The victory of parliament and its New Model Army, coupled with the abolition of monarchy, not only precipitated the search for a new constitution; it also unleashed the pent-up longings for drastic social, economic, religious, and law reforms. In this section a few representative samples have been selected from the flood of pamphlets and petitions that rushed from the busy London presses.

It is obvious that those who had fought, often enduring great hardships, for the final victory would want the fruits of that victory. But as we saw in Chapter IV, the views of the Levellers, often expressed in the language of the common man and with a certain virulence, tended to frighten the powers-that-be in parliament, and the "men of substance" in society at large. During the four years of the Commonwealth, 1649–53, Cromwell held a tight rein on himself and the army. He sincerely believed in parliamentary government, and the Rump was thus both tolerated and encouraged to take a lead in enacting some of the more moderate and necessary reforms. The Rump, however, seemed bent on nothing but the enjoyment of the fruits of office and its own perpetuation.

This stalemate of course was to drive the Levellers and

their allies to take an even more militant stance, which in turn raised anew the specter of anarchy. Finally Cromwell had had enough. When in April 1653 the Rump decided to hold by-elections to replenish its ranks, rather than call for a free general election, Cromwell did what Charles I had not dared to do and dissolved it. This event was another turning point in the Revolution. The last vestige of the old constitution was now gone—except for the courts; the Levellers were to disintegrate rapidly as an organized body, and Oliver Cromwell was to come out into the open and dominate the public stage until his death five years later. Of the multitude of reforms that were demanded, few had ever gotten beyond the hearing stage. But since Cromwell had expressed agreement with several of these reforms, the cause was not yet hopeless.

The bulk of the pamphlets and petitions calling for reform were quite specific as to what was wrong with the government of the Commonwealth, but rather vague as to how to remedy these wrongs. "The Humble Petition of Divers Free-born Englishmen" [1], the "Declaration of the Commons of England" [4], Lilburne's "Letter to a Dear Friend" [5], and "The Only Right Rule for Regulating Laws and Liberties" [6] are all typical of the popular cry that justice be done. These pleas emanated from the ranks of the Levellers and others on the radical side, who felt that, in essence the new Commonwealth was little different from the old monarchy. They represent the views of the politically disaffected.

However, some calls for reform were more specific as to remedies. The "Propositions" [3] and the "Bills Proposed for Acts" [2] by William Leach are typical of the flood of pamphlet literature demanding reform of the courts, imprisonment for debt, and of the antiquated and haphazard system for registering deeds. Attacks were also made on tithes, the court of chancery, and even the common law itself. The Nominated, or Barebone's, Parliament in the summer and fall of 1653 would debate most of these items, but to no practical effect. In fact this parliament was to come near to abolishing the common law itself in its eagerness for reform.

The ultimate validity of many of the reforms proposed at

this time was demonstrated by their adoption in the nineteenth century. But in the 1650s they had to labor under the handicap of their sponsorship.

1. THE HUMBLE PETITION OF DIVERS FREE-BORN ENGLISHMEN [1 September 1650]

How can we choose but bewail our own and the Nation's sad condition, when notwithstanding all those zealous ardent expressions for just Liberty, acknowledged to be due to the People: That yet it should be frequent to imprison *Englishmen* upon extrajudicial Prerogative-like Warrants, and that too in such places, and remote Castles, whereunto belongeth no legal Jail-delivery, but where they are detained during pleasure, examined against themselves, search to find matter against them, and some are used in a more barbarous manner, than those were called *Puritans* in the *Bishops'* time.

Whilst *Englishmen* are made liable to attachments, by *Messengers* and *Pursuivants*. To have their goods distrained without legal Proceedings, and by Persons not authorized by Law, to be tried in matters of property and estate, by Committees; and in cases of life, by an extraordinary Commission of *Oyer* and *Terminer*, or which is worse and far transcending all strain of the old *Prerogative* by a *High Court* of *Justice*, and *Trials* by *Jury*, of twelve sworn men, shall be withheld from any *Englishman*; how in the least is *Magna Charta*, or the *Petition of Right*, those ancient fundamental Rights, either in circumstance of substance made good.

Whilst Conscience is enforced to an *Engagement*, or the refuser to forgo all the comforts of life, and as an Out-Law, exposed to the wills of men, and that *Excise, Custom*, and *Taxes*, are exacted as they are upon all sorts of industrious People; Alas, what Liberty is left us? who is he that walks not in *Jeopardy* all his life long, if these things be continued (which God defend) enjoying neither any comforts of life, nor so much as life itself, but at the pleasures of Men. And therefore in Conscience to God (whose holy and dreadful name hath been often invocated to be a Witness of the reality of those Promises and Declarations we are constrained at this time in most humble manner, earnestly to beseech you, even by the mercies and forbearance of God) who yet vouchsafeth time and means to perform all your Vows.

2. BILLS PROPOSED FOR ACTS
by William Leach [10 June 1651]

1. That all Creditors may have their due of and against all their Debtors and Prisoners, out of all their Estates both real and personal of what nature soever; and that all Prisoners whatsoever (satisfying their Creditors rateable according to their abilities) may speedily be delivered out of prison, and not lie lingering there in misery and extremity.

2. That all Prisoners of ability may be compelled to discover the truth of their Estates to their Creditors, and not lie in prison wasting and spending in a riotous way among their keepers, and their agents, as much as would satisfy their Creditors.

3. And that such as shall be found faulty in concealing or so wasting their Estates, should be taken from the prison where they so lie rotting, and be put to some place, strictly (after allowance of their maintenance in an indifferent manner) to be held to work for the benefit of their Creditors; which course will cause those who usually contribute for such their liberty, and righteous and delicious maintenance and living, contribute more large[sse] to their Creditors to gain their favor for the liberty of such Prisoner.

3. PROPOSITIONS FOR RECORDING AND REGISTERING OF DEEDS AND CONVEYANCES
by William Leach [10 June 1651]

Forasmuch as great numbers of secret, fraudulent Deeds and Conveyances, and other frauds and deceits have been of late years contrived, and more frequent practiced than formerly (notwithstanding the good Act made and Enacted in the year of the Reign of the late Queen *Elizabeth* of England, for prevention of the same) by many wicked people, selling their Manors, Messuages, Lands, Tenements, Hereditaments, and other things; sometimes twice, other times thrice, four or five times over to several purchasers, for good and valuable consideration, whereby divers honest people of this Nation (who have purchased the same Leases, Rents, Annuities or charges, out of the same, for great sums of money) have been defrauded of all that which they carefully and honestly have labored for, the greatest part of their lives, and afterward lived in great misery and extremity the residue of the continuance of their time. And other of such Purchasers by reason of such frauds and deceits, have been troubled and turmoiled, and put to great excessive charges and tedious Suits; and especially in the Courts of Chancery, or in Courts called Courts of Equity, or English Courts, many years together; and yet in the end, by the means of aforesaid, have failed of recovery or obtaining that, for which they have justly and honestly paid, or any part of their money, which they have disbursed in that behalf.

4. *A DECLARATION OF THE COMMONERS OF ENGLAND to Cromwell* [13 February 1652]

The Government of a commonwealth is the uniting of the people of a Nation into one heart and mind; And blessed is that People, whose Earthly Government is the Law of Common Righteousness. When Israel was under a commonwealth's Government, they were a terror to all Oppressing Kings in all Nations of the World; and so will England be, if this righteous Law become our Governor: But when the Officers of Israel began to be covetous and proud, they made a breach; and then the Government was altered, and fell into the hand of Kings like other Nations, and then they fled before their Enemies and were scattered. But if we look upon the customs of the Law itself, it is the same it was in the King's days, only the name is altered; as if the Commoners of England had paid their Taxes, Free-quarter, and shed their blood, not to reform, but to baptize the Law into a new name, from Kingly Law, to State Law; by reason whereof the spirit of discontent is strengthened, to increase more

Suits of Law, than formerly was known to be; And so as the Sword pulls down Kingly power with one hand, the King's old Law builds up monarchy with the other.

. . . .

And now the Commoners of England in this Age of the world are risen up in an Army, and have cast out that Invasion of the Duke of Normandy, and have won their Land and Liberties again by the Sword, if they do not suffer their Councils to befool them into slavery again upon a new account. For if so be that Kingly Authority be set up in your Laws again, King CHARLES hath conquered you and your posterity by policy, and won the field of you, though you have seemingly cut off his head. For the strength of a King lies not in the visible appearance of his body, but in his Will, Laws, and Authority. But if you remove Kingly Government and set up true and free Commonwealth's Government, then you gain your Crown, and keep it, and leave peace to your Posterity.

5. "LETTER TO A DEAR FRIEND"
by John Lilburne [18 January 1653]

This kingdom of the Brambles now set up, viz. (Oliver Cromwell, and his purged little party in the House) being only able to scratch and tear, not to protect and govern, I further declare and protest, that this combined traitorous faction, have forced an Interregnum, and Justicium upon us, an utter suspension of all lawful government, Magistracy, Laws, and Judicatories, so that we have not *de jure*, any laws in force to be executed, any Magistrates or judges lawfully constituted to execute them; any court of justice wherein they can be judicially executed, any such instrument of the law, as a lawful great Seal, nor any authority in England that can lawfully condemn and execute a thief, murderer, or any other offender, without being themselves called murderers by the law; all legal proceedings being now *Coram non judice* [before a person not a judge]: nor can this remaining faction in the house of Commons, show any one precedent, law, reason or authority whatsoever, for their aforesaid doings, but only their own irrational tyrannical votes, and the swords of their Army.

6. THE ONLY RIGHT RULE FOR REGULATING LAWS AND LIBERTIES
by Divers Affectionate Persons to Parliament
[28 January 1653]

And you see likewise, that notwithstanding the many professions and Protestations of this Army, to maintain the Fundamental Laws and Liberties of this Nation, it yet remains under a greater degree of bondage, and fuller of just complaints than ever, because you have slackened your zeal, and there hath not been that diligent perseverance in all lawful endeavors until their plenary restoration and firm establishment: Your study ought not to be like Conquerors, to make things new, or innovate upon the Fundamental Laws (that never-failing means of trouble and confusion) but to clear them from those many encroachments, violations and abuses both upon the Laws themselves, and the execution of them, which have almost rendered them of no benefit, and full of vexation to the people of this Nation.

. . . .

You may please to observe, it is not the being of a Parliament that makes the Nation happy, but their maintaining of the fundamental Rights and Liberties, nor that in words only and Declarations, but in the real and effectual establishment of them; and when they either neglect those, or set up other things contrary, or oppose the establishing of them, they prove themselves enemies, and reduce this Nation into a condition of bondage.

. . . .

But as truth is more ancient than error, and righteousness was before sin, though error and sin have much to say for their antiquity, so is it answered in these and the like cases; though Kings, and Lords, and Bishops have been of long continuance, and have procured many Laws to be made in several times, by Parliaments in favor of them, yet upon due examination it will appear, that they are not of Fundamental Institution, no more than many other corrupt interests, yet extant, which time after time have one made way for another, until at length they got sway of all things, sat themselves upmost in all places, oft times filled the seats in Parliament, and then made Laws in favor of themselves, and each other's interest, and in subversion of the Fundamental Laws, endeavoring all they could utterly to root them up, and to blot the knowledge of them out of all remembrance.

. . . .

And therefore to find out what are truly Fundamental Institutions, you may please to look beyond Kings, and as you pass them, you will perceive that their original was either by force from without, or from confederacy within the Land, that of their confederates they made Lords and Masters over the people, created offices, and made their creatures officers for life, whereas the true mark of a Fundamental Institution is only one year's continuance in an office, by which mark it is evident, that neither Kings nor House of Lords are of Fundamental Institution, all true Fundamental Institutions ordaining elections to every office, which is another mark, and that by the Inhabitants of the place where the office is to be exercised; and another special mark is, that the main scope and intent of the office and business thereof, is of equal concernment to the general good of all the people, and not pointed to make men great, wealthy and powerful, all which undoubted marks exclude not only Kings, and Lords, and Bishops, but many other interests of men in this long enslaved and deluded Nation.

So that in removing these useless, burdensome and dangerous interests of Kings, Lords, and Bishops, no violence at all hath been done to the Fundamental Laws and Liberties of *England*, but they are so far cleared and secured from innovation, and many oppressions which attended them. Nor is there ground for any to suppose, that in restoring the true ancient fundamental Rights of *England*, there will be a necessity of maintaining any [of] the Courts in *Westminster*, or their tedious, burdensome or destructive way of proceeding in trial of Causes, both Chancery, and the rest being in all things (except the use of Juries) all of them of Regal institution except the Common Pleas, which is so a so, as to its being seated in *Westminster*: These have sometimes been strengthened by Laws made in Parliaments, which were ever to give place to Fundamentals, being indeed null and void, wherein any particular they innovate upon, or are contrary unto them: All causes by the Fundamental Laws being to be decided and finally ended, past all appeal, in the Hundreds, or County Courts, where parties reside, or where the complaint is made by Juries, without more charge or time than is necessary, so that until the Norman Conquest, the Nation never knew or felt the charge, trouble, or entanglements of Judges, Lawyers, Attorneys, Solicitors, Filers, and the rest of that sort of men, which get great estates by the too frequent ruins of industrious people, which is another mark to know that all such are not of Fundamental Institution, but Regal, and erected for the increase and defense of that interest.

. . . .

Had this rule [individual liberty] been observed of late years, it had ere this stopped the mouths of many Petitioners, and begot a better understanding amongst the people, who have been shattered into shivers for want of this principle to unite them, every man stirring and contending as for life for his own opinion; one will have the Parliament do this, another that; others gathering themselves together in knots, and boasting how many hands they had to their petition; a second sort of men to theirs, and so of the rest, how many friends they had in the House for this thing, how many for that; and thus like the builders of *Babel*, they have been divided for want of knowledge, and fixedness in and upon the Fundamentals, which only can give rest to the spirits of the English, the goodness whereof having been once tasted, would soon beget a reconcilement; and doubtless this way or none must come the true and lasting peace amongst ourselves, and by this means only can we ever be made considerable, either against obstinate corrupt interest at home, or against foreign pretenders abroad, who otherwise observing us to be a floating unbalanced people, and consequently divided and subdivided within ourselves, will never cease to disturb this Nation; whereas were we once again bound and knit together with this just and pleasant ligament of Fundamental Law, divide and reign would not be so frequent in their vanquished mouths, which indeed is the main ground of the hopes.

VII

THE PROTECTORATE

The dissolution of the Rump in April 1653 had left the initiative with Cromwell. He still believed in parliamentary government and in a modicum of social reform. A truly representative parliament might bring the Royalists back to power, but if all known supporters of monarchy and of the Anglican and Roman churches were disenfranchised, it was possible that the Levellers would win. To avoid both contingencies and to guarantee a co-operative and reforming parliament, Cromwell called the Nominated or Barebone's Parliament into session in July 1653. The members were all the nominees of the loyal congregations. But the events of the next few months proved to be a cruel blow to the lord general. The "fanatical" element quickly asserted its leadership and appointed several committees to prepare legislation which would implement a broad program of reform.

The Law Reform Committee, for example, introduced a bill totally abolishing the Court of Chancery, and putting nothing in its place. This meant that a vast number of private lawsuits each year would have no place to be tried. Other debates showed an interest in the total abolition of the common law and its replacement by a system based upon common sense. The abolition of tithes, which supported the independent clergy, was also proposed. These and other schemes, none of which were actually enacted, were to stretch Cromwell's patience to the breaking point. Finally, in December 1653, the Nominated Parliament went the way of the Rump.

First the Levellers and then the Saints in the Nominated Parliament drove a large and powerful segment of the population to look to Cromwell to provide a stable government, and to protect them from the reforms of the "fanatics." Following the dissolution of the Nominated Parliament, Cromwell and his officers promulgated "The Instrument of Government" [1], England's first and only paper constitution. The fact that the new system was reminiscent of the old constitution was a mark of the conservative reaction that had set in and was also its only hope for success.

The *True State of the Case of the Commonwealth* [2] provides us with one of the clearest and most intelligent justifications of the Instrument. The author (unknown) shows the basis of the fears that England would either fall into anarchy or that the Royalists would be restored to power unless Cromwell took effective action and saved the Revolution by providing stability in government and society.

These fond hopes for the success of the new constitution were to be dashed on the rocks of the new parliament's intransigence. The failure of the new parliament to co-operate with him, plus the revival of Royalist hopes, and even arms, led to the installation of the notorious rule of the Major Generals. England was now ruled by the naked power of the sword, which had been expressly forbidden without parliamentary consent as far back as 1628 in the Petition of Right. William Prynne, the inveterate opponent of tyranny, whether royal, parliamentary, or Cromwellian, now hurled his bitter invective against the Protectorate and its Major Generals [3]. Prynne had been one of the first and certainly one of the most consistent enemies of the tyranny of Charles I. He had been a loyal Parliamentarian, and now he was comparing the Protectorate unfavorably with the personal rule of Charles I. After Cromwell's death he became an avowed supporter of Charles II. His long and rambling pamphlet showed the deep sense of disillusionment that was taking hold in the mid-fifties. Prynne was too much a lover of freedom and the common law to be a true revolutionary. Yet it was the inability of the commonwealthsmen and Cromwell to win over such as Prynne that foreshadowed their ultimate downfall.

1. *THE INSTRUMENT OF GOVERNMENT*
[16 December 1653]

The government of the Commonwealth of England, Scotland, and Ireland, and the dominions thereunto belonging.

I. That the supreme legislative authority of the Commonwealth of England, Scotland, and Ireland, and the dominions thereunto belonging, shall be and reside in one person, and the people assembled in Parliament: the style of which person shall be the Lord Protector of the Commonwealth of England, Scotland, and Ireland.

II. That the exercise of the chief magistracy and the administration of the government over the said countries and dominions, and the people thereof, shall be in the Lord Protector, assisted with a council, the number whereof shall not exceed twenty-one, nor be less than thirteen.

III. That all writs, processes, commissions, patents, grants, and other things, which now run in the name and style of the keepers of the liberty of England by authority of Parliament, shall run in the name and style of the Lord Protector, from whom, for the future, shall be derived all magistracy and honors in these three nations; and have the power of pardons (except in case of murders and treason) and benefit of all forfeitures for the public use; and shall govern the said countries and dominions in all things by the advice of the council, and according to these presents and the laws.

IV. That the Lord Protector, the Parliament sitting, shall dispose and order the militia and forces, both by sea and land, for the peace and good of the three nations, by consent of Parliament; and that the Lord Protector, with the advice and consent of the major part of the council, shall dispose and order the militia for the ends aforesaid in the intervals of Parliament.

V. That the Lord Protector, by the advice aforesaid, shall direct in all things concerning the keeping and holding of a good correspondency with foreign kings, princes, and states; and also, with the consent of the major part of the council, have the power of war and peace.

VI. That the laws shall not be altered, suspended, abrogated, or repealed, nor any new law made, nor any tax, charge, or imposition laid upon the people, but by common consent in Parliament, save only as is expressed in the thirtieth article.

VII. That there shall be a Parliament summoned to meet at Westminster upon the third day of September, 1654, and that successively a Parliament shall be summoned once in every third year, to be accounted from the dissolution of the present Parliament.

VIII. That neither the Parliament to be next summoned, nor any successive Parliaments, shall, during the time of five months, to be accounted from the day of their first meeting, be adjourned, prorogued, or dissolved, without their own consent.

IX. That as well the next as all other successive Parliaments shall be summoned and elected in manner hereafter expressed; that is to say, the persons to be chosen within England, Wales, the Isles of Jersey, Guernsey, and the town of Berwick-upon-Tweed, to sit and serve in Parliament, shall be, and not exceed, the number of four hundred. The persons to be chosen within Scotland, to sit and serve in Parliament, shall be, and not exceed, the number of thirty; and the persons to be chosen to sit in Parliament for Ireland shall be, and not exceed, the number of thirty.

X. That the persons to be elected to sit in Parliament from time to time, for the several counties of England, Wales, the Isles of Jersey and Guernsey, and the town of Berwick-upon-Tweed, and all places within the same respectively, shall be according to the proportions and numbers hereafter expressed: that is to say,

Bedfordshire	5	Cambridge University	1
Bedford Town	1	Isle of Ely	2
Berkshire	5	Cheshire	4
Abingdon	1	Chester	1
Reading	1	Cornwall	8
Buckinghamshire	5	Launceston	1
Buckingham Town	1	Truro	1
Aylesbury	1	Penryn	1
Wycomb	1	East Looe and West Looe	1
Cambridgeshire	4	Cumberland	2
Cambridge Town	1	Carlisle	1

Derbyshire	4	Lincoln	2
Derby Town	1	Boston	1
Devonshire	11	Grantham	1
Exeter	2	Stamford	1
Plymouth	2	Great Grimsby	1
Clifton, Dartmouth, Hardness	1	Middlesex	4
		London	6
Totnes	1	Westminster	2
Barnstaple	1	Monmouthshire	3
Tiverton	1	Norfolk	10
Honiton	1	Norwich	2
Dorsetshire	6	Lynn-Regis	2
Dorchester	1	Great Yarmouth	2
Weymouth and Melcomb-Regis	1	Northamptonshire	6
		Peterborough	1
Lyme-Regis	1	Northampton	1
Poole	1	Nottinghamshire	4
Durham	2	Nottingham	2
City of Durham	1	Northumberland	3
Essex	13	Newcastle-upon-Tyne	1
Malden	1	Berwick	1
Colchester	2	Oxfordshire	5
Gloucestershire	5	Oxford City	1
Gloucester	2	Oxford University	1
Tewkesbury	1	Woodstock	1
Cirencester	1	Rutlandshire	2
Herefordshire	4	Shropshire	4
Hereford	1	Shrewsbury	2
Leominster	1	Bridgnorth	1
Hertfordshire	5	Ludlow	1
St. Alban's	1	Staffordshire	3
Hertford	1	Lichfield	1
Huntingdonshire	3	Stafford	1
Huntingdon	1	Newcastle-under-Lyne	1
Kent	11	Somersetshire	11
Canterbury	2	Bristol	2
Rochester	1	Taunton	2
Maidstone	1	Bath	1
Dover	1	Wells	1
Sandwich	1	Bridgwater	1
Queenborough	1	Southamptonshire	8
Lancashire	4	Winchester	1
Preston	1	Southampton	1
Lancaster	1	Portsmouth	1
Liverpool	1	Isle of Wight	2
Manchester	1	Andover	1
Leicestershire	4	Suffolk	10
Leicester	2	Ipswich	2
Lincolnshire	10	Bury St. Edmunds	2

Dunwich	1	East Riding	4
Sudbury	1	North Riding	4
Surrey	6	City of York	2
Southwark	2	Kingston-upon-Hull	1
Guildford	1	Beverley	1
Reigate	1	Scarborough	1
Sussex	9	Richmond	1
Chichester	1	Leeds	1
Lewes	1	Halifax	1
East Grinstead	1	**WALES**	
Arundel	1	Anglesey	2
Rye	1	Brecknockshire	2
Westmoreland	2	Cardiganshire	2
Warwickshire	4	Carmarthenshire	2
Coventry	2	Carnarvonshire	2
Warwick	1	Denbighshire	2
Wiltshire	10	Flintshire	2
New Sarum	2	Glamorganshire	2
Marlborough	1	Cardiff	1
Devizes	1	Merionethshire	1
Worcestershire	5	Montgomeryshire	2
Worcester	2	Pembrokeshire	2
YORKSHIRE		Haverfordwest	1
West Riding	6	Radnorshire	2

The distribution of the persons to be chosen for Scotland and Ireland, and the several counties, cities, and places therein, shall be according to such proportions and number as shall be agreed upon and declared by the Lord Protector and the major part of the council, before the sending forth writs of summons for the next Parliament.

XI. That the summons to Parliament shall be by writ under the Great Seal of England, directed to the sheriffs of the several and respective counties, with such alteration as may suit with the present government, to be made by the Lord Protector and his council, which the Chancellor, Keeper, or Commissioners of the Great Seal shall seal, issue, and send abroad by warrant from the Lord Protector. If the Lord Protector shall not give warrant for issuing of writs of summons for the next Parliament, before the first of June, 1654, or for the Triennial Parliaments, before the first day of August in every third year, to be accounted as aforesaid; that then the Chancellor, Keeper, or Commissioners of the Great Seal for the time being, shall, without any warrant or direction, within seven days after the said first day of June, 1654, seal, issue, and send abroad writs of summons (changing therein what is to be changed as aforesaid) to the several and respective Sheriffs of England, Scotland, and Ireland, for summoning the Parliament to meet at Westminster, the third day of September next; and shall likewise, within seven days after the said first day of August, in every third year, to be accounted from the dissolution of the precedent Parliament, seal, issue, and send forth abroad several writs of summons (changing therein what is to be changed) as aforesaid, for summoning the Parliament to meet at Westminster the sixth of November in that third year. That the said several and respective Sheriffs shall, within ten days after the receipt of such writ as aforesaid, cause the same to be proclaimed and published in every market-town within his county upon the market-days thereof, between twelve and three of the clock; and shall then also publish and declare the certain day of the week and month, for choosing members to serve in Parliament for the body of the said county, according to the tenor of the said writ, which shall be upon Wednesday five weeks after the date of the writ; and shall likewise declare the place where the election shall be made: for which purpose he shall appoint the most convenient place for the whole county to meet in; and shall send precepts for elections to be made in all and every city, town, borough, or place within his county, where elections are to be made by virtue of these presents, to the Mayor, Sheriff, or other head officer of such city, town, borough, or place, within three days after the receipt of such writ and writs; which the said Mayors, Sheriffs, and officers respectively are to make publication of, and of the certain day for such elections to be made in the said city, town, or place aforesaid, and to cause elections to be made accordingly.

XII. That at the day and place of elections, the Sheriff of each county, and the said Mayors, Sheriffs, Bailiffs, and other head officers within their cities, towns, boroughs, and places respectively, shall take view of the said elections, and shall make return into the chancery within twenty days after the said elections, of the persons elected by the greater number of electors, under their hands and seals, between him on the one part, and the electors on the other part; wherein shall be contained, that the persons elected shall not have power to alter the government as it is hereby settled in one single person and a Parliament.

xiii. That the Sheriff, who shall wittingly and willingly make any false return, or neglect his duty, shall incur the penalty of 2000 marks of lawful English money; the one moiety to the Lord Protector, and the other moiety to such person as will sue for the same.

xiv. That all and every person and persons, who have aided, advised, assisted, or abetted in any war against the Parliament, since the first day of January, 1641 (unless they have been since in the service of the Parliament, and given signal testimony of their good affection thereunto) shall be disabled and incapable to be elected, or to give any vote in the election of any members to serve in the next Parliament, or in the three succeeding Triennial Parliaments.

xv. That all such, who have advised, assisted, or abetted the rebellion of Ireland, shall be disabled and incapable for ever to be elected, or give any vote in the election of any member to serve in Parliament; as also all such who do or shall profess the Roman Catholic religion.

xvi. That all votes and elections given or made contrary, or not according to these qualifications, shall be null and void; and if any person, who is hereby made incapable, shall give his vote for election of members to serve in Parliament, such person shall lose and forfeit one full year's value of his real estate, and one full third part of his personal estate; one moiety thereof to the Lord Protector, and the other moiety to him or them who shall sue for the same.

xvii. That the persons who shall be elected to serve in Parliament, shall be such (and no other than such) as are persons of known integrity, fearing God, and of good conversation, and being of the age of twenty-one years.

xviii. That all and every person and persons seized or possessed to his own use, of any estate, real or personal, to the value of £200, and not within the aforesaid exceptions, shall be capable to elect members to serve in Parliament for counties.

xix. That the Chancellor, Keeper, or Commissioners of

the Great Seal, shall be sworn before they enter into their offices, truly and faithfully to issue forth, and send abroad, writs of summons to Parliament, at the times and in the manner before expressed: and in case of neglect or failure to issue and send abroad writs accordingly, he or they shall for every such offense be guilty of high treason, and suffer the pains and penalties thereof.

xx. That in case writs be not issued out, as is before expressed, but that there be a neglect therein, fifteen days after the time wherein the same ought to be issued out by the Chancellor, Keeper, or Commissioners of the Great Seal; that then the Parliament shall, as often as such failure shall happen, assemble and be held at Westminster, in the usual place, at the times prefixed, in manner and by the means hereafter expressed; that is to say, that the sheriffs of the several and respective counties, sheriffdoms, cities, boroughs, and places aforesaid within England, Wales, Scotland, and Ireland, the Chancellor, Masters, and Scholars of the Universities of Oxford and Cambridge, and the Mayor and Bailiffs of the borough of Berwick-upon-Tweed, and other places aforesaid respectively, shall at the several courts and places to be appointed as aforesaid, within thirty days after the said fifteen days, cause such members to be chosen for their said several and respective counties, sheriffdoms, universities, cities, boroughs, and places aforesaid, by such persons, and in such manner, as if several and respective writs of summons to Parliament under the Great Seal had issued and been awarded according to the tenor aforesaid: that if the sheriff, or other persons authorized, shall neglect his or their duty herein, that all and every such sheriff and person authorized as aforesaid, so neglecting his or their duty, shall, for every such offense, be guilty of high treason, and shall suffer the pains and penalties thereof.

xxi. That the clerk, called the clerk of the Commonwealth in Chancery for the time being, and all others, who shall afterwards execute that office, to whom the returns shall be made, shall for the next Parliament, and the two succeeding triennial Parliaments, the next day after such return, certify the names of the several persons so returned, and of the places for which he and they were chosen respectively, unto the Council; who shall peruse the said returns, and examine whether the persons so elected and returned be such as is agreeable to the qualifications, and not disabled to be elected: and that every person and persons being so duly elected, and being approved of by the major part of the Council to be persons not disabled, but qualified as aforesaid, shall be esteemed a member of Parliament, and be admitted to sit in Parliament, and not otherwise.

XXII. That the persons so chosen and assembled in manner aforesaid, or any sixty of them, shall be, and be deemed the Parliament of England, Scotland, and Ireland; and the supreme legislative power to be and reside in the Lord Protector and such Parliament, in manner herein expressed.

XXIII. That the Lord Protector, with the advice of the major part of the Council, shall at any other time than is before expressed, when the necessities of the State shall require it, summon Parliaments in manner before expressed, which shall not be adjourned, prorogued, or dissolved without their own consent, during the first three months of their sitting. And in case of future war with any foreign State, a Parliament shall be forthwith summoned for their advice concerning the same.

XXIV. That all Bills agreed unto by the Parliament, shall be presented to the Lord Protector for his consent; and in case he shall not give his consent thereto within twenty days after they shall be presented to him, or give satisfaction to the Parliament within the time limited, that then, upon declaration of the Parliament that the Lord Protector hath not consented nor given satisfaction, such Bills shall pass into and become laws, although he shall not give his consent thereunto; provided such Bills contain nothing in them contrary to the matters contained in these presents.

XXV. That Henry Lawrence, Esq., &c., or any seven of them, shall be a Council for the purposes expressed in this writing; and upon the death or other removal of any of them, the Parliament shall nominate six persons of ability, integrity, and fearing God, for every one that is dead or removed; out of which the major part of the Council shall elect two, and present them to the Lord Protector, of which he shall elect one; and in case the Parliament shall not nominate within twenty days after notice given unto them thereof, the major part of the Council shall nominate three as aforesaid to the Lord Protector, who out of them shall supply the vacancy; and until this choice be made, the remaining part of the Council shall execute as fully in all things, as if their number were full. And in case of corruption, or other miscarriage in any of the Council in their trust, the Parliament shall appoint seven of their number, and the Council six, who, together with the Lord Chancellor, Lord Keeper, or Commissioners of the Great Seal for the time being, shall have power to hear and determine such corruption and miscarriage, and to award and inflict punishment, as the nature of the offense shall deserve, which punishment shall not be pardoned or remitted by the Lord Protector; and, in the interval of Parliaments, the major part of the Council, with the consent of the Lord Protector, may, for corruption or other miscarriage as aforesaid, suspend any of their number from the exercise of their trust, if they shall find it just, until the matter shall be heard and examined as aforesaid.

xxvi. That the Lord Protector and the major part of the Council aforesaid may, at any time before the meeting of the next Parliament, add to the Council such persons as they shall think fit, provided the number of the Council be not made thereby to exceed twenty-one, and the quorum to be proportioned accordingly by the Lord Protector and the major part of the Council.

xxvii. That a constant yearly revenue shall be raised, settled, and established for maintaining of 10,000 horse and dragoons, and 20,000 foot, in England, Scotland and Ireland, for the defense and security thereof, and also for a convenient number of ships for guarding of the seas; besides £200,000 per annum for defraying the other necessary charges of administration of justice, and other expenses of the Government, which revenue shall be raised by the customs, and such other ways and means as shall be agreed upon by the Lord Protector and the Council, and shall not be taken away or diminished, nor the way agreed upon for raising the same altered, but by the consent of the Lord Protector and the Parliament.

xxviii. That the said yearly revenue shall be paid into the

public treasury, and shall be issued out for the uses aforesaid.

XXIX. That in case there shall not be cause hereafter to keep up so great a defense both at land or sea, but that there be an abatement made thereof, the money which will be saved thereby shall remain in bank for the public service, and not be employed to any other use but by consent of Parliament, or, in the intervals of Parliament, by the Lord Protector and major part of the Council.

XXX. That the raising of money for defraying the charge of the present extraordinary forces, both at sea and land, in respect of the present wars, shall be by consent of Parliament, and not otherwise: save only that the Lord Protector, with the consent of the major part of the Council, for preventing the disorders and dangers which might otherwise fall out both by sea and land, shall have power, until the meeting of the first Parliament, to raise money for the purposes aforesaid; and also to make laws and ordinances for the peace and welfare of these nations where it shall be necessary, which shall be binding and in force, until order shall be taken in Parliament concerning the same.

XXXI. That the lands, tenements, rents, royalties, jurisdictions and hereditaments which remain yet unsold or undisposed of, by Act or Ordinance of Parliament, belonging to the Commonwealth (except the forests and chases, and the honors and manors belonging to the same; the lands of the rebels in Ireland, lying in the four counties of Dublin, Cork, Kildare, and Carlow; the lands forfeited by the people of Scotland in the late wars, and also the lands of Papists and delinquents in England who have not yet compounded), shall be vested in the Lord Protector, to hold, to him and his successors, Lords Protectors of these nations, and shall not be alienated but by consent in Parliament. And all debts, fines, issues, amercements, penalties and profits, certain and casual, due to the Keepers of the liberties of England by authority of Parliament, shall be due to the Lord Protector, and be payable into his public receipt, and shall be recovered and prosecuted in his name.

XXXII. That the office of Lord Protector over these nations

shall be elective and not hereditary; and upon the death of the Lord Protector, another fit person shall be forthwith elected to succeed him in the Government; which election shall be by the Council, who, immediately upon the death of the Lord Protector, shall assemble in the Chamber where they usually sit in Council; and, having given notice to all their members of the cause of their assembling, shall, being thirteen at least present, proceed to the election; and, before they depart the said Chamber, shall elect a fit person to succeed in the Government, and forthwith cause proclamation thereof to be made in all the three nations as shall be requisite; and the person that they, or the major part of them, shall elect as aforesaid, shall be, and shall be taken to be, Lord Protector over these nations of England, Scotland and Ireland, and the dominions thereto belonging. Provided that none of the children of the late King, nor any of his line or family, be elected to be Lord Protector or other Chief Magistrate over these nations, or any the dominions thereto belonging. And until the aforesaid election be past, the Council shall take care of the Government, and administer in all things as fully as the Lord Protector, or the Lord Protector and Council are enabled to do.

xxxiii. That Oliver Cromwell, Captain General of the forces of England, Scotland and Ireland, shall be, and is hereby declared to be, Lord Protector of the Commonwealth of England, Scotland and Ireland, and the dominions thereto belonging, for his life.

xxxiv. That the Chancellor, Keeper or Commissioners of the Great Seal, the Treasurer, Admiral, Chief Governors of Ireland and Scotland, and the Chief Justices of both the Benches, shall be chosen by the approbation of Parliament; and, in the intervals of Parliament, by the approbation of the major part of the Council, to be afterwards approved by the Parliament.

xxxv. That the Christian religion, as contained in the Scriptures, be held forth and recommended as the public profession of these nations; and that, as soon as may be, a provision, less subject to scruple and contention, and more certain than the present, be made for the encouragement and maintenance of able and painful teachers, for the instructing the people, and for discovery and confutation of error, hereby, and whatever is contrary to sound doctrine; and until such provision be made, the present maintenance shall not be taken away or impeached.

xxxvi. That to the public profession held forth none shall be compelled by penalties or otherwise; but that endeavors be used to win them by sound doctrine and the example of a good conversation.

xxxvii. That such as profess faith in God by Jesus Christ (though differing in judgment from the doctrine, worship or discipline publicly held forth) shall not be restrained from, but shall be protected in, the profession of the faith and exercise of their religion; so as they abuse not this liberty to the civil injury of others and to the actual disturbance of the public peace on their parts: provided this liberty be not extended to Popery or Prelacy, nor to such as, under the profession of Christ, hold forth and practice licentiousness.

xxxviii. That all laws, statutes and ordinances, and clauses in any law, statute or ordinance to the contrary of the aforesaid liberty, shall be esteemed as null and void.

xxxix. That the Acts and Ordinances of Parliament made for the sale or other disposition of the lands, rents and hereditaments of the late King, Queen, and Prince, of Archbishops and Bishops, &c., Deans and Chapters, the lands of delinquents and forest lands, or any of them, or of any other lands, tenements, rents and hereditaments belonging to the Commonwealth, shall nowise be impeached or made invalid, but shall remain good and firm; and that the securities given by Act and Ordinance of Parliament for any sum or sums of money, by any of the said lands, the excise, or any other public revenue; and also the securities given by the public faith of the nation, and the engagement of the public faith for satisfaction of debts and damages, shall remain firm and good, and not be made void and invalid upon any pretense whatsoever.

xl. That the Articles given to or made with the enemy, and afterwards confirmed by Parliament, shall be performed and made good to the persons concerned therein; and that such appeals as were depending in the last Parliament for relief concerning bills of sale of delinquents' estates, may be heard and determined the next Parliament, any thing in this writing or otherwise to the contrary notwithstanding.

XLI. That every successive Lord Protector over these nations shall take and subscribe a solemn oath, in the presence of the Council, and such others as they shall call to them, that he will seek the peace, quiet and welfare of these nations, cause law and justice to be equally administered; and that he will not violate or infringe the matters and things contained in this writing, and in all other things will, to his power and to the best of his understanding, govern these nations according to the laws, statutes and customs thereof.

XLII. That each person of the Council shall, before they enter upon their trust, take and subscribe an oath, that they will be true and faithful in their trust, according to the best of their knowledge; and that in the election of every successive Lord Protector they shall proceed therein impartially, and do nothing therein for any promise, fear, favor or reward.

2. A TRUE STATE OF THE CASE OF THE COMMON-WEALTH [8 February 1654]

Look over all the Declarations, Remonstrances, and Protestations made by either, and it will appear that we never fought against the King, as King; nor for the Parliament or Representative considered purely as such. . . . And therefore (we say) Government under this or that Form, was not the moving Cause of this great Controversy, but those common ends of safety and Freedom, for which all sorts of Governments were instituted and appointed. . . . This was the Soul that animated their whole Undertaking; which was not by them intended to quarrel at the Kingly Form then established, but to regulate the disorders and excesses of the King and his Government, and reduce him within the due bounds of Authority. . . . And seeing it was impossible to secure the Interest of Religion and Liberty, with respect had any longer to the King himself, he was utterly laid aside;

the consideration of those great ends being superior to the
dignity of his Person.

. . . .

But when after the intercurrence of divers years, all our
hopes were blasted, in regard particular Members became
studious of Parties and private Interests, neglecting the public; and by reason of their dilatory Proceedings in the House,
and unlimited arbitrary decisions at committees, wholly perverted the end of Parliaments; so that the People being
delayed (and so in effect denied) Answers to their Petitions,
no door being open for the redress of Grievances, nor any
hope of easing the People of their burdens, it was found at
length by experience, that a standing Parliament was itself
the greatest Grievance.

. . . .

As to the *Laws* and *Civil Rights* of the Nation; When
the point of Law came into consideration in the House, the
one Party was for pruning away its exuberances and superfluities; the other, for a hewing down of the main Body:
The more sober Judgments were for a regulation of the
Law, by making it more succinct, intelligible, and certain,
as also to remedy the Abuses of it, and render it less tedious
and chargeable to the People; yet nothing would serve the
other, but a total eradication of the old, and introduction of
a new: And so the good old Laws of *England* (the Guardians
of our lives and Fortunes) established with prudence, and
confirmed by the experience of many ages and generations
(the preservation whereof was a principal Ground of our
late Quarrel with the King) having been once abolished,
what could we have expected afterward, but an enthroning
of arbitrary Power in the Seats of Judicature, and an exposing of our Lives, our Estates, our Liberties, and all that
is dear unto us, as a Sacrifice to the boundless appetite of
mere Will and Pleasure. For, it hath been said of old; *The
Law is that which puts a difference between Good and Evil,
between Just and Unjust: If you once take away the Law,
all things will fall into a confusion; every man will become
a Law unto himself, which in the depraved condition of
Human Nature must needs produce many great Enormities:*

Lust will become a Law, and Envy will become a Law, Covetousness and Ambition will become Laws; and what Dictates, what Decisions such Laws will produce, may easily be discerned. As for our parts, we in this Nation may easily perceive the event of such courses, having lived some years at the pleasure of a long-continued Parliament, who contrary to their Trust, and the nature of a Parliament (whose great work is to make Laws) took upon them ordinarily to administer Law and Justice, according to their own wills, and endeavored to perpetuate the Office of Administration in their own hands, against the will of the People: In which Acts of absolute and Lordly power, as they were followed to the heels by this last Assembly [Barebone's Parliament]; so these exceeded them in other dangerous attempts, which extended not only to the abolition of Law, but to the utter subversion of Civil Right and Property. For, there was a Party of men among them, who assumed to themselves only the name of Saints, from which Title they excluded all others that were not of their Judgment and opinion, and therefore seeing it is a name that shall be had in everlasting honor; we are heartily sorry to have seen it so wretchedly abused in this Age of light and godliness, as that the pretense of it hath by some men been intended for a Rise to advantages of worldly Power and glory, above the rest of their brethren.

For what else could be the intention of those in the last House? who were no sooner met, but they would have waved the way of Call upon a human account, and generally made pretense to an extraordinary Call from *Christ* himself, and to take upon them to rule the Nation by virtue of a supposed Right of Saintship in themselves; and upon this principle would have laid the foundation of a new platform, which was to go under the name of a *Fifth Monarchy*, never to have an end, but to war with all other Powers, and break them in pieces. In order whereunto, that they might make way for this *Fifth Kingdom*, they said their party having wrested and fitted Scriptures for their turn, professed and declared abroad (and into this principle and persuasion they baptized all their Proselytes) that the Powers in being were all branches of the *Fourth Monarchy*, which must be rooted up and destroyed; whereupon they took the confidence not only to asperse and judge whole States and Governments, and prophesy their ruin, but did, as much as in them lay, devote them to destruction, and thereby prepare the spirits of the people to embrace any opportunity to follow them and put their designs in execution. So that if their design of setting up the *Fifth Monarchy* according to the dreams they had of it, had taken effect, wherein men could have had no other Right but what they must have derived from them and their Party; it is no hard matter to discern how the common Interest of this Nation would have been swallowed up by a particular Faction, and what a pernicious Engine it must have proved to the perverting of all Order among Men; forasmuch as by turning the stream of Government out of its proper channel, it would have utterly confounded the whole course of Natural and Civil Right, which is the only Basis of foundation of Government in this world. And therefore seeing their design was of so high a nature, as it aimed at no less than the extirpation of Law, and Government itself, and of the main Rights and Interests of the People relating thereunto; it is the less needful to mention their intrenching upon other Rights which are of an inferior consideration, as in the matter of Tithes, and of Patronage and Presentation of Ministers to Livings: Concerning which we shall only say, that in this, as in all other things, nothing of moderation would content them. It was propounded, as the more sober and equitable way, the persons of eminent piety and fidelity might be appointed to judge of such Ministers as should be presented by Patrons: but they would admit of no such regulation, running out into the extreme, and quite voted away the whole Right of Presentation. And in the debate thereof they forbore not to discover the principle whereby they did it, judging all men to be carnal and Antichristian, that differed in opinion from them.

As concerning the *Army*, this being the great Impediment in the way of *their Monarchy*, they were not without their designs also upon it: which not being to be contended with by any open attempt, they proceeded towards it by other methods. For, when the necessary continuation of Assessments came to be debated in the House, they labored might and main (under specious pretenses) to have cast out the

Bill, and so at once to have cut all the sinews of the Army and their subsistence, the only visible support of the Nation's security: the consequence whereof would have been an exposing of the Soldiery to Free-quarter and disorder, and thereby the Country to rapine; all supplies must have been cut off likewise from the Navy, and our Affairs and Friends left to sink or swim in *Ireland* and *Scotland;* yea, and all this at such a time of unusual danger and necessity, when *Scotland* was unquiet, the Commonwealth engaged with Enemies abroad, and forced to an extraordinary Charge for the maintenance of our Fleets at Sea, which are as the walls and bulwarks of this Nation against Invasions of Foreigners. But the Bill of Assessments being past, and their intentions this way frustrated, their next method was to have altered the Government of the Army, and to have committed it to such hands as would have assisted them in their intended Transformations. As a Preparative hereto, all courses were taken to make the *Army* odious, the Officers aspersed with the title of *Janizaries,* and men set up in Pulpits, whose daily work was to cast dirt upon all persons in Trust and Power, in the Army and elsewhere, by proclaiming them to be *Pensioners of Babylon,* and the Government Anti-Christian: which licentious Tongues were not only encouraged herein by the presence, but assisted (many times) by the persons of some of their Patrons in the late Assembly. Nor did these men rest here: but not being able to serve their own wills and fanatasies within the House, so easily as they desired; then they resolved to divide and separate themselves from the other Members, who followed them not in their excesses, and to constitute themselves into a Power distinct from them. To this end, they led off divers well-meaning Gentlemen of the House along with them, to private Meetings of their own appointment, upon pretense of seeking the Lord by prayer for direction. But, to the great dishonor of God, and profanation of his holy Ordinances, the use that was made of those Meetings by the Contrivers of them, was, only for the better carrying on of things that they had beforehand resolved to act. And in order thereto, they took liberty to arraign and condemn the persons and proceedings of their fellow Members, and provoked others to Remonstrate against them; saying, That if the House then sitting should send for them, they ought not to obey them: Devising also at the same Meetings, which way to prepossess all the gathered Churches in *England* by Letters, and with Reports of their own to scandalize the Government in the opinion of our Brethren in those Churches, whose Liberties we tender as our own in the Lord, and for whose satisfaction this Discourse is chiefly intended; endeavoring thereby to lead aside the Godly of the Land into mistakes and offenses. And when they could not obtain a general consent to write unto the Churches, because many of the Meeting perceived the evil of this business, it was left to every man's discretion to write as he should see cause and occasion. Besides all this, direction was given at a Meeting, to pull down some of the great Officers, and put others in their places; thereby to create such discontents and emulations among the Soldiery, as would probably have divided and embrued them in each other's blood, and exposed them and the whole Nation for a prey to the common Enemy.

Things being at this pass, and the House (through these Proceedings) perfectly disjointed, and the two Parties wound up to such a height of animosity, that they were as much divided, as if they had been people of two distinct Nations, mutually contending for each other's Rights, it was in vain to look for a Settlement of this Nation from them thus constituted; but on the contrary, nothing else could be expected, but that the Commonwealth should sink under their hands, and the great Cause hitherto so happily upheld and maintained, be for ever lost, through their preposterous management of those Affairs wherewith they had been trusted. And therefore the major part of that Assembly being convinced, that they could sit no longer, without incurring the guilt of that destruction which was coming on the whole Land, did upon the 12th day of *December* 1653 by subscribing their Names to an Instrument in writing, resign up their Powers and Authorities to his now *Highness* (then Captain General of all the Forces of this Commonwealth).

3. A SUMMARY COLLECTION OF THE PRINCIPAL FUNDAMENTAL RIGHTS, LIBERTIES, PROPERTIES OF ALL ENGLISH FREEMEN
by William Prynne [6 November 1656]

The excellently connaturalness, conveniency of the Laws of England to Englishmen's tempers, is so fully expressed, demonstrated by Fortescue, in his Book *De Laudabus Legum Angliae*, Glanvil, Briton, and others of ancient, and by Sir John Davies in his Epistle to his *Irish Reports*, Sir Edward Coke in his Epistles to his *Reports*, *Institutes*, with others of later times: by the very New Modelers of our old hereditary Kingdom, into a puny Free-State, in their Remonstrance of March 17, 1649, and by Mr. John Pym, and Mr. Oliver Saint-John, in their late *Parliamentary Speeches*, printed by the Commons House special Orders; that I shall not spend waste-paper to commend them, being the most excellent Laws of all others in the world, as they all unanimously resolve. I shall only add to their Encomiums of them: That the extraordinary care, diligence of our Ancestors, and all our Parliamentary Councils in former ages, to maintain, preserve, defend and transmit to posterity those good old Laws we now do or should enjoy, with the last Long Parliament's impeaching, beheading Strafford and Canterbury for Arch-traitors for endeavoring to subvert them with their innovations on the one side, and the late King and his Partisans on the other side, in above 500 printed Declarations, Orders, Ordinances, Proclamations, Remonstrances; that the principal end of all their consultations, arms, wars, taxes, Impositions, expenses of infinite Treasure and Blood, in all the unhappy contests against each other; was inviolably to defend, maintain our Laws and the Subject's Liberties, secured by them as their best Patrimony, Birthright, and Inheritance; the inserting thereof into all their Generals and Military Officer's Commissions, and all Ordinances, to raise monies for the Army's pay; is an unswervable evidence of their transcendent excellency, utility, preciousness, value, esteem, in the eyes of our Parliament and whole Nation: And a convincing Discovery of the Jesuitical Infatuation, folly, frenzy, treachery of those Swordmen and their Confederates, who now revile, traduce, and endeavor all they may, to reform, alter, subvert those very Laws, and Liberties which they were purposely commissioned, waged, engaged inviolably to defend, both by the Parliament, and People, and for which end they formerly professed, declared in many printed Remonstrances of their own, they fought and hazarded their lives in the field; yet now would conquer, and trample under feet, as if they had only fought against them and our hereditary Liberties confirmed by them.

I must confess, there are some few Grievances, Abuses, not in the Theory, but Practice of our Laws (introduced by dishonest Attorneys and Solicitors for the most part) fit to be redressed by the Judges of the Law (as some of them have been upon complaint) which I myself had many years since reformed had not those Army-men violently pulled me with other Members out of the House [Pride's Purge]; and interrupted the settlement, peace, liberty, ease from taxes, excises, and good Government of the Kingdom, by a happy close [treaty] with the late King, upon more safe and honorable terms of Freedom and happiness to the whole Nation and our Parliaments, than ever we can hope for from our New Governors or Swordmen; to usurp the Sovereign Power of King and Parliament into their own hands, and perpetuate our Wars, Taxes, Excises, Armies, and Military Government upon us, from generation to generation, as experience now manifests beyond contradiction, not for the people's safety, ease, wealth, tranquillity, as they then pretended: which people though they then cried up, voted for the only Supreme Authority; their free elections for the only Basis of all lawful Magistracy, Power, in and over the Nation, and their safety as the Supreme Law; yet now they imperiously trample upon as their conquered slaves, and both by their public speeches, actions, proclaim to all the world, They now no more value them than they do the very Acorns of the Swine, or dust of their feet, no further than they are subservient to their own aspiring designs, and selfish ends.

For those few remaining Abuses in our Laws' execution yet unredressed by former Laws, as they no ways concern the Army, or Army officers as soldiers, being out of their calling, Commission, and fit only for Judges, or Parliaments in their defaults, to redress: So they concern not the generality of the People (many thousands of them having no suit at Law in all their lives, and the most of them very rarely) but for the most part only some Litigious, contentious persons, who out of their pride and animosity, occasion these abuses, and prolongations of suits in Law, which they and others complain against, and therefore are justly punished and rewarded them; the expensiveness and tediousness of their Law suits, being the best means to correct, cure their contentious malicious spirits: other suits between peaceable persons being soon determined without any great expense, or length of time, if diligently prosecuted by honest Lawyers, Attorneys, and Solicitors.

But the Grievances these Martial Reformers of our Laws have introduced, under pretext of reforming some petty Abuses in the practice of the Law and Lawyers, are of a far more grievous, general, and transcendent nature, subverting the very Fundamental Laws and Liberties of the whole Nation; and burdening them with two or three Millions of extraordinary Taxes, Expenses every year, whereas all the abuses in the Law if rectified, amount not above 5 or 6 thousand pounds a year at the most, and those voluntarily expended by litigious persons, not exacted from, or imposed upon any against their Wills, as Taxes, Excises, Imposts, Tunnage and Poundage now are by the Soldiers, without Act of Parliament gainst our Laws. Which if redressed by the Swordmen now, is not out of any affection towards, or design to ease the People, but out of spleen to the Profession and Professors of the Law, and to increase the People's monthly Taxes to the Soldiers, and maintenance of their new war, to tenfold the value every year at least, to what they now expend in Law suits by reason of these abuses they would now redress; which will be nothing so grievous, expensive to the People, as those alterations they intend to make in our Laws and legal conveyances, which will but multiply Suits, and draw all men's estates into sequestration in few years' space.

There are four things specially provided for by our Fundamental Laws, and the original constitution of our Government, which principally concern all the Freemen of England in General, above all things else.

1. The Privileges and Freedom of their Parliaments and their Members.

2. The safety and liberty of their Persons.

3. The property of their Estates.

4. The Free course of Common Law, Right, Justice.

All which our Army Reformers have lately violated in the highest degree, beyond the Precedents of the worst of former ages, against all Laws of God and the Land, their own Commissions, Trusts, Declarations, Protestations, Vows, Leagues, Covenants, Engagements, without any color of lawful Authority; to the whole Nation's intolerable Grievance, Injury, Oppression, Impoverishing, enslaving, and yet would be reputed the only just, upright, faithful, righteous, conscientious Protectors, Reformers of our Laws, Grievances, government, and God's most precious Saints; and all others mere Malignants or Disaffected persons to Liberty and Reformation, who oppose or dislike their proceedings, secluding them out of their New Parliaments as such, when elected most freely by the People.

1. For the Privileges, Freedom of Parliaments, and their Members, formerly held most sacred and inviolable, They have in their own and the Army's name, impeached, imprisoned, suspended from sitting, many Members of both Houses; marched up professedly against them; contrary to their Trusts, Commands, and the express Statutes . . . forced them to retract their own Orders, Votes, Ordinances; eject, imprison their own Members, and Vote what they prescribed them. Since which they imprisoned, close imprisoned myself, with sundry other Members, in remote Castles, sundry years, without any cause, hearing, or recompense for this transcendent injustice; And not content herewith, they contrary to both House's Votes seized, impeached, abused, condemned, beheaded the late King, *The head of the Parliament*; suppressed, abolished the whole House of Lords, the ancientest, chiefest Members of it; secured, secluded the greatest part of the Commons House; and forcibly dissolved the Parliament itself by the Sword, without any writ, contrary to an express act of Parliament. And how they have disturbed,

secluded, abused, dissipated, dishoused their own mock-Parliament, and their Members even in the like manner; How they and their new Instruments have New-modeled that they now call our Parliaments; how they have deprived many ancient Boroughs, Cities, of their right of electing Burgesses, or of so many Burgesses as they ought, contrary to their Charters, and the express Statutes . . . ; disabled many thousands of their Votes in Elections, who have Voices, and enabled others to be Electors who have no Votes by our Laws; incorporated Scottish, and Irish Knights, Burgesses as Members into their late Parliaments, and interrupted the Freedom of Elections, by Letters, Menaces, armed Troops, Soldiers, and other indirect means, against the Statute of 3 Elizabeth, I, c. 5, the great Charter, and Constitutions, Laws, Rights, Privileges of our Parliaments; (to make what Persons and Number of their own creatures they please, a pretended Parliament, to bind our three Nations (by color of a void, illegal Instrument, made suddenly by a few Privadoes of their own in a corner; having no more legal force to bind our three Nations or Parliaments, than a Fiddle string, or the new Cords wherewith the uncircumcised Philistines by their treacherous Delilah bound Samson of old; which he broke from off his arms like a thread). All which is so well known to themselves, and others, that I shall not insist any further thereon. And are not all and every of these far greater abuses, & of more general important concernment to the whole Nation, than any they would now reform, or declaim against in our Laws, or Lawyers? fit now to be redressed? being adjudged no less than High Treason in others; not only by the Parliaments . . . but likewise by the Army Officers themselves; yea the very groundwork of all the incapabilities, penalties, sequestrations, decimations, forfeitures, they have imposed on others for levying war, and adhering unto the late King against the Parliament; which they but mediately and indirectly opposed and warred against, but themselves immediately, actually, directly warred upon, seized, secured, dissolved, destroyed, against their Trusts, Commissions to defend both the Parliament and the Members of it from force and violence: and therefore are the far greater Delinquents, and incapable to give any voice to elect any Members, or to be elected or sit in the three next Parliaments, by their own self-condemning Censures, Declarations, New instruments, and Verdicts passed against others; and by St. Paul's own Verdict, . . . are inexcusable, and shall not escape the judgment of God: though they escape the sentence of all human Tribunals, or their offenses of this nature.

2. For the safety and liberty of their Persons, these Army Reformers have contrary to the Great Charter, all other Fundamental Laws, Statutes, the Petition of Right itself, and premised Votes in the Parliament of 3 [Charles I], in New-created Military Courts of Justice, impeached, condemned, executed not only the late King and sundry Nobles, but likewise Knights, Gentlemen, and other Freemen of all ranks, callings, without any lawful Indictment or Trial by their Peers, for offenses not capital by our known Laws; Forcibly apprehended by armed Troopers, the Persons of Parliament-men, Noblemen, and others of all sorts; imprisoned, close-imprisoned them in remote Castles, under Guards, and translated them from one Castle to another, and myself amongst others, without any legal examinations, accusation, hearing, or cause expressed; banished some, and imprisoned others (yea some of their own Military-officers, and greatest Friends) in those foreign Isles, Castles (whither the Prelates and Old Council-Table Lords, banished me and my fellow brethren heretofore) without any legal Sentences; imprisoned, close-imprisoned thousands at a time upon carnal fears and jealousies (unbeseeming Saints, Christians, or men professing so much faith, confidence in God, and such signal ownings both of their Persons and present Powers by God himself, as they have done in public or private from time to time, and having an whole Army to guard them) and dragging them out of their Houses, beds, in the night by Soldiers, and shutting them up in inconvenient places; banished multitudes from time to time, from London and other parts, for sundry months together; confined others to certain places; impressed thousands for Land and Sea-services, and foreign employment (as well Apprentices as others) against their wills, and carried them away perforce to, and others from foreign Plantations, to the Indies, where they have lost their limbs, lives, to the ruin of their families and Masters. De-

graded all our Nobles without any lawful cause or hearing, of all their personal, hereditary Powers, Trusts, Commands: Disfranchised, disofficed Judges, Justices, Recorders, Mayors, Aldermen, Common-councilmen, Freemen, Servants, and many such very lately even by Major Generals, and their Deputies at their pleasures, taking far more Authority upon them now in all places in this and other kinds, than ever any Kings of England did, in late or former ages. And that which transcends all Precedents, imprisoning Lawyers themselves, as grand Traitors, and Delinquents in the Tower of London, only for arguing their Client's Cases, according to their Oaths, Duties, in defense of their Common Fundamental personal Liberty and property, when illegally committed for refusing to pay unjust Excises and Imposts, without Act of Parliament, in the late case of Mr. Cony [a merchant], and threatening to imprison others for prosecuting lawful suits: when as the late King they beheaded for a Tyrant, freely permitted myself, and other Lawyers, to argue the cases of Knighthood, Loans, Ship-money, Imposts, Tunnage and Poundage, which so much concerned him, without imprisonment or restraint. And are not these, with the denying *Habeas Corpus* to some, stopping the returning, or benefit of them when returned, to others, far greater Grievances, Abuses (which concern every Subject alike, and strike at the Foundation of all our Liberties) than any these Swordmen dislike or declaim against in our Laws or Lawyers? fit now to be redressed. If any private person injure any Freeman in any of these kinds forementioned, he may be remedied and recover damages by an Action of the Case, Trespass, or false Imprisonments; but being thus injured by our New Whitehall Grandees, Swordmen, Soldiers, Committees, Excisemen, Major Generals, their Deputies, or Deputy Deputies, who all imprison, disfranchise, oppress men at their pleasures (which none of our Kings could do), he is now left destitute of all relief or recompense by Law, or ordinary course of Justice, and imprisoned by Committees of Indemnity, if he sue, and forced to desist, or release his action, having no Lawyer who durst to plead his cause, for fear of imprisonment, nor Judge to release him, for fear of displacing; such is our present, worse than Turkish Thralldom, under these Grand Reformers of our Laws, and New-found Guardians of our Liberties, crying aloud to Heaven and Earth for present redress.

3. For the Property of their Estates; so fenced, vindicated, secured by the fore-cited Parliamentary Votes, Acts, and Petition of Rights; alas what is become of it? Have not these Sword-Reformers forcibly disseized, disinherited not only our Kings, Nobles, and other Officers of their Hereditary Honors, Dignities, Offices, Franchises, but likewise them, and thousands more, their Heirs, Successors, Wives, Children, Kindred, of their Palaces, Manors, Houses, Lands, Possessions, Rents, Revenues, real and personal Estates, without any other Law or Title but (that of Thieves and Pirates, Turks and Mamelukes) the longest Sword? Against not only all Laws of the Land, but the very eighth and tenth Moral Commandments of God himself, now practically quite expunged out of their Decalogue? And do not all else hold their Lands and Estates as Tenants at will, to these supreme new Land-Lords, who upon any New-coined Delinquency, or pretended plots, really sequester, or confiscate them at their pleasures by the self-same Law and Title? Yea whereas all our Kings in former ages took Aids and Subsidies from our Ancestors only as their free Gifts and Grants in Parliament, and that in moderate proportions, to wit, one Fifteenth, Tenth or Subsidy, and no more in ancient times, and but two or three Subsidies and Fifteenths of later days, payable at sundry times, in divers years, for which our Kings returned them hearty thanks in their Answers to those Grants, and granted them New Confirmations of their Laws, Liberties and the Great Charter, when violated, together with beneficial General Pardons in recompense of these their Aids and Subsidies (though for public uses and defense) which they never claimed nor imposed in the Clergy or Laity, but by their several free Grants in full and free Parliaments, and Convocations of the Clergy (as all our Parliament Rolls, our imprinted Acts, Histories, and Sir Edward Coke at large inform us). Do not these our New Military Reforming Sovereigns (as if they were more than Kings) without any free gift, grant, or Act of Parliament in a full and free Parliamentary Assembly, by their own New-usurped Power (without any thanks at all to the People, or

confirmation of their violated Laws, Liberties, Privileges, or general Pardons) against all former Acts, and Parliamentary Votes, impose both on the Clergy and Laity, against their Wills (beyond all Precedents of former ages) what excessive heavy monthly Taxes, Excises, Imposts, Tunnage, Poundage, and other payments they please upon the whole Nation, without intermission (which their New-modeled Parliaments themselves must, nor alter nor control by the 27, 28, 29 Articles of their Instrument) and levy them by armed Soldiers, Violence, imprisonments, quartering, and other great penalties, fines inflicted on the Refusers of them, and dispose of them at their pleasures when levied, without giving any account thereof to the Nation? yea force them to pay their contributions some months before they grow due; when no Landlord can receive his Rents, nor Creditor his debts to pay these Taxes, till at, or after the time they become due? And all to enslave, impoverish the Nation, to carry on new Wars, without consent of Parliament, and gain new Conquests abroad, while in the meantime our Merchants are robbed, undone, our trading decayed by these taxes, wars, and for want of well-guarding the Seas at home. And not content with these ordinary Monthly contributions, excises, imposts, have not these Reformers, without any legal Trial, hearing, conviction of New Delinquency (oft endeavoring to take away all Ministers' Tithes, though due unto them *Jure divino*, as well as by the Laws of the Land) exacted the Tithes of all formerly sequestered persons, their heirs and Widows' estates, improved according to the best improved value, by a late Decimation (for which there is no divine nor human Law or Right) notwithstanding all former compositions, Pardons under Seal, Articles of War, their own Act of Oblivion, their late instrument of Government, and oath for its observance; besides all our ancient Laws, exempting them therefrom, yea notwithstanding this sacred Canon *Ezek.*, XVIII, 20. . . . when as yet many Sons, yea some Infants are merely decimated for their Fathers, and Wives' Jointures, Dowers charged for their Husbands' delinquencies; Nay which is yet more barbarous, illegal, hundreds of Orthodox, able, godly, learned, Protestant Ministers of our Church, without any hearing or crime at all, for their former expiated pardoned mistake, in being addicted to the late King's party, are not only turned out of all their livings, lectures, fellowships, schools at once; but likewise prohibited to preach, teach School, in public or private, or to be entertained as Chaplains in private Houses, to support themselves, wives, children; or to administer the Sacrament, or marry any, under pain of imprisonment, banishment: And may not all our other Protestant Orthodox Ministers, School Masters, Scholars be thus smitten down, and suppressed at once, by the like club-law and justice, of which this Precedent is a very sad presage? Moreover do not these Reformers seize men's Horses, Arms, Swords, fowling, birding pieces (yea the very Armorets, Chandlers, Arms and Ammunition, though their stock, wares, trade, livelihood) at their pleasures, upon every pretended plot, fear, jealousy? Yea do not Soldiers, Excisemen and their agents break open, search, ransack men's Homes, Studies, Trunks, Chests, both by day and night, and take away their Goods, Chattels, yea their Writings, Records, Papers (as they did mine) at their pleasures; against all Law, and many late Parliament Votes, Nay have not they forced thousands of all sorts to enter into great penal Bonds of late, with sureties, both for themselves and all their Servants, containing strange, unheard of illegal Conditions, and forced them to pay, some 10s, others 5s, others 2s.6d for every Bond (an unparalleled oppression), though many of them not worth so much, under pain of Imprisonment, sequestration, and banishment in case of refusal: to omit all other extorted fees by Marshals, Lieutenants, Officers of the Tower, and others, from Prisoners; by Soldiers for levying pretended arrears of Taxes, and of Excisemen, and their Instruments? And are not these more grievous abuses, fit to be redressed, than any corruptions, excesses, fees in Lawyers, or our Laws? No private Person or Lawyers can take one farthing from another against his will, nor do the least prejudice to his real or personal estate against Law, but he may have present remedy for it. But these New Reformers, by Excises, Imposts, Contributions, Decimations, Sequestrations, and new-invented forfeitures, can forcibly extort, and levy some Millions of pounds from the whole Nation, every year, against their wills, all our Laws, yea strip whole families of their Inheritances, without any remedy by Law or otherwise: yet this must be no grievance or injustice at all in them, though the *Highest Treason*, and unpardonable crying offenses, in Strafford, Canterbury, the old Council-Table, and beheaded King; but a most righteous proceeding, necessary to be still pursued if not now established by a New Law, enabling them still to tax and poll us at their pleasures, without any future Parliaments or redress.

4. For the free course of the Common Law, Right, and Justice, according to Magna Charta, c. 29, "We will deny, nor defer to no man Justice of Right." It was never so much obstructed in any age by any persons, as by these new Reformers of our Laws. Witness their unparalleled late Whitehall Ordinances, touching their legal Excises: which not only indemnify all Excisemen, and their Assistants against all actions to be brought against them, or other molestations by all parties grieved; but expressly requiring, enjoining all Courts of Justice of this Commonwealth, and all Judges and Justices of the same, Sheriffs, Counsellors, Attorneys, Solicitors, and all other persons to conform themselves accordingly, *without any opposition or dispute whatsoever*; So that now no Court of Justice, or Judge must or can write; nor any Lawyer, Attorney, Solicitor, or other person, plead, argue or prosecute any suit at Law against any illegal Excise, Tax or Imposition, though never so unjust and oppressive; nor against any Levier of them, or imprisoner of refusers of them, under pain of being dis-Judged (like Thorp, Nudigate, and Rolls of late), or being committed to the Tower. . . . A slavery worse than that of the English Jews of old; To omit all former enforcements of well-affected plundered persons and others, to release their Actions, Judgments, Executions against Cavaliers, Soldiers, and others, and to pay them damages, and costs of suit besides, to their undoing, by their Councils of War, and Committees of Indemnity, of which there are hundreds of sad Precedents; I shall only touch their new Major Generals', Captains', Lieutenants', and others' late Abuses of this kind, in sending for Lawyers, Attorneys, Solicitors, Parties, by Soldiers and other Messengers, and forcing them by menaces, terror, and threatened imprisonments to release their Actions, Judgments, Executions, and to

refer all suits depending in Courts of Equity or Justice, to their own hearing and determination. Their examining, controlling, reversing Orders, Judgments, Decrees, made not only by Judges, Justices, and others, in Courts of Law and Equity, but even by Committees of Parliament, and the Commons House itself: their sending for some persons in Custody who refused to attend them, upon references, and others sundry miles [knights], and making them dance attendance on them from day to day upon bare Petitions and false suggestions of clamorous persons, after several Judgments, Decrees in Courts of Justice, Equity, Parliaments, and former references by the late King, seconded with many years' quiet enjoyment, for lands recovered against them, to their intolerable expense and vexation. A preparative to engross all Law and Justice for the future into their own hands alone, and suppress all Courts of Justice, Judges, as *dull and useless tools*, as some of late have styled them. And are not these far heavier, sadder Grievances, abuses worthy redress, than any these Reformers complain of in our Laws or Lawyers?

VIII

THE RESTORATION

John Evelyn has recorded the joy with which London welcomed the young king back to "his own" [2]. The disintegration of the Protectorate had proceeded rapidly after the death of Oliver Cromwell in the late summer of 1658. He had chosen as his successor his eldest son Richard—"Tumbledown Dick"—rather than his abler fourth son Henry. The army refused to accept Richard as leader and he soon retired into the country, leaving the field to the army under Lambert and the newly restored Rump. At that point General George Monck brought his forces down from Scotland and recalled the old unpurged Long Parliament. This guaranteed a majority for the Presbyterian Royalists. The next step was inevitable—overtures went out to Charles.

In *The Declaration of Breda* [1] Charles demonstrated his desire to forget the past and to pardon his own and his father's enemies (with the approval of a new parliament). But while Charles was sincere in his desire to be magnanimous, the new Cavalier Parliament was not. Since the king got back his lands, his crown, and the constitution as it stood before civil war broke out in 1642, he could undoubtedly afford to be generous. Many Anglican gentry and clergy did not feel quite so forgiving since the mere return of the king was not considered sufficient redress of their grievances.

All acts of parliament, since 1642, all decrees of the Council of State, and proclamations of the Lord Protector were declared null and void, and Charles II's reign was officially said to have begun on the day his father died—January 30, 1649. The years from 1642 to 1660 were stricken from the books. Many generations were to pass before Englishmen would once again take pride in the "Good Old Cause."

Of course these eighteen years were not to have been for nothing. Charles II never forgot that there was a point beyond which he dared not go. The people also remembered that there was a point beyond which the opposition to the crown should not go. And in any case the crown that Charles II put on in 1660 was the reformed crown of 1642, not the divine right crown of the years of his father's personal rule. All had not been in vain.

The *Ready and Easy Way to Establish a Free Commonwealth* [4] was written by Milton early in 1660, when he thought that it might still be possible to avert a restoration of the Monarchy. By the time the manuscript was published the pre-Purge Long Parliament had reassembled and Milton's cause was all but hopeless. His choice of title does reflect, nonetheless, his hope that the Commonwealth could be quickly reconstituted.

1. *THE DECLARATION OF BREDA* [4 *April* 1660]

Charles R.

Charles, by the grace of God, King of England, Scotland, France and Ireland, Defender of the Faith, &c. To all our loving subjects, of what degree or quality soever, greeting.

If the general distraction and confusion which is spread over the whole kingdom doth not awaken all men to a desire and longing that those wounds which have so many years together been kept bleeding, may be bound up, all we can say will be to no purpose; however, after this long silence, we have thought it our duty to declare how much we desire to contribute thereunto; and that as we can never give over the hope, in good time, to obtain the possession of that right which God and nature hath made our due, so we do make it our daily suit to the Divine Providence, that He will, in compassion to us and our subjects, after so long misery and sufferings, remit and put us into a quiet and peaceable possession of that our right, with as little blood and damage to our people as is possible; nor do we desire more to enjoy what is ours, than that all our subjects may enjoy what by law is theirs, by a full and entire administration of justice throughout the land, and by extending our mercy where it is wanted and deserved.

And to the end that the fear of punishment may not engage any, conscious to themselves of what is past, to a perseverance in guilt for the future, by opposing the quiet and happiness of their country, in the restoration of King, Peers and people to their just, ancient and fundamental rights, we do, by these presents, declare, that we do grant a free and general pardon, which we are ready, upon demand, to pass under our Great Seal of England, to all our subjects, of what degree or quality soever, who, within forty days after the publishing hereof, shall lay hold upon this our grace and favor, and shall, by any public act, declare their doing so, and that they return to the loyalty and obedience of good subjects; excepting only such persons as shall hereafter be excepted by Parliament, those only to be excepted. Let all our subjects, how faulty soever, rely upon the word of a King, solemnly given by this present declaration, that no crime whatsoever, committed against us or our royal father before the publication of this, shall ever rise in judgment, or be brought in question, against any of them, to the least endamagement of them, either in their lives, liberties or estates, or (as far forth as lies in our power) so much as to the prejudice of their reputations, by any reproach or term of distinction from the rest of our best subjects; we desiring and ordaining that henceforth all notes of discord, separation and difference of parties be utterly abolished among all our subjects, whom we invite and conjure to a perfect union among themselves, under our protection, for the resettlement of our just rights and theirs in a free Parliament, by which, upon the word of a King, we will be advised.

And because the passion and uncharitableness of the times have produced several opinions in religion, by which men are engaged in parties and animosities against each other (which, when they shall hereafter unite in a freedom of conversation, will be composed or better understood), we do declare a liberty to tender consciences, and that no man shall be disquieted or called in question for differences of opinion in matter of religion, which do not disturb the peace of the kingdom; and that we shall be ready to consent to such an Act of Parliament, as, upon mature deliberation, shall be offered to us, for the full granting that indulgence.

And because, in the continued distractions of so many years, and so many and great revolutions, many grants and purchases of estates have been made to and by many officers, soldiers and others, who are now possessed of the same, and who may be liable to actions at law upon several titles, we are likewise willing that all such differences, and all things relating to such grants, sales and purchases, shall be determined in Parliament, which can best provide for the just satisfaction of all men who are concerned.

And we do further declare, that we will be ready to consent to any Act or Acts of Parliament to the purposes aforesaid, and for the full satisfaction of all arrears due to the officers and soldiers of the army under the command of General Monck; and that they shall be received into our service upon as good pay and conditions as they now enjoy.

> Given under our Sign Manual and Privy Signet, at our Court at Breda, this $\frac{4}{14}$[1] day of April, 1660, in the twelfth year of our reign.

2. John Evelyn's DIARY

May 29th [1660]: This day came in his Majesty Charles the Second to London after a sad and long exile and calamitous suffering both of the King and Church, being seventeen years. This was also his birthday, and with a Triumph of above 20,000 horse and foot, brandishing their swords and shouting with unexpressable joy. The ways strewed with flowers, the bells ringing, the streets hung with tapestry, fountains running with wine. The Mayor, aldermen, all the companies in their liveries, chains of gold, banners. Lords and nobles, cloth of silver, gold and velvet everybody clad in; the windows and balconies all set with ladies, trumpets, mu-

[1] April 4th—Old Style; April 14th—New Style. In the seventeenth century there was a difference of ten days between the Old (Julian) and the New (Gregorian) calendars.

sic; and myriads of people flocking the streets and ways as far as Rochester, so as they were seven hours in passing the city, even from two in the afternoon 'til nine at night. I stood in the Strand and beheld it and blessed God. And all this without one drop of blood, and by that very army which rebelled against him. But it was the Lord's doing, and wonderful to our eyes, for such a Restoration was never seen in the mention of any history ancient or modern, since the return from the Babylonian Captivity, nor so joyful a day and so bright ever seen in this nation. This happening when to expect or effect it was past all human policy.

3. A COUNTRY SONG, ENTITLED "THE RESTORA-TION" [1661]

Come, come away
To the temple, and pray,
And sing with a pleasant strain;
The schismatic's dead,
The liturgy's read,
And the king enjoys his own again.

The vicar is glad,
The clerk is not sad,
And the parish cannot refrain
To leap and rejoice,
And lift up their voice,
That the king enjoys his own again.

The country doth bow
To old justices now,
That long aside have been lain;
The bishop's restored,
God is rightly adored,
And the king enjoys his own again.

Committeemen fall,
And majors general,

No more do those tyrants reign;
    There's no sequestration,
    Nor new decimation,
For the king enjoys the sword again.

    The scholar doth look
    With joy on his book,
Tom whistles and plows amain;
    Soldiers plunder no more,
    As they did heretofore,
For the king enjoys the sword again.

    The citizens trade,
    The merchants do lade,
And send their ships into Spain;
    No pirates at sea
    To make them a prey,
For the king enjoys the sword again.

    The old man and boy,
    The clergy and lay,
Their joys cannot contain;
    'Tis better than of late
    With the church and the state,
Now the king enjoys the sword again.

    Let's render our praise
    For these happy days,
To God and our sovereign;
    Your drinking give o'er,
    Swear not as before,
For the king bears not the sword in vain.

    Fanatics, be quiet,
    And keep a good diet,
To cure your crazy brain;
    Throw off your disguise,
    Go to church and be wise,
For the king bears not the sword in vain.

Let faction and pride
Be now laid aside,
That truth and peace may reign;
Let every one mend,
And there is an end,
For the king bears not the sword in vain.

4. *THE READY AND EASY WAY TO ESTABLISH A FREE COMMONWEALTH by John Milton* [1660]

Although since the writing of this treatise, the face of things hath had some change, writs for new elections have been recalled, and the members at first chosen, readmitted from exclusion, yet not a little rejoicing to hear declared the resolution of those who are in power, tending to the establishment of a free Commonwealth, and to remove, if it be possible, this noxious humor of returning to bondage, instilled of late by some deceivers, and nourished from bad principles and false apprehensions among too many of the people, I thought best not to suppress what I had written, hoping that it may now be of much more use and concernment to be freely published, in the midst of our Elections to a free Parliament, or their sitting to consider freely of the Government; whom it behooves to have all things represented to them that may direct their judgment therein; and I never read of any State, scarce of any tyrant grown so incurable, as to refuse counsel from any in a time of public deliberation; much less to be offended. If their absolute determination be to enthrall us, before so long a Lent of Servitude, they may permit us a little Shroving-time first, wherein to speak freely, and take our leaves of Liberty. And because in the former edition through haste, many faults escaped, and many books were suddenly dispersed, ere the note to mend them could be sent, I took the opportunity from this occasion to revise and somewhat to enlarge the whole discourse, especially that part which argues for a perpetual Senate. The treatise thus revised and enlarged, is as follows:

The Parliament of *England*, assisted by a great number of the people who appeared and stuck to them faithfullest in

defense of religion and their civil liberties, judging kingship
by long experience a government unnecessary, burdensome
and dangerous, justly and magnanimously abolished it;
turning regal bondage into a free Commonwealth, to the admiration and terror of our emulous neighbors. They took
themselves not bound by the light of nature or religion, to
any former covenant, from which the king himself by many
forfeitures of a latter date or discovery, and our own longer
consideration thereon had more & more unbound us, both
to himself and his posterity; as hath been ever the justice
and the prudence of all wise nations that have ejected tyranny. They covenanted *to preserve the king's person and authority in the preservation of the true religion and our liberties*; not in his endeavoring to bring in upon our consciences
a Popish religion, upon our liberties thralldom, upon our
lives destruction, by his occasioning, if not complotting, as
was after discovered, the *Irish* massacre, his fomenting and
arming the rebellion, his covert leaguing with the rebels
against us, his refusing more then seven times, propositions
most just and necessary to the true religion and our liberties,
tendered him by the Parliament both of *England* and *Scotland*. They made not their covenant concerning him with
no difference between a king and a god, or promised him as
Job did to the Almighty, *to trust in him, though he slay us*:
they understood that the solemn engagement, wherein we
all forswore kingship, was no more a breach of the covenant,
than the covenant was of the protestation before, but a faithful and prudent going on both in the words, well weighed,
and in the true sense of the covenant, *without respect of
persons*, when we could not serve two contrary masters, God
and the king, or the king and that more supreme law, sworn
in the first place to maintain, our safety and our liberty.
They knew the people of *England* to be a free people, themselves the representers of that freedom; & although many
were excluded, & as many fled (so they pretended) from
tumults to *Oxford*, yet they were left a sufficient number to
act in Parliament; therefore not bound by any statute of
preceding Parliaments, but by the law of nature only, which
is the only law of laws truly and properly to all mankind
fundamental; the beginning and the end of all Government;

to which no Parliament or people that will thoroughly reform, but may and must have recourse; as they had and must
yet have in church reformation (if they thoroughly intend
it) to evangelic rules; not to ecclesiastical canons, though
never so ancient, so ratified and established in the land by
Statutes, which for the most part are mere positive laws,
neither natural nor moral, & so by any Parliament for just
and serious considerations, without scruple to be at any time
repealed. If others of their number, in these things were
under force, they were not, but under free conscience; if
others were excluded by a power which they could not resist, they were not therefore to leave the helm of government
in no hands, to discontinue their care of the public peace
and safety, to desert the people in anarchy and confusion;
no more than when so many of their members left them, as
made up in outward formality a more legal Parliament of
three estates against them. The best affected also and best
principled of the people, stood not numbering or computing
on which side were most voices in Parliament, but on which
side appeared to them most reason, most safety, when the
house divided upon main matters: what was well motioned
and advised, they examined not whether fear or persuasion
carried it in the vote; neither did they measure votes and
counsels by the intentions of them that voted; knowing that
intentions either are but guessed at, or not soon enough
known; and although good, can neither make the deed such,
nor prevent the consequence from being bad: suppose bad
intentions in things otherwise well done; what was well done,
was by them who so thought, not the less obeyed or followed
in the state; since in the church, who had not rather follow
Iscariot or *Simon* the magician, though to covetous ends,
preaching, than *Saul*, though in the uprightness of his heart
persecuting the gospel? Safer they therefore judged what they
thought the better counsels, though carried on by some perhaps to bad ends, than the worse, by others, though endeavored with best intentions: and yet they were not to learn
that a greater number might be corrupt within the walls of
a Parliament as well as of a city; whereof in matters of nearest concernment all men will be judges; nor easily permit,
that the odds of voices in their greatest counsel, shall more

endanger them by corrupt or credulous votes, than the odds of enemies by open assaults; judging that most voices ought not always to prevail where main matters are in question; if others hence will pretend to disturb all counsels, what is that to them who pretend not, but are in real danger; not they only so judging, but a great though not the greatest, number of their chosen Patriots, who might be more in weight, than the others in number; there being in number little virtue, but by weight and measure wisdom working all things: and the dangers on either side they seriously thus weighed: from the treaty, short fruits of long labors and seven years' war; security for twenty years, if we can hold it; reformation in the church for three years: then put to shift again with our vanquished master. His justice, his honor, his conscience declared quite contrary to ours; which would have furnished him with many such evasions, as in a book entitled *an inquisition for blood*, soon after were not concealed: bishops not totally removed, but left as it were in ambush, a reserve, with ordination in their sole power; their lands already sold, not to be alienated, but rented, and the sale of them called *sacrilege*; delinquents few of many brought to condign punishment; accessories punished; the chief author, above pardon, though after utmost resistance, vanquished; not to give, but to receive laws; yet besought, treated with, and to be thanked for his gracious concessions, to be honored, worshiped, glorified. If this we swore to do, with what righteousness in the sight of God, with what assurance that we bring not by such an oath the whole sea of blood-guiltiness upon our own heads? If on the other side we prefer a free government, though for the present not obtained, yet all those suggested fears and difficulties, as the event will prove, easily overcome, we remain finally secure from the exasperated regal power, and out of snares; shall retain the best part of our liberty, which is our religion, and the civil part will be from these who defer us, much more easily recovered, being neither so subtle nor so awful as a king reinthroned. Nor were their actions less both at home and abroad than might become the hopes of a glorious rising Commonwealth: nor were the expressions both of army and people, whether in their public declarations or several writings other than such as testified a spirit in this nation no less noble and well fitted to the liberty of a Commonwealth, than in the ancient *Greeks* or *Romans*. Nor was the heroic cause unsuccessfully defended to all Christendom against the tongue of a famous and thought invincible adversary; nor the constancy and fortitude that so nobly vindicated our liberty, our victory at once against two [of] the most prevailing usurpers over mankind, superstition and tyranny unpraised or uncelebrated in a written monument, likely to outlive detraction, as it hath hitherto convinced or silenced not a few of our detractors, especially in parts abroad. After our liberty and religion thus prosperously fought for, gained and many years possessed, except in those unhappy interruptions, which God hath removed, now that nothing remains; but in all reason the certain hopes of a speedy and immediate settlement for ever in a firm and free Commonwealth, for this extolled and magnified nation, regardless both of honor won or deliverances vouchsafed from heaven, to fall back or rather to creep back so poorly as it seems the multitude would to their once abjured and detested thralldom of kingship, to be our selves the slanderers of our own just and religious deeds, though done by some to covetous and ambitious ends, yet not therefore to be stained with their infamy, or they to asperse the integrity of others, and yet these now by revolting from the conscience of deeds well done both in church and state, to throw away and forsake, or rather to betray a just and noble cause for the mixture of bad men who have ill managed and abused it (which had our fathers done heretofore, and on the same pretense deserted true religion, what had long ere this become of our gospel and all protestant reformation so much intermixed with the avarice and ambition of some reformers?) and by thus relapsing, to verify all the bitter predictions of our triumphing enemies, who will now think they wisely discerned and justly censured both us and all our actions as rash, rebellious, hypocritical and impious, not only argues a strange degenerate contagion suddenly spread among us fitted and prepared for new slavery, but will render us a scorn and derision to all our neighbors. And what will they at best say of us and of the whole *English* name, but scoffingly as of that foolish builder, mentioned by our

Savior, who began to build a tower, and was not able to finish it. Where is this goodly tower of a Commonwealth, which the English boasted they would build to overshadow kings, and be another *Rome* in the west? The foundation indeed they laid gallantly; but fell into a worse confusion, not of tongues, but of factions, than those at the tower of *Babel*; and have left no memorial of their work behind them remaining, but in the common laughter of *Europe*. Which must needs redound the more to our shame, if we but look on our neighbors the United Provinces, to us inferior in all outward advantages; who notwithstanding, in the midst of greater difficulties, courageously, wisely, constantly went through with the same work, and are settled in all the happy enjoyments of a potent and flourishing Republic to this day.

Besides this, if we return to kingship, and soon repent, as undoubtedly we shall, when we begin to find the old encroachments coming on by little and little upon our consciences, which must necessarily proceed from king and bishop united inseparably in one interest, we may be forced perhaps to fight over again all that we have fought, and spend over again all that we have spent, but are never like to attain thus far as we are now advanced to the recovery of our freedom, never to have it in possession as we now have it, never to be vouchsafed hereafter the like mercies and signal assistances from heaven in our cause, if by our ingrateful backsliding we make these fruitless; flying now to regal concessions from his divine condescensions and gracious answers to our once importuning prayers against the tyranny which we then groaned under: making vain and viler than dirt the blood of so many thousand faithful and valiant *English* men, who left us in this liberty, bought with their lives; losing by a strange aftergame of folly, all the battles we have won, together with all *Scotland* as to our conquest, hereby lost, which never any of our kings could conquer, all the treasure we have spent, not that corruptible treasure only, but that far more precious of all our late miraculous deliverances; treading back again with lost labor all our happy steps in the progress of reformation; and most pitifully depriving ourselves the instant fruition of that free government which we have so dearly purchased, a free Commonwealth, not only held by wisest men in all ages the noblest, the manliest, the equalest, the justest government, the most agreeable to all due liberty and proportioned equality, both human, civil, and Christian, most cherishing to virtue and true religion, but also (I may say it with greatest probability) plainly commended, or rather enjoined by our Savior himself, to all Christians, not without remarkable disallowance, and the brand of *gentilism* upon kingship. God in much displeasure gave a king to the *Israelites*, and imputed it a sin to them that they sought one: but *Christ* apparently forbids his disciples to admit of any such heathenish government: *the kings of the gentiles*, saith he, *exercise lordship over them*; and they that *exercise authority upon them, are called benefactors: but ye shall not be so; but he that is greatest among you, let him be as the younger; and he that is chief, as he that serveth*. The occasion of these his words was the ambitious desire of *Zebede's* two sons, to be exalted above their brethren in his kingdom, which they thought was to be ere long upon earth. That he speaks of civil government, is manifest by the former part of the comparison, which infers the other part to be always in the same kind. And what government comes nearer to this precept of Christ, than a free Commonwealth; wherein they who are greatest, are perpetual servants and drudges to the public at their own cost and charges, neglect their own affairs; yet are not elevated above their brethren; live soberly in their families, walk the streets as other men, may be spoken to freely, familiarly, friendly, without adoration. Whereas a king must be adored like a Demigod, with a dissolute and haughty court about him, of vast expense and luxury, masks and revels, to the debauching of our prime gentry both male and female; not in their pastimes only, but in earnest, by the loose employments of court service, which will be then thought honorable. There will be a queen also of no less charge; in most likelihood outlandish and a Papist; besides a queen mother such already; together with both their courts and numerous train: then a royal issue, and ere long severally their sumptuous courts; to the multiplying of a servile crew, not of servants only, but of nobility and gentry, bred up then to the hopes not of public, but of court offices; to be stewards, chamberlains, ushers, grooms, even of the close-stool; and the lower their minds debased with court opinions, contrary to all virtue and reformation, the haughtier will be their pride and profuseness: we may well remember this not long since at home; or need but look at present into the *French* court, where enticements and preferments daily draw away and pervert the Protestant Nobility. As to the burden of expense, to our cost we shall soon know it; for any good to us, deserving to be termed no better than the vast and lavish price of our subjection and their debauchery; which we are now so greedily cheapening, and would so fain be paying most inconsiderately to a single person; who for any thing wherein the public really needs him, will have little else to do, but to bestow the eating and drinking of excessive dainties, to set a pompous face upon the superficial actings of State, to pageant himself up and down in progress among the perpetual bowings and cringings of an abject people, on either side deifying and adoring him for nothing done that can deserve it. For what can he more than another man? who, even in the expression of a late court-poet, sits only like a great cipher set to no purpose before a long row of other significant figures. Nay it is well and happy for the people if their king be but a cipher, being oft times a mischief, a pest, a scourge of the nation, and which is worse, not to be removed, not to be controlled, much less accused or brought to punishment, without the danger of a common ruin, without the shaking and almost subversion of the whole land. Whereas in a free Commonwealth, any governor or chief counselor offending, may be removed and punished without the least commotion. Certainly then that people must needs be mad or strangely infatuated, that build the chief hope of their common happiness or safety on a single person: who if he happen to be good, can do no more than another man, if to be bad, hath in his hands to do more evil without check, than millions of other men. The happiness of a nation must needs be firmest and certainest in a full and free Council of their own electing, where no single person, but reason only sways. And what madness is it, for them who might manage nobly their own affairs themselves, sluggishly and weakly to devolve all on a single person; and more like boys under age than men, to commit all to his patronage and disposal, who neither can perform what he undertakes, and yet for undertaking it, though royally paid, will not be their servant, but their lord? how unmanly must it needs be, to count such a one the breath of our nostrils, to hang all our felicity on him, all our safety, our well-being, for which if we were aught else but sluggards or babies, we need depend on none but God and our own counsels, our own active virtue and industry; *Go to the Ant, thou sluggard, saith Solomon; consider her ways, and be wise; which having no prince, ruler, or lord, provides her meat in the summer, and gathers her food in the harvest.* Which evidently shows us, that they who think the nation undone without a king, though they look grave or haughty, have not so much true spirit and understanding in them as a pismire: neither are these diligent creatures hence concluded to live in lawless anarchy, or that commended, but are set the examples to imprudent and ungoverned men, of a frugal and self-governing democracy or Commonwealth; safer and more thriving in the joint providence and counsel of many industrious equals, than under the single domination of one imperious Lord. It may be well wondered that any Nation styling themselves free, can suffer any man to pretend hereditary right over them as their lord; when as by acknowledging that right, they conclude themselves his servants and his vassals, and so renounce their own freedom. Which how a people and their leaders especially can do, who have fought so gloriously for liberty, how they can change their noble words and actions, heretofore so becoming the majesty of a free people, into the base necessity of court flatteries and prostrations, is not only strange and admirable, but lamentable to think on. That a nation should be so valorous and courageous to win their liberty in the field, and when they have won it, should be so heartless and unwise in their counsels, as not to know how to use it, value it, what to do with it or with themselves; but after ten or twelve years prosperous war and contestation with tyranny, basely and besottedly to run their necks again into the yoke which they have broken, and prostrate all the fruits of their victory for naught at the feet of the vanquished, besides our loss of glory, and such an example as kings or tyrants never yet had the like to boast of, will be an ignominy if it befall us, that never yet befell any nation possessed of their liberty; worthy indeed themselves, whatsoever they be, to be forever slaves: but that part of the nation which consents not with them, as I persuade me of a great number, far worthier than by their means to be brought into the same bondage. Considering these things so plain, so rational, I cannot but yet further admire on the other side, how any man who hath the true principles of justice and religion in him, can presume or take upon him to be a king and lord over his brethren, whom he cannot but know whether as men or Christians, to be for the most part every way equal or superior to himself: how he can display with such vanity and ostentation his regal splendor so supereminently above other mortal men; or being a Christian, can assume such extraordinary honor and worship to himself, while the kingdom of Christ our common King and Lord, is hid to this world, and such *gentilish* imitation forbid in express words by himself to all his disciples. All Protestants hold that Christ in his church hath left no vicegerent of his power, but himself without deputy, is the only head thereof, governing it from heaven: how then can any Christian-man derive his kingship from Christ, but with worse usurpation than the Pope his headship over the church, since Christ not only hath not left the least shadow of a command for any such vicegerence from him in the State, as the Pope pretends for his in the Church, but hath expressly declared, that such regal dominion is from the gentiles, not from him, and hath strictly charged us, not to imitate them therein.

I doubt not but all ingenuous and knowing men will easily agree with me, that a free Commonwealth without single person or house of lords, is by far the best government, if it can be had; but we have all this while say they [have] been expecting it, and cannot yet attain it. 'Tis true indeed, when monarchy was dissolved, the form of a Commonwealth should have forthwith been framed; and the practice thereof immediately begun; that the people might have soon been satisfied and delighted with the decent order, ease and benefit thereof: we had been then by this time firmly rooted past fear of commotions or mutations, & now flourishing: this care of timely settling a new government instead of the old, too much neglected, hath been our mischief. Yet the cause thereof may be ascribed with most reason to the frequent disturbances, interruptions and dissolutions which the Parliament hath had partly from the impatient or disaffected people, partly from some ambitious leaders in the Army; much contrary, I believe, to the mind and approbation of the Army itself and their other Commanders, once undeceived, or in their own power. Now is the opportunity, now the very season wherein we may obtain a free Commonwealth and establish it forever in the land, without difficulty or much delay. Writs are sent out for elections, and which is worth observing in the name, not of any king, but of the keepers of our liberty, to summon a free Parliament: which then only will indeed be free, and deserve the true honor of that supreme title, if they preserve us a free people. Which never Parliament was more free to do; being now called, not as heretofore, by the summons of a king, but by the voice of liberty: and if the people, laying aside prejudice and impatience, will seriously and calmly now consider their own good both religious and civil, their own liberty and the only means thereof, as shall be here laid before them, and will elect their Knights and Burgesses able men, and according to the just and necessary qualifications (which for aught I hear, remain yet in force unrepealed, as they were formerly decreed in Parliament) men not addicted to a single person or house of lords, the work is done; at least the foundation firmly laid of a free Commonwealth, and good part also erected of the main structure. For the ground and basis of every just and free government (since men have smarted so oft for committing all to one person) is a general council of ablest men, chosen by the people to consult of public affairs from time to time for the common good. In this Grand Council must the sovereignty, not transferred, but delegated only, and as it were deposited, reside; with this caution they must have the forces by sea and land committed to them for preservation of the common peace and liberty; must raise and manage the public revenue, at least with some inspectors deputed for satisfaction of the people, how it is employed; must make or propose, as more expressly shall be said anon, civil laws; treat of commerce, peace, or war with foreign nations, and for the carrying on some particular affairs with more secrecy and expedition, must elect, as they have already out of their own number and others, a Council of State.

. . . .

But admit, that monarchy of itself may be convenient to some nations; yet to us who have thrown it out, received back again, it cannot but prove pernicious. For kings to come, never forgetting their former ejection, will be sure to fortify and arm themselves sufficiently for the future against all such attempts hereafter from the people: who shall be then so narrowly watched and kept so low, that though they would never so fain and at the same rate of their blood and treasure, they never shall be able to regain what they now have purchased and may enjoy, or to free themselves from any yoke imposed upon them: nor will they dare to go about it; utterly disheartened for the future, if these their highest attempts prove unsuccessful; which will be the triumph of all tyrants hereafter over any people that shall resist oppression; and their song will then be, to others, how sped the rebellious *English?* to our posterity, how sped the rebels your fathers? This is not my conjecture, but drawn from God's known denouncement against the gentilizing *Israelites;* who though they were governed in a Commonwealth of God's own ordaining, he only their king, they his peculiar people, yet affecting rather to resemble heathen, but pretending the misgovernment of *Samuel's* sons, no more a reason to dislike their Commonwealth, than the violence of *Eli's* sons was imputable to that priesthood or religion, clamored for a king. They had their longing; but with this testimony of God's wrath; *ye shall cry out in that day because of your king whom ye shall have chosen, and the Lord will not hear you in that day.* Us if he shall hear now, how much less will he hear when we cry hereafter, who once delivered by him from a king, and not without wondrous acts of his providence, insensible and unworthy of those high mercies, are returning precipitantly, if he withhold us not, back to the captivity from whence he freed us. Yet neither shall we obtain or buy at an easy rate this new guilded yoke which thus transports us: a new royal-revenue must be found, a new episcopal; for those are individual: both which being wholly dissipated or bought by private persons or assigned for service done, and especially to the Army, cannot be recovered without a general detriment and confusion to mens' estates, or a heavy imposition on all mens' purses; benefit to none, but to the worst and ignoblest sort of men, whose hope is to be either the ministers of court riot and excess, or the gainers by it: But not to speak more of losses and extraordinary levies on our estates, what will then be the revenges and offenses remembered and returned, not only by the chief person, but by all his adherents; accounts and reparations that will be required, suits, indictments, inquiries, discoveries, complaints, informations, who knows against whom or how many, though perhaps neuters, if not to utmost infliction, yet to imprisonment, fines, banishment, or molestation; if not these, yet disfavor, discountenance, disregard and contempt on all but the known royalist or whom he favors, will be plenteous: nor let the new royalized presbyterians persuade themselves that their old doings, though now recanted, will be forgotten; whatever conditions be contrived or trusted on. Will they not believe this; nor remember the pacification, how it was kept to the *Scots;* how other solemn promises many a time to us? Let them but now read the diabolical forerunning libels, the faces, the gestures that now appear foremost and briskest in all public places; as the harbingers of those that are in expectation to reign over us; let them but hear the insolencies, the menaces, the insultings of our newly animated common enemies crept lately out of their holes, their hell, I might say, by the language of their infernal pamphlets, the spue of every drunkard, every ribald; nameless, yet not for want of license, but for very shame of their own vile persons, not daring to name themselves, while they traduce others by name; and give us to foresee that they intend to second their wicked words, if ever they have power, with more wicked deeds. Let our zealous backsliders forethink now with themselves, how their necks yoked with these tigers of Bacchus, these new fanatics of not the preaching but the sweating-tub, inspired with nothing holier than the Venereal pox, can draw one way under monarchy to the establishing of church discipline with these new-disgorged atheisms: yet shall they not have the honor to yoke with these, but shall be yoked under them; these shall plow on their backs. And do they among them who are so forward to bring in the single person, think to be by him trusted or long regarded? So trusted they shall be and so regarded, as by kings are wont reconciled enemies; neglected and soon after discarded, if not prosecuted for old traitors; the first inciters, beginners, and more than to the third part actors of all that followed; it will be found also, that there must be then as necessarily as now (for the contrary part will be still feared) a standing army; which for certain shall not be this, but of the fiercest Cavaliers, of no less expense, and perhaps again under *Rupert*: but let this army be sure they shall be soon disbanded, and likeliest without arrear or pay; and being disbanded, not be sure but they may as soon be questioned for being in arms against their king: the same let them fear, who have contributed money; which will amount to no small number that must then take their turn to be made delinquents and compounders. They who past reason and recovery are devoted to kingship, perhaps will answer, that a greater part by far of the Nation will have it so; the rest therefore must yield. Not so much to convince these, which I little hope, as to confirm them who yield not, I reply; that this greatest part have both in reason and the trial of just battle, lost the right of their election what the government shall be: of them who have not lost that right, whether they for kingship be the greater number, who can certainly determine? Suppose they be; yet of freedom they partake all alike, one main end of government: which if the greater part value not, but will degenerately forego, is it just or reasonable, that most voices against the main end of government should enslave the less number that would be free? More just it is doubtless, if it come to force, that a less number compel a greater to retain, which can be no wrong to them, their liberty, than that a greater number for the pleasure of their baseness, compel a less most injuriously to be their fellow slaves. They who seek nothing but their own just liberty, have always right to win it and to keep it, whenever they have power, be the voices never so numerous that oppose it. And how much we above others are concerned to defend it from kingship, and from them who in pursuance thereof so perniciously would betray us and themselves to most certain misery and thralldom, will be needless to repeat.

Having thus far shown with what ease we may now obtain a free Commonwealth, and by it with as much ease all the freedom, peace, justice, plenty that we can desire, on the other side the difficulties, troubles, uncertainties, nay rather impossibilities to enjoy these things constantly under a monarch, I will now proceed to show more particularly wherein our freedom and flourishing condition will be more ample and secure to us under a free Commonwealth than under kingship.

The whole freedom of man consists either in spiritual or civil liberty. As for spiritual, who can be at rest, who can enjoy anything in this world with contentment, who hath not liberty to serve God and to save his own soul, according to the best light which God hath planted in him to that purpose, by the reading of his revealed will and the guidance of his holy spirit? That this is best pleasing to God, and that the whole Protestant Church allows no supreme judge or rule in matters of religion, but the scriptures, and these to be interpreted by the scriptures themselves, which necessarily infers liberty of conscience, I have heretofore proved at large in another treatise, and might yet further by the public declarations, confessions and admonitions of whole churches and states, obvious in all history since the Reformation.

This liberty of conscience which above all other things ought to be to all men dearest and most precious, no government more inclinable not to favor only but to protect, than a free Commonwealth; as being most magnanimous, most fearless and confident of its own fair proceedings. Whereas kingship, though looking big, yet indeed most pusillanimous, full of fears, full of jealousies, startled at every umbrage, as it hath been observed of old to have ever suspected most and mistrusted them who were in most esteem for virtue and generosity of mind, so it is now known to have most in doubt and suspicion them who are most reputed to

be religious. Queen *Elizabeth* though herself accounted so
good a Protestant, so moderate, so confident of her Subjects'
love would never give way so much as to Presbyterian reformation in this land, though once and again besought, as
Camden relates, but imprisoned and persecuted the very
proposers thereof; alleging it as her mind & maxim unalterable, that such reformation would diminish regal authority.
What liberty of conscience can we then expect of others, far
worse principled from the cradle, trained up and governed
by *Popish* and *Spanish* counsels, and on such depending
hitherto for subsistence? Especially what can this last Parliament expect, who having revived lately and published the
covenant, have re-engaged themselves, never to readmit
Episcopacy: which no son of *Charles* returning, but will
most certainly bring back with him, if he regard the last and
strictest charge of his father, *to persevere in not the doctrine
only, but government of the church of* England; *not to neglect the speedy and effectual suppressing of errors and
schisms*; among which he accounted Presbytery one of the
chief: or if notwithstanding that charge of his father, he
submit to the covenant, how will he keep faith to us with
disobedience to him; or regard that faith given, which must
be founded on the breach of that last and solemnest paternal
charge, and the reluctance, I may say the antipathy which is
in all kings against Presbyterian and Independent discipline?
for they hear the gospel speaking much of liberty; a word
which monarchy and her bishops both fear and hate, but a
free Commonwealth both favors and promotes; and not the
word only, but the thing itself. But let our governors beware
in time, lest their hard measure to liberty of conscience be
found the rock whereon they shipwreck themselves as others
have now done before them in the course wherein God was
directing their steerage to a free Commonwealth, and the
abandoning of all those whom they call *sectaries*, for the
detected falsehood and ambition of some, be a willful rejection of their own chief strength and interest in the freedom of all Protestant religion, under what abusive name
soever calumniated.

The other part of our freedom consists in the civil rights
and advancements of every person according to his merit:

the enjoyment of those never more certain, and the access
to these never more open, than in a free Commonwealth.
Both which in my opinion may be best and soonest obtained,
if every county in the land were made a kind of subordinate
Commonalty or Commonwealth, and one chief town or
more, according as the shire is in circuit, made cities, if they
be not so called already; where the nobility and chief gentry
from a proportionable compass of territory annexed to each
city, may build, houses or palaces, befitting their quality,
may bear part in the government, make their own judicial
laws, or use those that are, and execute them by their own
elected judicatures and judges without appeal, in all things
of civil government between man and man. So they shall
have justice in their own hands, law executed fully and finally
in their own counties and precincts, long wished, and spoken
of, but never yet obtained; they shall have none then to
blame but themselves, if it be not well administered; and
fewer laws to expect or fear from the supreme authority; or
to those that shall be made, of any great concernment to
public liberty, they may without much trouble in these commonalties or in more general assemblies called to their cities
from the whole territory on such occasion, declare and publish their assent or dissent by deputies within a time limited
sent to the Grand Council: yet so as this their judgment declared shall submit to the greater number of other counties
or commonalties, and not avail them to any exemption of
themselves, or refusal of agreement with the rest, as it may
in any of the United Provinces, being sovereign within itself, ofttimes to the great disadvantage of that union. In
these employments they may much better than they do now,
exercise and fit themselves, till their lot fall to be chosen
into the Grand Council, according as their worth and merit
shall be taken notice of by the people. As for controversies
that shall happen between men of several counties, they
may repair, as they do now, to the capital city, or any other
more commodious, indifferent place and equal judges. And
this I find to have been practiced in the old *Athenian* Commonwealth, reputed the first and ancientest place of civility
in all *Greece*; that they had in their several cities, a peculiar;
in *Athens*, a common government; and their right, as it be-

fell them, to the administration of both. They should have here also schools and academies at their own choice, wherein their children may be bred up in their own sight to all learning and noble education not in grammar only, but in all liberal arts and exercises. This would soon spread much more knowledge and civility, yea religion through all parts of the land, by communicating the natural heat of government and culture more distributively to all extreme parts, which now lie numb and neglected, would soon make the whole nation more industrious, more ingenuous at home, more potent, more honorable abroad. To this a free Commonwealth will easily assent; (nay the Parliament hath had already some such thing in design) for of all governments a Commonwealth aims most to make the people flourishing, virtuous, noble and high spirited. Monarchs will never permit: whose aim is to make the people, wealthy indeed perhaps and well fleeced, for their own shearing and the supply of regal prodigality; but otherwise softest, basest, vitiousest, servilest, easiest to be kept under; and not only in fleece, but in mind also sheepishest; and will have all the benches of judicature annexed to the throne, as a gift of royal grace that we have justice done us; whenas nothing can be more essential to the freedom of a people, than to have the administration of justice and all public ornaments in their own election and within their own bounds, without long traveling or depending on remote places to obtain their right or any civil accomplishment; so it be not supreme, but subordinate to the general power and union of the whole Republic. In which happy firmness as in the particular above mentioned, we shall also far exceed the United Provinces, by having, not as they (to the retarding and distracting ofttimes of their counsels or urgentest occasions) many Sovereignties united in one Commonwealth, but many Commonwealths under one united and entrusted Sovereignty. And when we have our forces by sea and land, either of a faithful Army or a settled Militia, in our own hands to the firm establishing of a free Commonwealth, public accounts under our own inspection, general laws and taxes with their causes in our own domestic suffrages, judicial laws, offices and ornaments at home in our own ordering and administration, all distinction of lords and commoners, that may any way divide or sever the public interest, removed, what can a perpetual senate have then wherein to grow corrupt, wherein to encroach upon us or usurp; or if they do, wherein to be formidable? Yet if all this avail not to remove the fear or envy of a perpetual sitting, it may be easily provided, to change a third part of them yearly or every two or three years, as was above mentioned; or that it be at those times in the people's choice, whether they will change them, or renew their power, as they shall find cause.

I have no more to say at present: few words will save us, well considered; few and easy things, now seasonably done. But if the people be so affected, as to prostitute religion and liberty to the vain and groundless apprehension, that nothing but kingship can restore trade, not remembering the frequent plagues and pestilences that then wasted this city, such as through God's mercy we never have felt since, and that trade flourishes no where more than in the free Commonwealths of *Italy, Germany,* and the Low Countries before their eyes at this day, yet if trade be grown so craving and importunate through the profuse living of tradesmen, that nothing can support it, but the luxurious expenses of a nation upon trifles or superfluities, so as if the people generally should betake themselves to frugality, it might prove a dangerous matter, lest tradesmen should mutiny for want of trading, and that therefore we must forgo & set to sale religion, liberty, honor, safety, all concernments Divine or human to keep up trading, if lastly, after all this light among us, the same reason shall pass for current to put our necks again under kingship, as was made use of by the *Jews* to return back to *Egypt* and to the worship of their idol queen, because they falsely imagined that they then lived in more plenty and prosperity, our condition is not sound but rotten, both in religion and all civil prudence; and will bring us soon, the way we are marching, to those calamities which attend always and unavoidably on luxury, all national judgments under foreign or domestic slavery: so far we shall be from mending our condition by monarchizing our government, whatever new conceit now possesses us. However with all hazard I have ventured what I thought my duty to speak in season, and to forewarn my country in time: wherein I doubt not but there be many wise men in all places and degrees, but am sorry the effects of wisdom are so little seen among us. Many circumstances and particulars I could have added in those things whereof I have spoken; but a few main matters now put speedily in execution, will suffice to recover us, and set all right: and there will want at no time who are good at circumstances; but men who set their minds on main matters and sufficiently urge them, in these most difficult times I find not many. What I have spoken, is the language of that which is not called amiss *the good Old Cause*: if it seem strange to any, it will not seem more strange, I hope, than convincing to backsliders. Thus much I should perhaps have said though I were sure I should have spoken only to trees and stones; and had none to cry to, but with the Prophet, *O earth, earth, earth!* to tell the very soil itself, what her perverse inhabitants are deaf to. Nay though what I have spoke, should happen (which Thou suffer not, who didst create mankind free; nor Thou next, who didst redeem us from being servants of men!) to be the last words of our expiring liberty. But I trust I shall have spoken persuasion to abundance of sensible and ingenuous men: to some perhaps whom God may raise of these stones to become children of reviving liberty; and may reclaim, though they seem now choosing them a captain back for *Egypt*, to bethink themselves a little and consider whether they are rushing; to exhort this torrent also of the people, not to be so impetuous, but to keep their due channel; and at length recovering and uniting their better resolutions, now that they see already how open and unbounded the insolence and rage is of our common enemies, to stay these ruinous proceedings; justly and timely fearing to what a precipice of destruction the deluge of this epidemic madness would hurry us through the general defection of a misguided and abused multitude.

APPENDIX I
BRIEF BIOGRAPHIES

COKE, SIR EDWARD (1552–1634)

Coke was the most famous and influential figure in English legal history. His *Reports* and his *Institutes of the Laws of England* became the textbooks for judges and lawyers for generations after his death. Into the struggle for power between the crown and parliament, Coke introduced the principle of the supremacy of the common law of England—and the law was what the judges said it was.

During his long life he reached the top in all three arenas of government. He was speaker of the House of Commons in 1593 and then attorney-general in 1594. As the chief legal officer of the crown, he was a forceful prosecutor and upholder of the prerogative. In 1606 James I made him chief justice of common pleas. From the supporter of prerogative he now became the great spokesman for and champion of the common law. James I and his theories of divine right monarchy were frequently to clash with the contrary opinions of Coke. The king hoped to side-step Coke by promoting him to the chief justiceship of King's Bench, thinking that its more restricted criminal jurisdiction would give him less opportunity to tilt at the prerogative. This, however, was not to be. Coke continued his struggle and was finally removed from office.

In later years he served again in parliament under Charles I and championed its cause against the crown. In 1628 he was one of the principal architects of the Petition of Right.

Coke's familiarity with the law and its precedents was vast, but his great knowledge was not unmixed with fiction. It was not possible completely to separate the law from the constitution, and in his interpretations of the latter he often, unknowingly, misread history to serve the cause of the opposition. His adherence to the principle of the law's supremacy over crown and parliament has had a much greater influence in America than in England. For it was in the United States that the principle of a "fundamental" law was enshrined in the constitution. In England it was the sovereignty of parliament that was to triumph.

CROMWELL, OLIVER (1599–1658)

Cromwell was a landowner with moderate holdings in Huntingdon and a justice of the peace during the years of Charles I's personal rule. In the latter role he showed great concern for the problems of the poor under his jurisdiction. He also exhibited a keen interest in Puritanism and actively supported the Puritans' rights to teach and preach. He first entered parliament in 1628–the year of the Petition of Right –but played no active role. In 1638 he claimed a "religious experience" when he was "being given to see the light."

He was sent to the Long Parliament for Cambridge (town) and became a supporter of John Pym. When civil war broke out in 1642 he became a captain of horse and quickly rose to the rank of lieutenant-general of horse in the New Model Army. His military and political prowess were rewarded when parliament voted to defer holding him to the Self-Denying Ordinance. By the end of the first civil war (1646) Cromwell was the effective leader of the New Model, militarily and politically, although nominally he was under the command of General Fairfax. In addition to his difficulties in negotiating a settlement with the defeated Charles, there were the increasingly bitter splits in the parliamentary ranks. Cromwell came to be the champion of the Independents against the increasingly pro-Royalist Presbyterians.

When the Scots openly supported the king in the second civil war (1647–48), Cromwell broke completely with the Presbyterians and with the previous policy of affecting a compromise with the king. Both these actions strengthened his hold on the men in the army ranks, as well as on the officers. In quick succession came Pride's Purge (barring the Presbyterians from the House of Commons) and the trial and execution of the king.

The death of the king ushered in new opportunities and problems for Cromwell, for he was now without question the most powerful man in England. Until his death he sought to achieve an England based on parliamentary government and independent religious congregations. However, in his attempt to work with the Rump of the Long Parliament he found himself becoming increasingly alienated both from the parliament and the Levellers and sects on his left. During the four years that remained of the Rump's life, he conquered Scotland, Ireland (wreaking a terrible vengeance, not yet forgotten) and eliminated the Levellers as a contender for power. In April 1653 he forcibly dissolved the Rump and never again let the reins of power slip from his firm grasp. Assuming the lord protectorship under the Instrument of Government (and later under the Humble Petition and Advice), he was consciously moving ever closer to the restoration of a monarchical system of government. In these years he was to find his parliaments as difficult to work with as any of his royal predecessors had.

Oliver Cromwell was without doubt the ablest ruler England had in the seventeenth century. In foreign affairs he championed England's economic interests against the Dutch and the interests of Protestantism against continental Catholicism. England's voice in international circles was more respected than at any time since the death of Elizabeth I. In domestic affairs he failed to achieve his goals, but the fault was not his alone. He sought to further the centralization of government that had started under the Tudors. By uniting Ireland and Scotland into the Commonwealth of England he presaged the creation of the United Kingdom in 1801. The Protectorate parliaments were elected with a wider franchise and with the constituencies more equally distributed than at any time prior to the nineteenth-century reform bills. In religion he was certainly one of the few men of his age who sincerely believed in liberty of conscience. Yet his Independent, or Congregational system was not acceptable to the majority, who continued to favor episcopacy. As really free elections would undoubtedly have returned the Royalists to power, so complete religious freedom might have restored Anglicanism.

It is easy to see Cromwell as a hypocrite; yet he was no more so than most men. He sought religious freedom, free elections, and parliamentary government in an England that was not ready for any of these things. Rather than logically pursue these goals and see the revolution destroyed, he used his great power to create a Protectorate through which, in time, a true commonwealth might be created. He constantly had to battle the commonwealthsmen on his left and the "men of substance" on his right. In the end he could trust no one and nothing but himself and the swords of his soldiers. Before his death the old monarchy had been largely restored in all but name.

CROMWELL, RICHARD (1626–1712)

Richard was Oliver Cromwell's oldest surviving son and was designated his successor as lord protector. Unlike his younger brother Henry, Richard had shown little interest in anything but a life of pleasure. He held no important posts prior to his appointment to the chancellorship of Oxford University and to the Council of State the year before his father's death. As he was not a soldier, the officers refused to accept him as their leader, and thus his power as lord protector was quickly undermined. Heavily in debt, he secured the permission of parliament and the army to resign and fled to France in 1660.

ELIOT, SIR JOHN (1592–1632)

Sir John Eliot was the outstanding supporter of the privileges of parliament in the seventeenth century prior to the Long Parliament. Once a friend of the Duke of Buckingham, he led the attack on him in the parliament of 1626. This resulted in Eliot's being sent to the Tower, only to be released when Commons claimed that his imprisonment was a violation of their privileges. In 1627 he was one of the knights imprisoned for refusing to subscribe to a "forced" loan. The following year he actively assisted in the passage of the Petition of Right. Perhaps his greatest moment was in 1629. Charles I ordered an adjournment of parliament, to which Eliot and others objected. The speaker was forcefully restrained from vacating his seat while Eliot urged the House to accept several resolutions aimed at the king and the pope. For his participation in this extraordinary scene he was convicted in King's Bench and sent to the Tower, to remain there until he repented. He died in the Tower three years later.

FAIRFAX, THOMAS, LORD (1612–71)

Fairfax was a landowner and soldier in Yorkshire who joined the parliamentary forces at the beginning of the war. His brilliant feats as a cavalry officer, coupled with his rank as an heir to a barony, led to his appointment as commander-in-chief of the New Model Army in 1645. Always more at home on the battlefield than at the conference table, he took little part in the negotiations with the king at the end of the first civil war, although he did support those who wanted a settlement with Charles. With the end of the first war his influence declined, although he struggled to maintain discipline in the army on one hand and to get parliament to pay the soldiers' wages on the other. During the second civil war he was reluctant to fight the Scots and quickly found Cromwell assuming command of the army in all but name.

Pride's Purge took him by surprise, but he did indicate his approval of the trial and deposition of the king and was named as one of the judges on the High Court of Justice. He then refused to take part in the trial and Lady Fairfax loudly protested from the gallery when his name was read from the list of judges at the opening session. During the trial he remained available to Cromwell and his faction and also to the Dutch ambassadors and others who pleaded with him to save the king. Fairfax's role during these days shows him to have been either a coward or a political incompetent, or both. He would do nothing to stop the trial and execution, nor would he take responsibility for it.

In the following year he refused to sign the Engagement and to take part in the war with Scotland. After announcing his general support for the Rump, he resigned his post as commander-in-chief and went into retirement. Until Cromwell's death he emerged into public life only once—to serve as a member of the first parliament of the Protectorate. During the last days of Richard Cromwell's rule he once again came out of retirement and urged General Monck to support both a restoration and the calling of a free parliament. The Convention Parliament sent him to The Hague to negotiate with Charles II. On this occasion he proved to be successful, but he was never to receive any reward for his efforts. On the other hand, he was not to be punished for his brilliant leadership during the first civil war.

Fairfax's Royalist sympathies had been suspected as early as 1648 and there were rumors to that effect all during the Commonwealth and Protectorate. In fact, he was just one of many moderates who knew how to win the war but not what to do with victory once it was in his grasp.

IRETON, HENRY (1611–51)

Ireton was one of the most politically minded officers in the parliamentary army. He began his military service as a captain of the horse in the town of Nottingham. By 1646 he was commissary-general of the horse and had become close personally and professionally to Cromwell. As the first civil war drew to a close, he entered into negotiations with the king, thereby winning a reprimand from his friend Cromwell for mixing politics with soldiering. He entered parliament in a by-election in 1645, but took no active role, preferring to immerse himself in army politics. In fact, he became an ardent supporter of the soldiers' grievances against parliament.

In 1647 he played a key role in drawing up "The Heads of the Proposals." His goal during the next two years (1647–48) seems to have been the firm establishment of a mixed government—king, lords, and Commons, and throughout, he seems to have been more concerned with getting the king's support for his scheme than that of parliament. His marriage to Cromwell's daughter Bridget cemented his already close ties with Cromwell and guaranteed him a certain freedom of maneuver.

In late 1648 he helped prepare the second "Agreement of the People" but only succeeded in alienating both the Levellers and parliament. He accompanied his father-in-law to Ireland in 1649 and died there two years later.

LAUD, WILLIAM (1573–1645)

Laud was bishop of St. David's (Wales) at the time of

Charles's accession, and his rise to even greater power was swift and sure; Charles made him bishop of Bath and Wells in 1626, bishop of London in 1628, chancellor of Oxford University in 1629, and archbishop of Canterbury in 1633. Not only was he the king's chief ecclesiastical adviser; he also exercised a great influence in secular affairs, even serving for a year as a lord commissioner of the treasury (while archbishop).

Put simply, Laud's policies were three: (1) the rigid enforcement of the Book of Common Prayer and the Thirty-Nine Articles upon all the clergy, without exception; (2) the restoration of the recently lost church properties and the impropriated tithes that laymen had acquired, together with the reintroduction of the clergy into secular government; (3) the need for obedience—active and passive—to the king by all his subjects, lay and clerical. He used every organ of power at his command—Court of High Commission, Star Chamber, Court of Canterbury—to enforce the ritual and teachings of the church. He was single-minded in his opposition to anything that smacked of Puritanism, or challenged his or the king's authority. While not particularly interested in theology as such, he was associated in the public mind with the Dutch theologian Arminius. Laud's authoritarian practices and his enforcement of a Catholic-like ritual quite naturally led his opponents to accuse him of leading England back to Rome. There was, however, no truth to this charge—belief in the royal supremacy was one of his cardinal principles, after all.

Laud contributed, perhaps more than any other man, to the emergence of the opposition that controlled the Long Parliament in its first months. If anti-Laudianism equaled Puritanism, then the majority of the nation had become Puritan. His efforts to enforce the Prayer Book in Scotland led to the ruin of all that Charles and Laud had stood for.

In 1640 he was placed in the Tower and was executed in 1645. He and the Earl of Strafford were the principal enemies upon whom the Long Parliament wreaked vengeance.

LENTHALL, WILLIAM (1591–1662)

Lenthall was speaker of the House of Commons in the Long Parliament and of the first Parliament of the Protectorate (1654). While officially a supporter of parliament, the Commonwealth, and the Protectorate, he was probably a Royalist at heart, and in any case was a self-confessed coward. Since all his lands were in Royalist hands during the civil war, parliament granted him money to meet his expenses. In 1643 he was made Master of the Rolls, an office he held until 1660, and from 1646 to 1648 he served as one of the Commissioners of the Great Seal. He (reluctantly) supported the trial and execution of Charles I, but in 1660 he supported General Monck's efforts to restore the Stuarts. His greatest moment came in 1642 when Charles I went to the House to arrest the five members. Lenthall won the approval of the Commons by this statement to the king; "May it please Your Majesty, I have neither eyes to see nor tongue to speak in this place but as the House is pleased to direct me whose servant I am here; and humbly beg Your Majesty's pardon that I cannot give any other answer than this to what Your Majesty is pleased to demand of me."

LILBURNE, JOHN (1614–57)

"Free-born John" was the most famous agitator and pamphleteer of the Puritan Revolution. As a young man he printed attacks on the church and the lords, for which he was whipped and imprisoned. Released by parliament in 1641, he took a commission in the parliamentary army. For the next decade a torrent of words issued from his pen. Although he was an ardent Puritan and Calvinist, his great interest was in social and constitutional reform. With Walwyn and Overton he was a leader of the Leveller party, which some historians regard as the first political party in the modern organizational sense.

Lilburne was nothing if not a true believer. The passion and zeal with which he defended liberty and attacked the corruptions of society won him a large following among the common soldiers and the artisan class of London. He was personally fearless; indeed, he seemed to court martyrdom. His lack of a sense of humor, common sense, and a willingness to compromise led to his own and the Levellers' ruin once they began to attack Cromwell in 1648. Subsequently Lilburne spent much of his time in prison and after 1649 he and the movement lost importance. Before his death he became a Quaker.

Lilburne's failure, however, was as much the fault of his program as of his personality and character. The dominant forces in parliament and in the nation sought an England where the common law and the rights of subjects and of property would be secure from tyranny. Lilburne condemned the whole legal system that had evolved since the Conquest, likening it to a yoke that the Normans had forced upon the shoulders of the innocent Saxon. Not many Englishmen consciously wished to see the destruction of that law upon which all their rights and properties depended. By way of rebuttal the Levellers were accused of wanting to level all men's estates. This was actually not true; Lilburne believed in social and political, but not economic, equality.

It was John Lilburne and his Levellers who provided the real possibility of social revolution during this era. They were also a principal reason why the rest of society turned back from the precipice with horror.

LUDLOW, EDMUND (1617?–92)

An officer in the parliamentary army, Ludlow entered the Long Parliament in a by-election in 1646. He supported Pride's Purge in 1648 and was one of the judges at the king's trial. From 1650 to 1655 he was largely concerned with Irish affairs. He then lived in retirement until the recall of the Long Parliament in 1659.

Ludlow was a convinced republican and opposed Cromwell's assumption of the lord protectorship. His *Memoirs* provide us with one of the more useful accounts of the Puritan Revolution and are especially useful in chronicling the commonwealthmen's opposition to Cromwell during the years of the Protectorate.

MONCK, GEORGE, later DUKE OF ALBEMARLE (1608–70)

Monck was a professional soldier who fought for the king in the Irish rebellion in 1642 and subsequently against parliament. Having been captured and put in the Tower, he switched his allegiance and returned to Ireland in 1647 as the leader of the parliamentary forces. In 1649 the Commons reprimanded him for signing an unfavorable truce with the

Irish enemy. Following this, he was sent to Scotland, where he served well and loyally, becoming commander-in-chief there.

When Richard Cromwell resigned the protectorship, Monck worked for a Stuart restoration. He had a fine army, received the co-operation of Fairfax, who was in retirement, and met no opposition on his way to London. Upon his arrival there, he ordered the recently reassembled Rump to recall all those excluded in Pride's Purge eleven years before. The peaceful return of Charles II was now inevitable. Monck was rewarded with the title of Duke of Albemarle, the last Englishman to go from commoner to duke in one step.

OVERTON, RICHARD (dates unknown)

Overton first came into prominence as a pamphleteer against the bishops in the 1630s. In 1643 he was attacked in the House of Commons for publishing a treatise stating that the body and soul were one mortal substance. He joined Lilburne in publishing tracts and in the prison sentences that followed. He refused to sign the Engagement and went into opposition to the Commonwealth. In 1654 he offered to spy on the Royalists and the following year he was implicated in a Leveller rising. After this he fled to Flanders and obtained a commission from Charles II. Now a Royalist, he returned to England and attempted to foment insurrections, being frequently jailed for his efforts. After the Restoration he seems to have continued his habit of being in and out of jail. He then disappeared from history.

PARKER, HENRY (1604–52)

Henry Parker's principal claim to fame rests upon his speech in the early days of the Long Parliament in which he issued the first clear call for parliamentary sovereignty. He was never again to be in the center of affairs.

After receiving his B. A. and M. A. degrees from Oxford, he was called to the Bar from Lincoln's Inn in 1637. At the beginning of the Long Parliament he was a Presbyterian but soon became identified with the Independents. In 1642 he was appointed secretary to the Earl of Essex, the commander of the parliamentary army. In 1645 he became secretary to the House of Commons and in 1646 he took the post of secretary to the Merchant Adventurers in Hamburg. Parker remained at his post in Hamburg until after the execution of the king and then took up his appointment as secretary to the army in Ireland, where he died in 1652.

Parker was a prolific writer on both political and religious topics, but his views on parliamentary sovereignty constitute his most important contribution to the literature of the Puritan Revolution.

PRYNNE, WILLIAM (1600–69)

Lawyer, Puritan, and inveterate writer of books and pamphlets, William Prynne spent most of his life in opposition to the powers-that-be. His book *Histrio-Mastix* (1633), an attack on the theater, music, etc., was regarded as an attack on the king and his court. Consequently he was committed to the Tower of London, fined £5,000, and had his ears clipped. While in the Tower he wrote "News from Ipswich," attacking Laud. Again he was fined and what remained of his ears was cut off. Finally, the Long Parliament restored him to freedom and fortune.

As a Presbyterian and a bitter opponent of royal and clerical tyranny he supported the Parliamentary cause. In 1648, however, he opposed Cromwell's efforts to bring the king to trial and was removed from his seat in the Commons. From that point on he became as bitter an opponent of Cromwell as he had earlier been of Charles I and Laud, and in fact seemed to look upon the old days with a certain nostalgia, even though his treatment upon the two occasions he was imprisoned by Cromwell was less harsh than that meted out by the Star Chamber. After the Restoration he became keeper of the records in the Tower.

For a man who wrote so much, he never developed a good style. His flair for the rhetorical was better geared to the platform than the printed page.

PYM, JOHN (1583?–1643)

Pym was one of the few men of the early seventeenth century who could be called a professional member of parliament. He first entered the Commons in 1614 and sat in every subsequent parliament until his death. Beginning with his support of the impeachment of the Duke of Buckingham in

1626, he was one of the members actively engaged in institutionalizing parliamentary opposition to the royal prerogative and to Laudian Anglicanism.

Until his death he was unquestionably the most important figure in the Long Parliament. With his concerted attacks on Strafford, Laud, and the prerogative courts, he immediately placed the crown on the defensive and himself in the position of leadership in the Commons. Deeply suspicious of the king's motives, Pym refused to compromise with Charles even after his original program had been enacted. To undermine the position of the radicals to his left, and that of the king, he kept up the pressure on Charles and pushed through "The Grand Remonstrance." In the event, however, this document created strong support for the king.

Pym refused to concede to the king any control over the military forces needed to crush the Irish rebellion. The king's attempt to capture the Five Members (of whom Pym was one) and his refusal to accept the Militia Bill precipitated civil war. Pym then helped to mold the Parliamentary alliance with Scotland, culminating in the adoption of "The Solemn League and Covenant." J. H. Hexter has aptly called the early years of the Long Parliament "the reign of King Pym."

VANE, SIR HENRY, the Elder (1589–1655)

The Vanes, father and son, were among the most controversial figures of the Puritan Revolution. The father early became a favorite at the court of James I and retained this position in the reign of his son Charles I. In 1630 he was appointed to the Privy Council and early in 1640 he was also made secretary of state. It was largely on his testimony that the Earl of Strafford was charged with treason. Vane insisted that he had heard Strafford suggest the use of force to reduce "this kingdom." In spite of having played a key role in the destruction of the king's favorite, Vane sought to retain his position at court. Charles I delayed his retribution for a year and then dismissed Vane from all of his offices. Vane now retaliated by joining the forces of John Pym, being rewarded in 1642 with the appointment of the lord lieutenancy of the county of Durham. Since Durham was quickly seized by the

Royalists, some in parliament accused him of treachery. Pym supported him and appointed him to the Committee of Both Kingdoms in 1644. In 1645 he was one of the Parliamentary representatives to the Scottish army.

From this point on he ceased to play a vital role and gradually lost the confidence of the parliament. In 1649 he sought a place on the new Council of State (the successor to the Privy Council) but parliament rejected the appointment. He died in 1655 amid Royalist rumors that he had committed suicide.

VANE, SIR HENRY, the Younger (1613–62)

The younger Vane ended his career with the reputation of being one of the most consistent supporters of the Commonwealth, but from 1640 to 1660 his actions and, even more important, his motives were constantly under a cloud of suspicion. He was considered tricky and self-seeking.

Young Henry had an entrée at court through his father and was generally favorably regarded, but he was known to harbor anti-episcopal views. In 1635 he emigrated to Boston and quickly immersed himself in colonial politics. From 1636 to 1637 he served as governor of the colony and was continually embroiled in controversy over both Indian and ecclesiastical affairs.

In 1639 he returned to England and became a joint treasurer of the navy, thus being required to handle the controversial Ship Money. By the time the Long Parliament convened he was still acceptable at court, although his Puritan views were never a secret. While going through his father's papers, with the latter's permission, he found the notes of Strafford's remarks to the Privy Council. While reading the notes John Pym entered his room and Vane showed him the papers. It was thus the son who first revealed the evidence damning Strafford.

Vane sat in both the Short and Long Parliaments for Hull and consistently supported Cromwell and Oliver St. John in their opposition to episcopacy. Finally in 1641 the king removed him from all of his offices. His reputation for trickery began when he served as one of the negotiators for The Solemn League and Covenant. Even though openly in favor of

Presbyterianism, he was in fact an Independent. He secured the inclusion in the treaty of a phrase that would later give the Independents a chance to back out of the commitment to support the establishment of Presbyterianism in England.

Upon the death of John Pym Vane became a leader of the War Party, but became increasingly distrusted by the Presbyterians and later the Levellers. In 1648 he supported negotiations with the king and after Pride's Purge he voluntarily absented himself from the House of Commons. He took no part in the trial of the king nor in the abolition of monarchy, but was appointed without opposition to the Council of State in 1649. Upon taking up this new appointment he refused to swear his support of the execution of the king and the abolition of monarchy, as required, but instead swore to uphold the new government. With the dissolution of the Long Parliament in 1653 he retired to the country and became increasingly critical of Cromwell, both politically and religiously. From this point on he consistently supported the supremacy of a free parliament, and a free Independent church, not the state imposed Independency supported by Cromwell.

After Cromwell's death and the recall of the Long Parliament he was accused of intriguing with General Lambert in the hope of coming to power to save the Commonwealth. From this point on no one trusted him. He was one of the few men whom the Convention Parliament denied a pardon at the Restoration and he was executed on Tower Hill, June 14, 1662. His opposition to Cromwell and to the Restoration earned him his reputation as an uncompromising Commonwealthsman.

WALWYN, WILLIAM (1600?– ?)
Little is known of William Walwyn before or after the years of the Levellers' prominence. He was a stanch supporter of the freedom and dignity of the individual conscience and worked closely with Lilburne. He participated in the meetings when the second "Agreement of the People" was being drawn up and joined with Lilburne in attacking both its final draft and Cromwell. He spent most of 1649 in

the Tower, and, except for one pamphlet in 1651, disappeared from history after his release.

WENTWORTH, THOMAS, Earl of Strafford (1593–1641)

Strafford, together with Laud, was the principal promoter of the policy of "Thorough." In the parliament of 1628 he was a strong supporter of the Petition of Right. Shortly after its passage, the king created him a baron and then a viscount and privy councillor. From an opponent of prerogative he became one of its most ardent supporters. His work as president of the Council of the North and later in Ireland won the enthusiastic support of Charles and Laud, but created a great fear and opposition to him in England.

One of the first acts of the Long Parliament was Strafford's impeachment. He was accused, by Sir Henry Vane, of suggesting to the king that his army in Ireland could be used to reduce "this kingdom" (England). Since impeachment is a charge in law, it was necessary for the Commons to prove its accusations of treason before the Lords, its case being legally weak, Commons resorted to a bill of attainder, which carried both houses. While it was true that Strafford's policies were destructive of the "fundamental laws" of England, yet it was also true that he was not in law a traitor. His real crimes were political, and so it was necessary to resort to a political device—the attainder—to bring him low. (The term "fundamental law" was frequently referred to, but its meaning was vague. To Pym and his followers in parliament it at least meant a "mixed" monarchy or a sharing of power by king and parliament, and the "rights of Englishmen" guaranteed by the common law. Even if it was difficult to prove that Strafford had violated the law, there was no doubt that he wholeheartedly supported the royal prerogative at the expense of any meaningful role for parliament. Thus he had violated the "fundamental" laws, if not the particular laws, of England.)

Strafford absolved the king from his promise to protect him, and so Charles signed the bill, but the king's acquiescence in Strafford's death did not appease the Commons. Rather it was taken as a sign of weakness, and the refusal to save his friend was as politically disastrous for the king as his earlier support of him had been.

WILSON, SIR THOMAS (1560–1629)

Wilson was keeper of the records at Whitehall and an inveterate traveler. While on trips to the continent, he gathered intelligence for Sir Robert Cecil and the Privy Council. In addition to *The State of England*, he probably wrote the *Book on the State of Ireland*, and he translated, from the Spanish, on which was based *Two Gentlemen of Verona*.

WINSTANLEY, GERRARD (1609?–60?)

Of Gerrard Winstanley, little is known beyond his authorship of several tracts. He first came to public notice when, with William Everard and others, he began to cultivate the common waste land on St. George's Hill, Walton-on-Thames, Surrey. When the parliamentary authorities removed him and his "Diggers," Winstanley and Everard countered with the publication of the *True Levellers' Standard*. This led to Everard's imprisonment and the fining of Winstanley and the others.

Even in comparison with Lilburne and the Levellers, Winstanley and Everard were beyond the bounds of seventeenth-century thought and society. They preached a true rural communism—no land-lords, no lawyers, no manors, no tithes to support the clergy, no money in circulation. Religiously, Winstanley seems to have been the first English Universalist, and some thought that he was in fact the real founder of the Quakers.

APPENDIX II
SUGGESTED READINGS

NARRATIVE HISTORIES

Clarendon, Earl of, *History of the Rebellion,* 6 vols., 1888.
Davies, Godfrey, *The Early Stuarts, 1603–1660,* 1959.
Firth, C. H., *The Last Years of the Protectorate, 1656–58,* 2 vols., 1909.
Gardiner, Samuel Rawson, *History of the Commonwealth and Protectorate,* 4 vols., 1893.
——, *History of the Great Civil War, 1642–49,* 4 vols., 1893.
Wedgwood, C. V., *The King's Peace, 1637–1641,* 1956.
——, *The King's War, 1641–1647,* 1959.

CHAPTER I: ENGLAND ON THE EVE OF THE CIVIL WAR

Barnes, T. G., *Somerset, 1625–1640,* 1961.
Brinton, Crane, *The Anatomy of Revolution,* New York, 1952.
Campbell, Mildred, *The English Yeoman under Elizabeth and the Early Stuarts,* 1959.
Hexter, J. H., *Reappraisals in History,* 1961.
Hill, Christopher, *Intellectual Origins of the English Revolution,* 1965.
Jordan, W. K., *Philanthropy in England, 1480–1660,* 1959.
Mathew, David, *The Age of Charles I,* 1951.
Notestein, Wallace, *The English People on the Eve of Colonization, 1603–1630,* 1954.
Pocock, J. G. A., *The Ancient Constitution and the Feudal Law,* 1957.

Stone, Lawrence, *The Crisis of the Aristocracy, 1558–1641,* 1965.

Supple, B. E., *Commercial Crisis and Change in England, 1600–1642,* 1959.

Tawney, R. H., "The Rise of the Gentry, 1558–1640," *Economic History Review,* XI (1941), 1–38.

Trevor-Roper, H. R., "The Gentry, 1540–1640," *Economic History Review,* Supplement I, 1953.

CHAPTER II: SEEDS OF CONFLICT

A. POLITICAL

Gough, J. W., *Fundamental Law in English Constitutional History,* 1955.

Hexter, J. H., *The Reign of King Pym,* 1941.

Judson, M. A., *The Crisis of the Constitution,* 1949.

Tanner, J. R., *English Constitutional Conflicts of the Seventeenth Century, 1603–89,* 1957.

Zagorin, Perez, *A History of Political Thought in the English Revolution,* 1954.

B. RELIGIOUS

Haller, William, *The Rise of Puritanism,* 1938.

Simpson, Alan, *Puritanism in Old and New England,* 1955.

Trevor-Roper, H. R., *Archbishop Laud,* 1962.

Yule, George, *The Independents in the English Civil War,* 1958.

CHAPTER III: THE RIVAL ARMIES

Firth, C. H., *Cromwell's Army,* 1921.

Solt, Leo, *Saints in Arms, Puritanism and Democracy in Cromwell's Army,* 1959.

Woodhouse, A. S. P. (ed.), *Puritanism and Liberty, being the Army Debates (1647–48),* 1951.

Woolrych, Austin, *Battles of the English Civil War,* 1961.

CHAPTER IV: THE LEVELLERS AND THE DIGGERS

Berens, Lewis H., *The Digger Movement in the Days of the Commonwealth*, 1906.

Brailsford, H. N., *The Levellers and the English Revolution*, 1961.

Coltman, Irene, *Private Men and Public Causes*, 1962.

Frank, Joseph, *The Levellers*, 1955.

Gregg, Pauline, *Free-born John*, 1961.

Haller, William (ed.), *Tracts on Liberty in the Puritan Revolution, 1638–1647*, 3 vols., 1934.

Pease, Theodore C., *Leveller Movement*, 1916.

Wolfe, Don M. (ed.), *Leveller Manifestoes of the Puritan Revolution*, 1944.

CHAPTER V: THE "ROYAL MARTYR"

Higham, F. M. G., *Charles I*, 1932.

Underdown, David, *Royalist Conspiracy in England, 1649–1660*, 1960.

Wedgwood, C. V., *A Coffin for King Charles*, 1964.

CHAPTER VI: THE COMMONWEALTH

James, Margaret, *Social Problems and Policy during the Puritan Revolution, 1640–1660*, 1930.

Prall, Stuart E., *The Agitation for Law Reform during the Puritan Revolution, 1640–1660*, 1966.

Schenk, W., *The Concern for Social Justice in the Puritan Revolution*, 1947.

CHAPTER VII: THE PROTECTORATE

Abbott, W. C., *The Writings and Speeches of Oliver Cromwell*, 4 vols., 1938–47.

Ashley, Maurice, *The Greatness of Oliver Cromwell*, 1957.

Buchan, John, *Oliver Cromwell*, 1934.

Firth, C. H., *Oliver Cromwell*, 1909.

Morley, John, *Oliver Cromwell*, 1901.

CHAPTER VIII: THE RESTORATION

Bryant, Sir Arthur, *King Charles II*, 1936.
Davies, Godfrey, *The Restoration of Charles II, 1658–1660*, 1955.
Turberville, A. S., *Commonwealth and Restoration*, 1936.

INDEX